Phonology in English Language Teaching

APPLIED LINGUISTICS AND LANGUAGE STUDY

General Editor
Professor Christopher N. Candlin, Macquarie University

For list of titles see pp. viii–ix

Phonology in English Language Teaching: An International Approach

Martha C. Pennington

LONGMAN
LONDON AND NEW YORK

Addison Wesley Longman Limited,
Edinburgh Gate,
Harlow, Essex CM20 2JE, United Kingdom
and Associated Companies throughout the world.

*Published in the United States of America
by Addison Wesley Longman, New York*

© Addison Wesley Longman Limited 1996

First published 1996

ISBN 0 582 22571X PPR

British Library Cataloguing-in-Publication Data
A catalogue record for this book is available from the British Library

Library of Congress Cataloging-in-Publication Data
Pennington, Martha Carswell.
    Phonology in English language teaching : an international approach
/ Martha C. Pennington.
        p.   cm. — (Applied linguistics and language study)
    Includes bibliographical references and index.
    ISBN 0–582–22571–X (pbk.)
    1. English language—Study and teaching—Foreign speakers.
    2. English language—Phonology, Comparative.   I. Title.
    II. Series.
PE1128.A2P38   1996   95–31239
421'.52—dc20   CIP

Set by 8 in 10/12 pt Times
Produced through Longman Malaysia, VVP

Contents

General Editor
Professor Christopher N. Candlin, Macquarie University

Error Analysis
Perspectives on second
language acquisition
JACK C. RICHARDS (ED.)

Stylistics and the Teaching of
Literature
HENRY WIDDOWSON

Contrastive Analysis
CARL JAMES

Language and Communication
JACK C. RICHARDS AND
RICHARD W. SCHMIDT (EDS)

Learning to Write: First Language/
Second Language
AVIVA FREEDMAN, IAN PRINGLE
AND JANIC YALDEN (EDS)

Reading in a Foreign Language
J. CHARLES ALDERSON AND
A.H. URQUHART (EDS)

An Introduction to Discourse
Analysis
New Edition
MALCOLM COULTHARD

Language Awareness in the
Classroom
CARL JAMES AND
PETER GARRETT

Bilingualism in Education
Aspects of theory, research and
practice
JIM CUMMINS AND
MERRILL SWAIN

Second Language Grammar:
Learning and Teaching
WILLIAM E. RUTHERFORD

The Classroom and the Language
Learner
Ethnography and second-language
classroom research
LEO VAN LIER

Vocabulary and Language Teaching
RONALD CARTER AND MICHAEL
McCARTHY (EDS)

Observation in the Language
Classroom
DICK ALLWRIGHT

Listening to Spoken English
Second Edition
GILLIAN BROWN

Listening in Language Learning
MICHAEL ROST

An Introduction to Second Language
Acquisition Research
DIANE LARSEN-FREEMAN AND
MICHAEL H. LONG

Language and Discrimination
A study of communication in
multi-ethnic workplaces
CELIA ROBERTS, TOM JUPP AND
EVELYN DAVIES

Translation and Translating:
Theory and Practice
ROGER T. BELL

Process and Experience in the
Language Classroom
MICHAEL LEGUTKE AND HOWARD
THOMAS

Rediscovering Interlanguage
LARRY SELINKER

Language as Discourse
Perspectives for Language Teaching
MICHAEL McCARTHY AND
RONALD CARTER

Analysing Genre – Language Use in
Professional Settings
V.K. BHATIA

From Testing to Assessment
English as an International
Language
CLIFFORD HILL AND KATE PARRY
(EDS)

Second Language Learning
Theoretical Foundations
MICHAEL SHARWOOD SMITH

Interaction in the Language Curriculum
LEO VAN LIER

Phonology in English Language Teaching
An International Approach
MARTHA C. PENNINGTON

Measuring Second Language Performance
T.F. McNAMARA

Theory and Practice of Writing
An Applied Linguistic Perspective
WILLIAM GRABE AND
ROBERT B. KAPLAN

General Editor's Preface

Martha Pennington's book represents a further extension of what is a new departure for the *Applied Linguistics and Language Study Series*, to focus on the interrelationship between theory, description and practice in areas of language form. To say this, of course, immediately raises not only central issues of such an interrelationship for Applied Linguistics as a discipline, but also foregrounds and questions the ways in which language form does engage with contexts of language function, particularly, as here in the international pedagogic context of the teaching and learning of English. Seen in this way, form becomes immediately a problematic and in no ways a neutral concept. All the important and currently struggled over issues are placed on the table: whose forms? whose functions? whose models? what curricular selections and priorities? what room and place for teachers' pedagogic choices? what buying power in the linguistic market place of those choices and selections that are made? At once, phonology, perhaps *par excellence*, becomes a critical site for applied linguistic debate.

From the outset, Professor Pennington makes her position clear: variationist and not prescriptivist, international and accent neutral, and socially relative to the users and uses of English as an international language. Moreover, she drives her arguments from a bidirectional approach to the pedagogy of phonology in terms of production and interpretation, rather than one only focused on the formal description of pronunciation varieties. Her goals are similarly commendably clear: in taking her international English stance, she is able to motivate the need to explicate the relationship between phonetics and phonology, and to do so through an extremely clear analytical and descriptive apparatus influenced by issues of classroom applicability. Indeed, in the best and most usable sense, the book takes on the nature of a compendium of techniques through the regular tasks that are included throughout the chapters. These tasks are themselves carefully designed not only to provide a resource for the self-study of the reader and the instructional program but also indirectly as an action-research curriculum for the classroom teacher. Issues of learner assessment and feedback are cyclically linked to particular pedagogic actions, themselves drawn from particular exercise and task-types informed by experimental and classroom-based research. In this way, the book becomes much more than merely an exploration of its phonological subject-matter; it offers a worked-through and coherent model of applied linguistic research in action, sited appropriately in the pedagogic workplace of the classroom. Such subject-matter and such action research could, of course, be narrowly construed; a curriculum focus on form and a focus by the teacher on the instruction and assessment of particular performance features. There are many such books in this topic area which achieve such goals admirably. Here in this book, however, we have something quite different in both design and execution. From the outset the reader is asked to manage the entire range of potential perspectives on phonology: that of the linguistic environment (and here very much including the discoursal as well as the segmental), the acoustic as well as the articulatory, the sociological and the contextual, the sociopsychological as well as the biological and cognitive, and the pedagogic and acquisitional. In short, addressing that complexity which any learner, any teacher indeed any speaker, necessarily confronts, as it were in a naturalised way, in every uttering of language and in its didacticising. The issue for the author, as for the trainer, is how to represent this complexity and make it engageable by the reader and the student. Here Professor Pennington's book is masterly; note for example, how she achieves this accessibility by choosing an issue, like that of the so-called 'critical period' in language acquisition, and demonstrates how these perspectives all interweave to offer a much richer and more explanatory treatment from her phonological viewpoint, of what is itself a contentious construct.

The author rightly emphasises, as I have done here also, the relevance of her book's content and organisation to teachers of English phonology internationally. The tasks throughout the book and the whole chapter devoted to pronunciation in the language curriculum are ample evidence of this. There are, however, important other audiences that will draw benefit from the multidisciplinarity inherent in the stance taken in *Phonology in English Language Teaching: An International Approach*. Teachers of literacy necessarily must engage with phonology in their work on orthography; what is less well understood is that if they seek to draw on their students' spoken language competence in an attempt to improve their control of written text and texture, they need also to understand how prosody serves to mark subject position and agency, what is given and what is new in an utterance's messages, and more broadly, how conversation is prosodically marked for meaning. In a related way, professional phoneticians both articulatory and instrumental, need to acknowledge the influence of second language acquisition research on the learnability of phonology and to include the contexts of the personal and the social as fundamental to their work. Just such an example is provided in the field of psychotherapy by the need to include social psychological data as a basis for the interpretation of the phonology of affect. Further audiences with a similar need for a multidisciplinary approach are not difficult to find: the creation in Australia, for example, of a spoken language database by speech scientists engaged in speech generation and recognition systems necessarily required in the context of that multilingual and multicultural community an orientation to a pluricentric model of English phonology, in many ways similar to the position adopted by Professor Pennington in this book.

In sum, this latest contribution to the *Applied Linguistics and Language Study Series* fully matches the aspirations of the series as a whole: to offer a broadly based study of a key applied linguistic subject matter, demonstrating how the linguistic, the social, the cognitive and the pedagogic are not adventitiously yoked together but each necessary to the other and contributive to the theoretical understanding and practical application of the field.

Professor Christopher N Candlin
General Editor
Macquarie University,
Sydney

Acknowledgements

The Publishers are indebted to the following for permission to reproduce copyright material:

Cambridge University Press for our Figures 2.6, 2.7 and 2.8 from 'Social Differentiation in Ottawa English' by H B Woods in *English Around the World* edited by J Cheshire (1991) and our Figure 4.4 from *Variation in Australian English: The sociolects of Sydney* by B M Horvath (1985); and Edward Arnold for our Tables 3.10, 3.11, 3.12 and 3.13 from 'Belfast: Change and variation in an urban vernacular' by Jim and Lesley Milroy from *Sociolinguistic patterns in British English* edited by Peter Trudgill (1978).

We have been unable to trace the copyright holders of the poem by T.S.W. in the *Sunday Times* 3 January 1965, and our tables 3.2, 3.3 and 3.4, and would appreciate any information which would enable us to do so.

Author's Preface

This text is the result of a fascination on my part, beginning in high school, with the study of language. It is no doubt significant for my interest in accents that when I was thirteen, my family moved from Jacksonville, Florida, which is located in a southern dialect area of the United States, to Nashua, New Hampshire, located in a very different dialect area near Boston, in the extreme Northeast. After more than thirty years, I can still vividly recall being chastised by my seventh grade history teacher when, standing in front of the class to give a report on Magellan, I rhymed *route* with *out* rather than with *root*.

My interest in phonology was more formally aroused in graduate school and soon became a focus of my study. The foundation for this text was laid in the 1970s at the University of Pennsylvania, where I received instruction and guidance in research on phonetics and phonology during master's and doctoral studies in the Department of Linguistics. In particular, I am indebted to Professors John Fought, William Labov, Zellig Harris, Henry Hoenigswald and Leigh Lisker. In addition, while a student at Penn I attended the Summer Institute of the Linguistic Society of America and became acquainted with Michael Halliday, whose work I have eagerly followed from then until now. The impact of each of these linguists on my knowledge, my linguistic skills, my thinking and my teaching is incalculable.

At the University of Hawaii, I was privileged to come into contact with several phonologists of stature, including David Stampe, Patricia Donegan and Timothy Vance, as well as with Suzanne Romaine when she taught summer courses there. From each of these scholars I have learned many and varied things. I have been greatly influenced, too, by the work in phonetics and phonology by Dwight Bolinger, Peter Ladefoged, John Laver, Alan Cruttenden, John Esling, Björn Hammarberg, David Brazil, Gillian Brown, D. Robert Ladd and Steve Weinberger.

In all its practical aspect, the book derives most immediately from my interactions during the last two decades with teachers and graduate students in ESL in many locations around the world. I wish to express my gratitude to the hundreds of teachers and graduate students who inspired my work in phonology classes and workshops, first at the University of California at Santa Barbara and later, at the University of Hawaii at Manoa. Thanks are also due to the students and teachers at Nagoya Gakuin University in Japan, the MATESL students at Temple University Japan, and the BATESL and MATESL students at the City University of Hong Kong, who inspired me to go through additional revisions of my material in an attempt to increase its relevance for teachers who are themselves non-native speakers and who work in a country where the majority language is not English.

I have benefited much since 1990 from a close association at my present institution with Graham Lock, who always seems to have a different and enlightening perspective on everything linguistic and whose point of view has substantially influenced my thinking about second language phonology and many other matters. Graham has also been most generous in his willingness to read drafts of the material, and he has given me many useful suggestions for improvements. I also gratefully acknowledge the supportive response and feedback from Dick Schmidt and Suzanne Romaine on sections of an earlier draft of this material.

Finally, I must give credit to two individuals without whose support this book would never have been published. I am grateful, first of all, to Chris Candlin for his unflagging interest in and assistance with the project – in particular, for his valuable conceptual and editorial input, which stimulated and helped me to go far beyond the original concept for the book. I would also like to acknowledge a general debt of gratitude to Jack Richards, whose encouragement helped me to bring this project to a successful completion and whose guidance and inspiration have made a big difference in my professional life over the many years that I have been associated with him.

Martha C. Pennington
Hong Kong
1996

To the Reader

This book is intended as a comprehensive introduction to English phonology set in the social and international context of language learning and language teaching around the world. The book is principally geared to teachers of English as a second or foreign language (ESL/ EFL), though the material will also be of value for teachers of other languages, as well as for language researchers in various fields. The course examines phonology from a variationist, accent-neutral and international point of view, explicitly comparing the major varieties of English around the world and using a system of description and transcription which is relatively generic. The book is therefore usable in non-English speaking as well as English speaking countries.

The text blends theory and practice in phonetics, phonology, English linguistics, sociolinguistics and language teaching. The subject matter of the course centers on the details of English phonology in the categories of consonants, vowels and prosody, with additional material on the relationship of phonology to orthography and to the larger language curriculum. Its practical component includes pedagogical activities, ideas for carrying out classroom action research, and a final chapter addressing classroom issues, needs analysis and lesson design. With slight modifications, most of the teaching ideas and action research projects could be adapted to the phonology of languages other than English.

Goals and objectives

The major goals of this material are to provide:

(1) an understanding of general principles of phonetics and phonology;
(2) knowledge of the nature of English phonology;
(3) applications of phonology in the language classroom;
(4) skills for pronunciation diagnosis and needs analysis.

As a secondary goal, the material aims to provide:

(5) a summary of the relationship of the English spelling system to its sound system.

The coverage of the book offers language teachers and other interested readers the background and experience necessary for:

(a) assessing students' pronunciation and related aspects of listening proficiency;
(b) giving useful feedback on students' pronunciation;
(c) designing original classroom materials for teaching pronunciation;
(d) reading published literature on the teaching of phonology.

It also supplies the necessary background and skills for:

(e) conducting investigations that explore English phonology in its social context or in the teaching and learning of pronunciation, including action research in their own classes.

Organization

The design of the book presents the sometimes daunting content of phonology in a way that will be interesting, useful and accessible to language teachers. Therefore, the discussion throughout the book returns with regularity to the concerns of practitioners. The material is also presented in a structured and orderly fashion appropriate for self-teaching or classroom use in teacher preparation courses. Thus, each chapter ends with activities to help reinforce the chapter content. The activities, which may be carried out individually or comparatively in a class or small group, include suggestions for classroom action research and community-based or classroom-based sociolinguistic mini-research projects.

At the same time as it aims for high interest and "user-friendliness", the material is also meant to provide a thorough, integrated coverage of English phonology and the teaching of pronunciation. It is therefore organized as six comprehensive chapters, each beginning with an overview of the core material, which lays a foundation for the theoretical and practical points that follow.

Chapter 1 provides a philosophical framework and subject matter background for the whole book. The next three chapters (Chapter 2–4) overview the phonology of English consonants, vowels and prosody. Each of these chapters is organized in two parts. The first part presents the core material on English phonology. The second part is oriented to applications of the chapter content in the way of introspective exercises, action research and sociolinguistic mini-research project ideas, and teaching materials.

Chapter 5 addresses the topic of orthography in relation to English phonology from both a historical and a present-day perspective. Like the preceding chapters, it ends with introspective review activities as well as practical ideas for teaching and research activities related to the chapter content. The final chapter discusses the nature of second language learning and the place of phonology in the language classroom, offering principles for needs analysis and lesson design, sample material to critique, and practical advice on diagnosing and responding to students' pronunciation difficulties.

Uniqueness

The present book is unique in the following respects:

- the treatment of phonology in a context of internationalism, language variation and social factors affecting speech;
- inclusion of basic phonetics in a treatment of phonology geared for language teachers;
- the provision of a wide range of material related to classroom concerns;
- the inclusion of a separate chapter on lesson design and pronunciation diagnosis.

Its content and organization make the book suitable for a wide range of needs of phonology, including (a) graduate students in TESL/TEFL seeking a general overview of English phonology geared to their concerns, (b) language teachers looking for practical activities for teaching and for giving feedback on pronunciation, and (c) language researchers looking for guidance in conducting research on the phonology of speakers whose first or second language is English. It may also prove to be of value to speech pathologists and others who specialize in communication problems of native or non-native speakers.

1 Introduction to phonology in language teaching

Phonology in the context of language teaching

What is phonology?

This is a course in English, the language which developed in England and has been spreading in the last three centuries as a medium for communication around the globe. It is also a course in phonology, as viewed from at least three different perspectives. In this book, the term **phonology** is used in the senses of:

(a) the sound patterns of language;
(b) the pronunciation patterns of speakers;
(c) the study of (a) and/or (b).

In one sense, we speak of the phonology of a language or language variety (e.g. a dialect) as the system of sounds, or sound patterns, of that language or language variety. In other words, English phonology is a description of the sounds of English and their relationships and contrasts with each other. More concretely, we can view the phonology of English – or of any language or language variety – as the pronunciation patterns of those who speak it. Additionally, phonology can be described as the study of the sound patterns of languages or of the pronunciation patterns of speakers.

The subject of phonology, when viewed from these different perspectives, addresses questions such as the following:

(1) How do the sound patterns of languages change over time?
(2) What are the similarities and differences in the sound patterns of languages?
(3) How do individual speakers differ in their pronunciation patterns?
(4) How do people learn the pronunciation patterns of a language?

This is a course in English phonology for current or prospective language teachers. The course does not require any background in linguistics or teaching methodology, although those who have such backgrounds may have a slight advantage. On the other hand, the

1

perspective of the book and much of the content, particularly in its practical aspect, will probably be new even for those who have already had coursework in English phonology or related areas. The teaching ideas which are included in the book are generally not available in other texts and so are likely to be new for most or all readers.

Types of meaning conveyed by phonology

Although the course is designed for language teachers, some readers may have reservations at the outset about the need for instruction in phonology or for attention to this aspect of language in their own present or future classes. Yet phonology is one of the most all-encompassing, pervasive phenomena of language. Phonology provides the basis for all other aspects of language, in that all higher units (e.g. words, phrases, sentences) are ultimately analyzable as sounds. Moreover, phonology is associated with a wide variety of symbolic functions in human interaction such as different types of linguistic meaning, personal and group identity, and affect (mood or emotion).

As Stevick (1978) observes: *"Pronunciation is the primary medium through which we bring our use of language to the attention of other people"* [italics in original] (p. 145). It is also a primary medium for communication of information about ourselves as individuals and as representatives of different groups. Since it opens the way to a better understanding of how language works and how the different aspects of linguistic and social meaning are interrelated, an understanding of the phonology of a language is a necessary basis for fully effective teaching of a spoken language.

Since sounds are the basis of all higher linguistic units, phonological differences can signal differences at several levels of language, e.g. differences in:

- lexical meaning;
- grammatical meaning;
- utterance meaning.

The difference between *pin* and *pen* and that between *pen* and *pan* are lexical differences signaled by the difference in pronunciation of the central sound of the words, i.e. the **vowel** sounds. Analogously, the contrast in meaning of the lexical items *tin* and *sin* and of *sin* and *shin* is in each case signaled by the difference in one sound – in these cases, the initial **consonant** sounds.

As an example of a grammatical difference signaled by phonology, consider the difference between the verb *use* and the noun *use*. This is signaled by a difference in the last sound of the word. The same contrast of final sounds differentiates *advise* and *advice*. To take a different sort of example, the difference between the noun and verb forms of *object* is signaled by the amount of energy expended to produce the first part of the word, the **prefix** *ob-*, as compared to the **stem** part, *-ject*. In the noun form of *object*, the prefix is more forcefully pronounced than the stem; in the verb form, the stem is more forcefully pronounced than the prefix. The same contrast in pronunciation of noun–verb pairs recurs in a large group of words in English.

Differences in sentence-level or utterance-level meaning can also be signaled by phonology. For example, the difference between a statement and a question can often be indicated by a falling voice at the end of an utterance, as in (a), whereas a rise, as in (b), indicates questioning.

(a) He left.   (b) He left?

Besides these differences in meaning, phonology may indicate something about the speaker's personal or group identity, or his/her temporary affective state.

Personal identity is signaled by the general phonological properties of a person's voice, i.e. the person's unique **voice quality** (**voice set**). While people in the same family will often sound similar, particularly if they are the same sex, it is generally an easy matter to tell any two people apart by overall voice quality after only a very short exposure to their voices.

Identification with or membership in various types of groups is also signaled by phonology. Group identity as symbolized by phonology may be primarily geographical or primarily social. The general principle in both cases is that people who have a great deal of contact with each other and/or who identify closely with each other's values will tend to talk in much the same way. Accordingly, children pick up the speech patterns of their relatives and playmates.

People who come from the same country or region will have similar pronunciation patterns, while those coming from different countries or regions will differ in their phonology to a greater or lesser degree. After only a brief exposure, one can notice great differences in national and regional accents.

These national and regional accents are generally associated with some sociocultural differences among people in the geographical areas where they occur, and with traditional views or stereotypes of such sociocultural differences. As a result of these perceived sociocultural differences, national and regional varieties carry social meaning. The differences in perception may be based on the listener's interpretation of linguistic differences between groups of speakers in relation to stereotypes of how those groups behave. Speakers from some areas may, for example, characteristically speak more slowly or with a greater range in voice quality as compared to speakers from other regions. In such cases, it may be that these differences in tempo, or **speech rate**, and voice quality come to symbolize stereotyped differences in the behavior of the different groups of people.

In big cities throughout the world, speakers who live in different neighborhoods often have noticeably different accents. In general, these differences in local accent are not merely geographical but signify social differences, both perceived (e.g. stereotyped behaviors or traits) and actual (e.g. economic level), between the residents of the different neighborhoods as well. In fact, various types of social group – including many cases in which people belong to the same social grouping but do not reside in the same geographical area – are identified by their phonology and other speech characteristics.

When people adjust their pronunciation style towards that of another speaker or social group, i.e. when their pronunciation converges on that of the other speaker or group, they are said to be **accommodating** themselves to a greater or lesser degree to those speakers and their style of pronunciation. In the opposite case, that of **non-accommodation**, a person diverges from the pronunciation of the other speaker or group (Giles and Powesland 1975). On the whole, people adopt the pronunciation of a certain social group less through conscious choice and more through unconscious initation based on such feelings as empathy or admiration.

To take one recurrent example of the way in which socially defined groups residing in different geographical areas can be identified by their phonology, different ethnic groups, even in the same geographical community, often maintain distinctive pronunciation patterns. For example, residents of Greek, Italian and Northern European descent in Sydney, Australia, each have recognizably different pronunciation patterns (Horvath 1985). Conversely, speakers of the same ethnic group who live in different cities or regions of the same country may have recognizably similar phonology, which distinguishes their speech to some degree from that of their neighbors belonging to different ethnic groups. For example, Black speakers in different parts of the US sometimes share a cluster of phonological and grammatical features which are not common among speakers of other groups (Wolfram 1991: 106–11). What this means is that the signaling of ethnic group identity by phonology can supersede a geographical accent.

Other kinds of social identity such as socioeconomic class or gender may be signaled to some extent by phonology. People who can be classified into different socioeconomic categories (e.g. those with and without a university education, or those in the upper, middle and lower income brackets) generally have somewhat different pronunciation patterns. Males and females – even those who belong to the same ethnic group, who live in the same geographical area and who belong to the same socioeconomic class – will generally orient their pronunciation somewhat differently. Thus, the pronunciation patterns of males and females are to some extent divergent. In all such cases, different groups of speakers maintain a distinctive identity to some extent through linguistic means, including their pronunciation. (They may also use some differences in syntax, lexical items, expressions, or the meaning of words or grammatical patterns for the same purpose.)

Differences in phonology that signal differences in group identity are not only differences in overall voice quality, but also differences in the pronunciation of individual sounds. A pronunciation of a certain sound that signals membership in a particular group is termed a **phonological marker** of identity in that group. Use of phonological markers thus signals a speaker's conscious or unconscious desire to accommodate to and to be identified with the values and social roles of a particular group.

A good example of differences in pronunciation patterns across groups of speakers is the pronunciation of the English vowel termed **short-a**, which occurs in a large group of words, e.g. in *class, bath, plan, sad, at, and, can, daddy*. The pattern of a person's pronunciation in a representative sample of short-a words has been shown to be a fairly reliable indicator of geographical region – e.g. in different parts of North America and the British Isles – and of socioeconomic class within that region. Pronunciation patterns in short-a words also show some systematic differences among different ethnic groups, between males and females, and between older and younger speakers.

The style of phonology that is adopted also signals affective information about the speaker's momentary mood, emotions or attitude towards the listener or to some aspect of the topic of conversation. For example, a speaker who is depressed generally shows this in a depressed style of phonology, i.e. weak (indistinct or mumbled) pronunciation of individual sounds and weak (low) tone of voice or colorless (unvarying) voice quality. A speaker likewise shows heightened emotion, whether intentionally or unintentionally, through heightened phonological characteristics, such as exaggerated length of consonant and vowel sounds, loudness and high voice. If the speaker regards some aspect of the topic or discourse as especially important or wishes to attract the listener's attention, the speaker can highlight the message by using careful or emphatic pronunciation, a loud or high voice, or an attractive and colorful voice quality.

As the basis of all higher linguistic units and as the bearer of many different kinds of symbolic meaning, phonology is an important aspect of fluency and therefore of **discourse competence,** i.e. the ability to construct extended stretches of speech appropriate to different contexts. To ignore phonology means to ignore an aspect of language which is central to the production, the perception and the interpretation of many different kinds of linguistic and social meaning.

The description of grammatical speech, fluent speech, social roles, and the different kinds of language spoken by different groups and under different circumstances all require a close examination of phonology. To be ignorant of the nature of the phonology of the language being taught, i.e. the **target language,** is to risk being unable to respond appropriately to student needs in this area. The study of phonology can therefore not easily be dismissed as an unnecessary "frill" in the second language classroom and in the professional preparation of language teachers. Whether or not they choose to teach phonology explicitly, language teachers are in a sense always teaching phonology whenever they teach anything at all. And, like other areas of instruction, a solid knowledge base can be seen as the minimum requirement for effective teaching.

Native and non-native accent

For those who might be teaching adolescent or adult learners, the question of whether it is possible to eradicate a so-called "foreign accent" is an inevitable one. In order to approach this question objectively, one must carefully define the term "foreign accent" – something which, perhaps surprisingly, has hardly been attempted. Although the received wisdom is that we can tell a "foreign accent" as soon as we hear it, there is no universally accepted definition of "foreign accent", nor has anyone systematically tested the ability to discriminate unfamiliar accents as "foreign" and "non-foreign".

For a language such as English, for which many very different native accents exist, there is the considerable problem, given the spread of English around the globe, of establishing in a principled, non-subjective manner just which accents count as "native". Even if a principled basis for such a categorization could be developed, it is possible that native speaker judges would not be able to distinguish reliably those varieties labeled "native" and "non-native" – especially if (1) the non-native speakers whose accents were to be judged had advanced competency in English and (2) if the native speakers whose voices were to be judged spoke with accents that were unfamiliar to the judges.

The difficulty of defining "foreign accent" is an important point which has largely been overlooked by scholars and which is related to the difficult of defining terms such as **language, dialect**, and the like. In spite of these problems of definition, we can see that a great variety of explanations for "foreign accents" have been put forth in the literature on first and second language learning, as reviewed in Scovel (1988) and in Singleton (1989). This literature discusses the question of an age-related advantage in acquiring "accent-free" speech.

According to Scovel and many others in the fields of linguistics, psychology and human biology, the period up to puberty (around age twelve) is a **critical period** for acquisition of a language without a foreign accent. Singleton, however, argues that the critical period and other age-related arguments have been overstated, as there is evidence of continuous acquisition of language into old age. However, most people would probably admit that there is a clear difference in the linguistic performance of children and adults, particularly in relation to phonology, and that this difference must be explained.

One plausible explanation for age-related factors in language acquisition is that the child, being a naive and inexperienced learner, acquires language in a more direct and basic manner than the adult speaker, who has greater sophistication and experience in learning language – and many other things as well. The adult therefore tends to tackle the learning of a new language in a more organized and analytical manner than the child, drawing on previous learning experiences and previously acquired knowledge, including knowledge of the mother tongue. While the adult's way of learning language may have some advantages in terms of mastering grammatical rules and vocabulary, it may in fact not be the most effective way to acquire the sound system of a language.

The key to the difference in child and adult acquisition of phonology may lie in the fact that the child perceives and produces language in a holistic manner, attending primarily to its most obvious and salient, surface-level characteristics. For this reason, children may be better equipped than adults to imitate and reproduce speech as they hear it. In contrast, adults tend to process speech at a deeper, more abstract and more sophisticated level – i.e. at a level that is more removed from direct experience.

By this line of reasoning, the acquisition of phonology – at least in the way that a child goes about it – is essentially a matter of acquiring an undifferentiated type of experience through holistic, surface-oriented attention. Adults, while at an advantage for acquiring other kinds of experience, are at a disadvantage as compared to children for acquiring anything in a naive, unthinking, non-analytical way: such learning very literally **goes against the grain** of the adult's nature and experience. This is a reality which we must contend with when teaching a second language to older learners. It does not by any means follow, however, that adults cannot learn the phonology of a second language – only that we have to consider their nature as learners when devising appropriate instructional approaches.

Language varieties and English

Speech norms

This book treats English from an international perspective, in all its forms, rather than narrowing the focus to one dialect, or variety, of the language as spoken by a particular group of speakers or in one country. The orientation of the book is thus **variationist** rather than **prescriptivist**.

The description of individual languages and language standards can be related to the notion of **speech community**. A speech community is describable in geographic terms as a region or a neighborhood; or it is describable in terms of ethnic or other types of affiliations which bind people together under common values, even though they are separated geographically. Thus, a speech community does not necessarily have definable physical borders and may in fact be geographically discontinuous. In such cases, we may perhaps speak more accurately of a community of speakers who share certain values but who do not actually live in the same area.

A speech community or community of speakers can then be defined as a group of speakers who share a common set of values, or norms, for the production and evaluation of speech (Hymes 1974). These shared norms make up the **rules of speaking** that apply within a particular community of speakers. In other words, a speech community is defined as a group of speakers who tend to agree on what counts as an appropriate or inappropriate style of speaking in a given circumstance. For example, the utterance of (b) is recognized by native speakers of English as more polite than (a):

(a) Get me a drink!
(b) Would you mind getting me a drink?

Certain styles of pronunciation are negatively or positively valued within a particular speech community and considered more or less appropriate depending on circumstances. A speaker who pronounces a certain word, or a certain vowel or consonant, in one way rather than another will produce a certain effect on the listener by that (conscious or unconscious) choice. For example, drawing out the final vowel sound of the word *so* while raising the voice somewhat can signal that the speaker is nearing the conclusion of a narrative or other type of discourse and is offering the listener a chance to take a conversational turn. The following exchange shows how the first speaker's use of the drawled *so* signals that s/he is about to give up the floor. The fact that Pat recognizes Marty's signal and takes the floor indicates that Pat understands this rule of speaking.

Marty: So-o-o-o, that's my big news.
Pat: Well, I have some news, too.

Based on the rules of speaking, the choice of a casual or formal style of pronunciation overall makes a certain impression on the listener, depending on the circumstances surrounding the communication. For example, in a typical context for English speech, we would expect two teenage boys to use a relaxed, casual style of pronunciation when speaking to each other. At the same time, we would not be surprised to hear a teenage boy speaking more carefully and formally when required to meet with the principal or headmaster of the school.

Imagine the odd or special effect if one of the boys adopted the careful, formal style that he had used with the principal when speaking to the other boy. He might appear to be imitating the principal, as when relating to the other teenager what happened when he spoke to the principal. On the other hand, if he used his most casual style of pronunciation in his meeting with the principal, he might appear, at best, immature or, at worst, disrespectful. We can also imagine the unusual effect if the principal used a very casual style of pronunciation in a disciplinary action when addressing the student offender.

By pronouncing according to the norms of a particular community of speakers, whether socially or geographically defined, a speaker expresses solidarity with the other members of that group or community. Such pronunciation is associated with group and local identity and serves as a symbolic claim to group membership and to certain rights and privileges such as being able to participate in local clubs and societies (Labov 1972). The value attached to a local accent is a kind of locally oriented prestige (Rickford 1985) or **covert prestige** (Labov 1972; Trudgill 1974) in which members of a speech community intuitively, often subconsciously, esteem a style of speaking that is not socially valued outside that community.

The local and sometimes covert prestige attached to the style of speaking within a tightly knit group of speakers – whether bound together geographically or not – defines a local accent, a specific or localized variety, or **vernacular language**, as against a more generalized variety, or **standard language**, that cuts across individual speech communities and has a more generalized and overt type of prestige.

Standards and varieties, old and new

Historically, standard languages often begin as the variety used in a certain locale by a particular group of people who are recognized as having power, prestige and social advantage. After a period of time, this prestige variety becomes disseminated to other locales and groups of speakers through imitation and deliberate choice, as those speakers seek to gain the rights and privileges associated with its use, or through governmental decree, as the socially advantaged group wields power over others in the community.

For both of these reasons, English has been spreading dramatically around the globe – sometimes by choice and sometimes by imposition of the government as an official standard alongside or in place of a local language – as a strong second (or third, etc.) language and as a language of international communication. As Trudgill and Hannah (1985) note: "In many parts of the world, particularly in Africa, Malaysia, Philippines, Singapore, Hong Kong and the Indian sub-continent, English is widely used as an official language, as the language of education and as a means of wider communication by people who are native speakers of some other language" (pp. 100–1).

A standard language is a national linguistic norm employed for such formal and "external" (non-intimate) purposes as education, government and news media. For many people in many communities, it is not the variety that is learned in childhood within the family for the in-formal and "internal" (intimate) functions of the home and the neighborhood. Rather, it is acquired through schooling, as either a second language or second dialect. For example, in the United States, children from rural areas of the South and from many inner-city neighborhoods in large urban areas such as Los Angeles, Chicago, New York and Philadelphia must master a new dialect of English, especially for writing, when they go to school. Similarly, all over the Chinese-speaking areas of Asia, ethnic Chinese children learn to write Standard Written Chinese, which diverges considerably from some of the varieties of Chinese found in different regions, especially in the southern region which includes Guangdong (formerly Canton) province and Hong Kong.

Most Hong Kong Chinese school children additionally learn English, which is still employed as the main standard in education (especially at tertiary level), in law, in business at the higher levels of management and to some extent in government as well. The large majority of these students use Cantonese at home and for virtually all communication other than some limited use of English in school. When English is used by native Cantonese speakers in Hong Kong, it is sometimes spoken with recognizably local features of phonology, syntax and lexis (Bolton and Kwok 1990), as is the case in many other communities where English has historically been an official language – e.g. Singapore, India and Sri Lanka, in Asia (Kandiah 1991; Kachru 1982, 1984; Sahgal 1991); Kenya, Tanzania and Zambia, in East Africa (Abdulaziz 1991; Hancock and Angogo 1984; Kanyoro 1991; Schmied 1991); and Cameroon, Gambia, Ghana, Liberia, Nigeria and Sierra Leone, in West Africa (Bokamba 1991; Todd 1984). The varieties of English – e.g. Hong Kong English, Singaporean English, Indian English, and Nigerian English or West African English – which developed during this century and the previous one in different parts of the world and which incorporate features of the local language(s), are sometimes referred to as **localized** or **nativized** varieties of English.

Although many of these localized varieties have few (if any) native speakers, they are often spoken (and written) by a large proportion of the community as a second language. In some cases, such as in Hong Kong and Singapore (but not in India), the localized varieties of English exist side-by-side with non-local varieties of English (e.g. British or American English), with each variety spoken by groups with different socioeconomic characteristics.

The new varieties of English (NVEs), or **New Englishes** (Pride 1982), have properties which differentiate them from the speech of language learners, often termed **learner language** or **interlanguage** (Selinker 1972, 1992). The new English varieties are described by D'Souza (1992) as follows:

> The NVEs are varieties of English that have emerged as a result of the colonial experience. This fact is important because it contributes

a great deal to making the NVEs what they are. Colonialism has led to the institutionalization of English in . . . countries like India, Sri Lanka, Singapore, Nigeria, etc. . . . English has to function in what may be called 'un-English' contexts covering a very wide territory, and is used in a variety of domains – social, cultural, educational, media-related, administrative and literary. It is used primarily for intranational communication. English has a time-depth in these . . . countries (at least 200 years in the case of India) and also a depth of penetration in that it is not restricted to the upper classes but is used by all levels of society, albeit in varying degrees. The range and depth of English has resulted in its nativization and, therefore, the NVEs differ from the OVEs (old varieties of English, i.e. British, American, etc.) and from each other in terms of lexis, semantics, syntax, phonology and pragmatics. The NVEs are fairly stable and speakers can articulate the norms of usage of the variety they speak. Creativity is another feature of these varieties. . . (pp. 217–18)

Considering all of these new varieties of English, Cheshire (1991a) contends that "the distinction that has been drawn conventionally between the 'native speaker' and the 'non-native speaker' is becoming blurred and increasingly difficult to operationalise" (p. 2). Cheshire's (1991a) collection, which consists of sociolinguistic descriptions of the "Old Englishes" as well as a large number of the New Englishes, stands as evidence that the NVEs are not merely examples of non-native or non-proficient English, but serve a wide range of communicative functions and exhibit systematic variation according to such features as the socioeconomic status of speakers and the formality of speech in the communities where they occur.

In acquiring English as a second language – including the new varieties of English – the divergences from the most generalized English standard often embody features from the speakers' mother tongue(s), as well as the effects of natural processes of learning and development. In the former category falls the phenomenon known as **transfer**, or production based on native language forms. In the latter category fall various types of natural phonological processes as well as natural learning processes such as generalization and simplification to ease the mental processing of difficult information. In acquiring English as a language of wider communication – e.g. as an **international** or **auxiliary** community language – features added to the local variety of English through transfer and simplification do not merely represent errors but also embody facts about the identity of the speakers of that variety. By incorporating distinctive local features – either derived "directly" from the native language(s) of the region or developed as innovations – the speakers of English in each region maintain or develop a distinctive social identity.

To the extent that each new variety of English is modeled on the local language(s) and to the extent that it is simplified in regular ways, to that extent will the localized variety become more accessible and learnable by a larger group of speakers within that community. It therefore becomes more valuable to the community as a language of wider communication. In addition, those who speak another variety as their main **in-group** language have a disincentive to introduce or to maintain in their second language the degree of complexity that obtains in a variety that is intended to be difficult for **out-group** speakers (non-members of the in-group) to fully understand or master. Thus, the speaker of English as a second language may have little motivation to introduce or to maintain complex variation and subtle phonological features in the language for intricate social identification.

As an illustration of this potential tendency to avoid complexity, Milroy (1982) has noted that the range of variation in short-a words is much less in speakers outside the inner city of Belfast than among those inside the inner city. As Milroy (1991) observes:

> It is to be expected that within the wider social structure of a city, social distance between groups will develop. In such circumstances, the norm enforcement mechanisms that maintain the complex structure of inner-city phonology (and other patterns of language use) will be weakened, and simplification is likely. (p. 80)

Analogously, it is to be expected that the norms of English as a second language or world language will be weaker and/or more general than those for English as a native variety or primary language, so that systematic variation may be reduced.

On the other hand, the addition of new varieties – whether "simplified" in any sense or not – expands the stock of English repertoires available to the world's population. Moreover, as soon as a new variety becomes codified, its forms become potential sites within the community of speakers of that variety for the forces of innovation, diversification and complexification associated with pronunciation-based identity to begin to operate.

To recapitulate, it is natural that when English is adapted for communication around the world, a local variety will develop which exhibits characteristics of the native language(s) and varieties of the members of that community but which gradually evolves in a new direction independent of both. Hence, the localized variety of English spoken in India is recognizably different from that spoken in the

Philippines, Hong Kong, Singapore, Malaysia, Sri Lanka, Nigeria, Tanzania, the West Indies and Guyana – and from that spoken in Scotland and Québec. Indeed, just as happened comparatively recently in many countries, when English spread in previous centuries from England to other parts of the world, distinctive varieties developed in Canada, the United States, Australia, New Zealand and South Africa.

In England, the generalized standard can be referred to as British English. According to Trudgill and Hannah (1985):

> As far as grammar and vocabulary are concerned, this generally means Standard English as it is normally written and spoken by educated speakers in England and, with minor differences, in Wales, Scotland, Northern Ireland, The Republic of Ireland, Australia, New Zealand and South Africa. As far as pronunciation is concerned, it means something much more restrictive, for the RP ('Received Pronunciation') accent which is taught to foreigners is actually used by perhaps only 3 per cent to 5 per cent of the population of England. The RP accent has it origins in the south-east of England but is currently a social accent associated with the BBC, the Public Schools in England, and with members of the upper-middle and upper classes. (pp. 1–2)

RP is a prestige accent of British English particularly fostered by certain English "public" (i.e. private) schools and spoken by those in the higher socioeconomic strata of English society. All other varieties spoken in England – and the same holds true by and large for Wales – are by definition regional dialects, though Irish English and Scottish English are national varieties with their own regional and class accents and separate identities (Wells 1982: 15). Scottish English in particular has established an identity, often one of some prestige, outside of Britain. Within England and Wales, the regional varieties are to some extent negatively valued, as non-RP accents, yet they also have local (sometimes covert) prestige. Nowadays, a sort of reverse-prestige or new prestige is coming to be associated with the non-RP accents of the major urban centers of England such as Liverpool and Manchester, which are establishing their own unique and positive identities at home and abroad.

In the United States, the generalized standard is referred to as General American or (Standard) American English. As compared to Britain, the standard language in the United States is representative more of the middle class than the upper class and is also tied to a particular geographical region – the part of the country other than the Northern, Eastern, Southern and Western perimeter (including Hawaii and Alaska), i.e. the Central section. It is the accent of "Middle America" in both a social and a geographical sense. Speakers who are not Middle Americans – i.e. those who are in the lower or higher social strata and who live in coastal or border states, or outside the contiguous United States – have the most recognizable regional accents, though with some differences among social strata.

Apart from Newfoundland and the French-speaking areas, with respect to pronunciation, Canada forms one large regional dialect area (Chambers 1991: 93; Wells 1982: 492). Canadian English is quite similar to American English, with which it forms a common North American variety. In Australia and New Zealand, as well as in South Africa, different accents – "broad" vs. "mild" ("cultivated") – are associated more with rural vs. urban origin and with social distinctions than with geographical locale (Trudgill and Hannah 1985: 16). As compared to the situation in Britain or the US, "what seems to be the preeminent characteristic of [Australian and New Zealand] forms of English is their overall uniformity, particularly on a regional basis, which may partly be explained by the heavy concentration of the population in a few centers" (Eagleson 1984: 427).

Because they are expressions of the speakers' identity and membership in the local speech community, vernacular languages and local varieties such as Southern American English, Southern British English, Black English, "Broad" New Zealand or Australian English, West Indian English, Indian English and Hong Kong English are to a large extent the speakers' preferred varieties of English. Though the speakers of these varieties recognize that the official or standard language has institutionalized prestige, they also understand that their unique local variety affords them the privileges of membership in their own communities and sets them apart from all other groups. In cases where English is not the primary local language, as in Hong Kong, people may see it as appropriately used only in certain well-defined circumstances.

For many speakers of local vernacular or nativized varieties, the traditionally recognized prestige standard may in fact be considered affected when spoken by most community members under most circumstances. Thus, for instance, a study by Poynton (1979) on the evaluation of Australian English found that the "cultivated" variety (based to some extent on a British English norm) was judged as "good speech used by phony people" while the relatively informal "broad" (vernacular) variety was viewed as "bad speech used by real people" (Horvath 1985: 24). Somewhat analogously, students in Hong Kong may describe Chinese who speak English in inappropriate circumstances (e.g. in non-academic contexts where no Westerners are present) as being pretentious, as showing off or as emulating the West (Gibbons 1987: 30).

Thus, a formal standard language may not be relevant to many people in their everyday life and communication, outside of school and a few other restricted circumstances. For the many individuals in the English speaking world who would nowadays judge the "cultivated" norm outside their own local community as unnatural and who are uncomfortable with a formal standard for speech, it is more realistic to posit an **informal standard** as "applied to spoken language; determined by actual usage patterns of speakers . . . ; [with] multiple norms of acceptability, incorporating regional and social considerations; [and] defined negatively by the *avoidance* of socially stigmatized linguistic structures" (Wolfram 1991: 12).

Because of the existence of both more localized and more generalized norms and because the phonology of a language or speech community is open to many influences and changes over time, the standards or rules of speaking are not entirely fixed, or absolute, but rather vary according to individual circumstances such as the following:

- **The area in which a person grew up**: rural or urban, the specific neighborhood of a city, the region of the country, and the country.
- **The speaker's age**: young people are more likely than older people to adopt innovations spreading into a local speech community from outside.
- **The social network of people that the speaker spends time with and the speaker's socioeconomic status**: speakers who are less socially mobile and who have a relatively homogeneous network of friends and associates tend to be more conservative and more oriented to localized speech norms than those who are more socially mobile and who associate with a more diverse network of people.
- **The sex of the participants**: males generally orient their speech more to localized norms than do females.
- **The circumstances surrounding the speech event**: e.g. the relationship of the participants and the formality of the situation.
  (Labov 1972; Milroy 1980; Trudgill 1974)

When describing a national standard language such as American, British or Australian English, it is important to recognize the existence of both the generalized variety and other more specific or localized varieties. A correct description will refer to the most generalized form while identifying the patterns of variation from this norm in different varieties. Such an approach, which emphasizes the social dimensions of language, falls into the field of **sociolinguistics**.

The non-prescriptive orientation of this book means that no one variety of English is seen as inherently superior to any other. Nevertheless, it must be noted that the variety of a language which is spoken by those who are most educated and/or who hold social and political power is often viewed as the most prestigious variety and the one which non-native speakers would most like to acquire. The definition of standard language in terms of this kind of prestige is an important guidepost for many non-native speakers who want to know the most generalized prestige form of the language in the community where they live and work (or plan to live and work in the future), i.e. the one that will have the greatest social advantage for them. As in all teaching, it is important in planning instruction to consider the student's expressed needs and desires. At the same time, it is important to consider the benefits for the student of being exposed to a wider range of experience in the phonology of the second language.

A variationist approach to teaching phonology

The approach to phonology taken in this book is opposed to more traditional approaches in the importance it assigns to variation in a complete and realistic account of language for descriptive or pedagogical purposes. It also emphasizes the centrality of phonology to other aspects of social and linguistic meaning. As part of this larger complex of social and linguistic meaning (Pennington and Richards 1986), phonology cannot correctly be viewed as incidental to language learning.

Based on its variationist orientation to English phonology, the philosophy of teaching of this book, as developed in Chapter 6 as well as in the Teaching Ideas offered at the end of each of the other chapters, is also non-prescriptivist. A variationist teaching philosophy suggests that learners should be given choices in their learning activities. It also suggests that learners' individual circumstances should dictate the targets of language learning. As Esling (1987) maintains, "attempting to teach students to sound exactly like one particular group as opposed to another is counter-productive, and not consistent with the need to provide as much input as possible in order for cognitive processes [of the learner] to select modes of performance that are appropriate for the individual learner" (pp. 468–9).

Consistent with the variationist philosophy of this book, it is advocated that learners be provided with multiple models of English phonology and that they be actively involved in deciding what they will learn and in developing their own learning process. A major part of the language teacher's job then becomes one of providing the students with a broad range of experiences within the language and a diversity and quantity of input in the way of speech samples on which to base their own phonology, under the principle of "collection not correction" (Esling 1987: 469).

Perception and production of speech

Levels of analysis

In a sense, phonology is the first impression we have when exposed to a new language. Before we understand anything that is being said, we are exposed to an undifferentiated babble of speech sounds. These are at first uninterpretable **auditory** impressions; only gradually do we learn how to break up, or break down, the stream of speech into interpretable units. At first, all that is heard by one unfamiliar with a new language is a kind of babble (though to the speaker it is sensible language) that I will represent as semi-random (i.e. partially repeated) strings of utterables as follows:

balabalabalee ablabla bloblee blablee papeepa blablablee

What is it that differentiates language from babbling or other kinds of **vocalizations** which would not normally be considered language? It is the possibility of tying the sounds (and the accompanying silent periods) to regular patterns of meaning. Spoken language is a combination or interplay of noises and silences generated by the speech mechanism and mutually arranged in regular and meaningful patterns. At a very early stage of acquiring their first language, children learn how to use 'babbling-like sounds' to express their feelings and other 'broad' communicative meanings such as 'request' or 'interest' (Vihman 1993: 67). At a later stage, speech sounds are combined in regular ways into meaningful units such as words, phrases, clauses and sentences.

Phonology is describable as (the study of) the regular, meaningful patterning of vocalizations in language. Phonology includes two levels, or aspects, of analysis and description. On one level, the phonology of a language can be described in terms of the individual sounds which speakers use to form words and larger utterances. When we describe the phonology of a language in this way, we are taking a **segmental** perspective. The segmental features, or segments, of a language are its consonants and vowels and any component sounds of which these are made. Chapters 2 and 3 focus on consonants and vowels, respectively.

Although this way of describing spoken language matches well with the facts of written language – which for English employs individual alphabetic symbols to represent sounds, as illustrated in detail in Chapter 5 – it is in fact a considerable abstraction from the reality of pronunciation, which is an essentially continuous and non-discrete phenomenon. Although it is quite convenient to be able to record and describe spoken language in terms of a string of symbols, a segmental description in fact artificially breaks up the relatively continuous stream of sound that is language and arbitrarily assigns small bits of ever-shifting sound waves to individual symbols.

From a broader, more global – and more physically accurate – perspective, the phonology of a language can be described in terms of features which span more than one segment. In this style of description, spoken language is characterized in terms of its **transsegmental** (or **suprasegmental**) properties, or **prosodics**. The prosodic aspects of speech include such properties as **duration**, **rhythm**, **stress**, **pitch**, **intonation** and **loudness**. These and related properties of connected speech will be dealt with in Chapter 4. A complete **phonological description** of a language will comprise descriptions of both its segmental and transsegmental characteristics.

The two levels of phonology are hierarchically related in that the prosodic, or transsegmental, aspect forms the framework and the basis for the segmental aspect. This is because the transsegmental properties of speech span more than one segment, across stretches of speech. Thus, while explicit attention in teaching to the segmental aspects of phonology can make only piecemeal improvements, attention to the prosodic aspects can make global and sequential improvements to the whole stream of speech, i.e. across neighboring segmental sounds.

The prosodic aspect can also be thought of as a deeper and more primal aspect of phonology because it is more directly related to the breath stream which drives the whole speech mechanism. This is because the amount of breath produced and the exact nature of the breath stream coming up from the lungs and entering the vocal tract directly determines the prosodic properties of speech (within the limits of a given individual's voice). From this perspective, the most basic unit of speech production is taken to be the **breath group** (Lieberman 1967), which defines a continuous stretch of speech produced on one breath. According to Lieberman (1986):

> The *breath-group* is the primary element that people use to segment the flow of speech into sentence-like units. The breath-group is organized about . . . constraints of respiration and the physiology of the lungs and layrnx. Its primary elements can be seen in the initial

cries of the newborn infants [sic] and follow from the articulatory and respiratory maneuvers that are necessary to sustain life. Its full linguistic expression, however, involves behavioral patterns that are not present at birth, i.e., a complex pattern of articulatory control that involves reference to the probable length of a sentence **before** a sound is uttered. . . . [italics and boldface in original] (p. 240)

A message is therefore planned in relation to an expiration of breath, which delimits the amount of speech that will be produced and perceived as a unified utterance under one prosodic contour (e.g. intonational and rhythmic pattern). Once the prosodic aspect is determined, then the breath stream is further modified within the vocal tract, beginning at the larynx, to make all of the modifications needed to produce individual sounds and modifications of these. The hierarchical relationships of these three components of breath, prosodic phonology and segmental phonology can be represented as in Figure 1.1.

The speech mechanism

Speech can be described in a general way as a human form of communication in which the organs of speech, the **vocal organs**, are used to generate patterns of sound that have meaningful associations. On a very basic level, all speech starts out as "silent air", i.e. as a breath stream. In

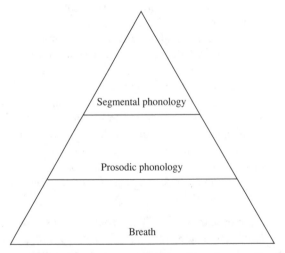

FIGURE 1.1 Hierarchical relationship of breath, prosodic phonology and
            segmental phonology

the production of speech, molecules of air coming up from the lungs are rearranged by the movement of the vocal organs and exit the vocal tract as a type of **pressure wave** called a **sound wave**. This sound wave travels through the air surrounding the speaker and may reach the ears of another person, creating a sensation of sound, before it degenerates to become plain air again. The sounds which make up speech can therefore be described on one level as:

(a) a column of air
(b) whose shape or character is modified
(c) by the shape and the other properties of the surfaces that it meets and the spaces that it passes through
(d) as it travels along a path to become, ultimately, just air again.

At a very basic level, the speech mechanism has just three components: **air**, some type of **resistance** or **obstruction** which impinges on the air and so makes a sound of some kind, and some kind of **amplification** to make the sound loud enough for humans to hear it easily. To be a little more specific, speech can be modeled in terms of the diagram in Figure 1.2.

The air starts out in the lungs of the speaker, then travels up through the **trachea**, or windpipe, through the **larynx**, past the **epiglottis**, and into the **pharynx**. As the air moves through the larynx and into the pharynx, it passes into the **vocal tract**, which comprises the air passageways used for speech. From the pharynx, the airstream goes into either the mouth or the nose. The organs within the vocal tract, the **articulators**, may be used to modify the shape and character of the airstream coming up from the lungs. This column of air, which has now been altered in its journey from the lungs and through the vocal tract, exits the nose or the mouth and travels into the surrounding air, where it may reach the ears of some other person and be heard as language.

To summarize, the speech mechanism is an air-driven mechanism. Two basic categories of sounds are possible, depending on where the air exits the vocal tract: **nasal** and **oral**. In the production of nasal sounds such as [m] (as in the initial sound of *mouth*) and [n] (as in the initial sound of *nose*), air exits the nose. In the production of oral

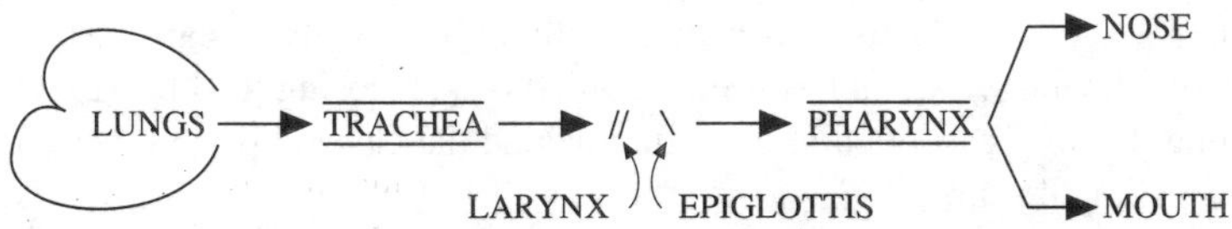

FIGURE 1.2 Simplified model of the speech mechanism

sounds such as [f] (as in the initial sound of *face*) and [g] (as in the initial sound of *give*), the air coming up from the lungs exits the mouth.

The mouth is much more flexible and malleable than the nose, and, as a consequence, is used in the production of nearly all variations in human speech sounds. Humans can make very precise modifications in the place and shape of the **articulation** of sounds by variably using different parts of the tongue, the lips, the teeth and the upper surfaces of the mouth which lie between the teeth and the back of the throat. We will learn more about these possibilities in the next chapter.

The larynx and voicing

The **larynx** is a very important vocal organ which contains two very tiny muscles down in the throat that can create a sound – though a very faint, weak sound – by vibrating. Though it is a tiny organ, all speech is described with reference to what the larynx is doing. The larynx itself or the muscles inside it are called by several different terms, including **voice box**, **vocal bands**, **vocal folds** and **vocal cords**. The vocal cords are housed inside the protective cartilage familiarly known as the "Adam's Apple".

You can see in the alternate names for the muscles of the larynx the analogy to rubber bands or to the cords of a musical instrument. Raising the pitch of the voice involves tightening the muscles of the larynx, and lowering the pitch of the voice means loosening them. If you loosen them too much, you will actually lose voice completely, as the cords are too slack to sustain vibration.

The larynx is completely closed when swallowing. When breathing normally or resting, it is slack and open, so that air can go in and out of the space between the muscles. The space, or opening, between the muscles is called the **glottis**. The shape and size of the glottis has a dramatic effect on the sound which is produced and ultimately heard as speech. An oval-shaped elastic band is a good visual model of the vocal cords, with the hole in the middle representing the glottis.

For some segmental speech sounds, the larynx is open and air just passes through the slack vocal cords. The air is later modified in the mouth to make a particular sound. An example is the consonant [p], as in *put* or *supper*. This consonant is nothing but air (the **breath stream** from the lungs) which has been modified by (1) closing the lips, (2) letting the air pressure build up a little behind the closed lips and then (3) expelling the air.

The type of sound represented by [p], which involves only a modification of the shape of the column of air coming up through the open glottis, is called **voiceless**. Another example of a voiceless consonant is [f]. Like [p], [f] is nothing but a breath of stream with a certain modification of that column of air in the mouth. This time the modification involves not the two lips, but rather the top teeth and the bottom lip.

For another major class of speech sounds, the vocal folds are brought close together and tightened, narrowing the glottis. When air passes through the narrowed glottis, the vocal folds vibrate and make a sound, called a **vocal buzz**. This is a very faint sound caused by the vibrating vocal cords. This basic vocal buzz is later amplified in the **resonance chamber** – of the mouth (the **oral chamber**) and/or the nose (the **nasal chamber**). Speech sounds produced with vibrating vocal cords are referred to as **voiced**.

An example of a voiced consonant is [b]. Like [p], [b] is produced by bringing the two lips together and then releasing the air built up behind that closure. Unlike [p], however, the vocal folds are vibrating during the production of [b]. Similarly, [v] differs from [f] only in the fact that [f] is produced without vocal fold vibration, while [v] requires vocal fold vibration for its production. If you put your hands over your ears or touch your Adam's Apple as you alternate prolonged productions of [f] and [v], you should be able to hear and feel the vocal cords turning on and off their vibration (Ladefoged 1982: 2). You can also hear the difference between voiced and voiceless sounds very clearly by producing a sustained vowel sound such as [aaaa] and then pronouncing the same vowel in a whispered manner. The normal vowel is voiced; the whispered vowel is voiceless. When not whispered, all vowels in English (and most languages) are voiced. Consonants may be either voiced or voiceless.

For both voiced and voiceless sounds, the nature of the basic sound at the glottis – either the buzz or the naked puff of air coming up from the lungs – is modified in the oral chamber, with or without coupling to the nasal chamber. There are many, many possible modifications, as will be introduced in the next three chapters.

Phonetics and phonology

Phonology is the study and description of the patterning of the noises and silences of speech in regular ways within particular languages. **Phonetics** is the study and description of the nature of the raw noises and silences of speech. Phonetics is thus the basis for phonology, and phonology can be said to build on phonetics and to be a more general and abstract pursuit than phonetics.

We language teachers are primarily interested in phonology, that is, in the patterns of sounds which make up speech. However, we must also concern ourselves with phonetics, which is the basis for phonology. If the characteristics of individual speech sounds are carefully investigated and precisely described phonetically, then we will be on a firm basis for investigating and describing how the individual sounds pattern within a given language.

Phonetic differences large and small are important in the phonology of languages. Consider the production of the initial consonant sounds, or **phones**, below:

sip/ship   a small difference in lip and tongue position

For English, the distinction between the initial consonant phones in these words forms a **minimal pair**, i.e. a pair of words which differ in lexical meaning based on a difference in one sound. This difference in sound is said to be **phonemic**, and not merely phonetic, because it is tied to lexical meaning differences in the language in question, which in this case is English. In general, speakers of a language do not notice differences in sound which are not tied to meaning, i.e. which are not phonemic.

Now although the distinctions among the initial consonants of these examples are important from the point of view of meaning distinctions in English, i.e. when viewed **phonemically**, those distinctions are rather small from a phonetic point of view. In addition, the phonemic distinction between this pair of consonant phones does not necessarily exist in other languages. For speakers of such languages wanting to acquire English phonology, the distinction has to be learned.

The same differences in pronunciation represented by the contrast *ship/sip* is only phonetic, and not phonemic, in some other languages. In such cases, the difference in sound does not signal a difference in lexical meaning (though it may signal some kind of difference in social meaning). For example, the difference in pronunciation of the initial sounds of *ship* and *sip*, while phonemic for English, is not for Japanese. As a consequence, a Japanese learner will only gradually come to detect and to produce a difference in the initial sounds of these words.

A **phoneme** is a phone or a group of phones which contrasts with another phoneme in a minimal pair. Phones, written between square brackets, represent the exact pronunciation of a sound. Phonemes, written between slant lines, represent the category of a sound and are an abstraction from the details of actual pronunciation. The phonemes of a language are the basic units, or building blocks, of all higher units, i.e. individual morphemes and longer utterances.

The initial sounds of *ship* and *sip* are two different phonemes in English, written /š/ and /s/. In Japanese, they are two different phones, [š] and [s], which are **phonetic variants** (or **allophones**) of the same phoneme, /s/. The Japanese phoneme /s/ is pronounced [š] before certain vowels and [s] before other vowels. This means that [š] and [s] are **positional variants** of /s/ in Japanese. In contrast, in English both [š] and [s] can occur before any vowel. They are therefore two separate categories of consonants, i.e. two separate phonemes. An English speaker can therefore easily distinguish the difference between these sounds in any context, while a Japanese speaker may not be able to.

Points of contrast with the native language – either in terms of its inventory of phonemes or in terms of the exact phonetic details of pronunciation of a certain phoneme, i.e. its phonetic variants – are bound to cause problems for those learning a new language. In many cases, the second language has two phonemes where the native language has only one, as in the case of /š/ and /s/ just discussed. As another example, while English has both /r/ and /l/ phonemes, many Asian languages have only one of these – often one which combines the phonetic properties of [r] and [l] phones into one phoneme. In such cases, the language learner must learn to make new meaningful distinctions between sounds.

Even when two languages have the same phonemes in common, the phonemes in the first language may be phonetically close but not identical to the phonemes in the second language, so that the language learner tends to substitute the native language sounds for the slightly different second language sounds. For example, /t/ and /d/ are pronounced in some languages and some varieties of English with the tip of the tongue touching the back of the upper front teeth, whereas in other languages and varieties of English, the usual pronunciation of these sounds is with the tip of the tongue on the gum ridge just behind the upper front teeth, rather than touching them. As another example, in the initial position in a word, English /p/, /t/ and /k/ tend to be rather breathy as compared to these same phonemes in some other languages. Learning to recognize and to produce such distinctions can make the difference between a non-native and native-like accent.

Since learning is an incremental process which builds on previous knowledge, in an early stage of second language acquisition, the pronunciation of a language learner is likely to be heavily influenced by transfer of the native phonological patterns to the pronunciation of the target language. During the period of second language development, we can expect that the non-native speaker will for a time show variation between those phonetic variants transferred from the native language and those which are being learned through exposure to the second language. In the case of speakers who have already learned one or more languages beyond the native language, transfer from those languages can be expected as well. Only gradually can the learner be expected to acquire the patterns of the target language phonology, including the **range of variation** (e.g. between casual and formal styles of speaking) that is typical of native speech.

The effect of linguistic context on pronunciation

Coarticulation and assimilation

In addition to the general effects of communicative context on pronunciation, the strictly linguistic context of neighboring sounds influences the pronunciation of a given segment or stretch of speech. In connected speech, sounds are **coarticulated** to a greater or lesser degree. **Coarticulation** means that one sound, rather than being produced entirely distinctly from other sounds with which it occurs, tends to blend imperceptibly into the next.

To take a historical case, the Latin prefix *in-* ('not') was attached to a number of adjectives in the history of the English language, forming the negative of the original word, or stem. The combination of *in-* + Adjective proceeded according to phonological principles dictating that the prefix *in-* would be altered for ease of pronunciation when attached to adjectives beginning with certain sounds. For example:

(1) *in-* + an adjective beginning with *p*, *b* or *m* became *im-*, as in *impossible*, *imbalance*, *immature*;
(2) *in-* + an adjective beginning with *r* became *ir-*, as in *irrational*, *irredeemable*, *irregular*;
(3) *in-* + an adjective beginning with *l* became *il-*, as in *illiterate*, *illogical*, *illegitimate*.

As these examples show, historically the prefix *in-* was altered in certain specifiable environments according to the preferred sound patterns of the language. The regularity of the attachment process matching the pronunciation of the final consonant of the prefix to the initial consonant of the adjective to which it was attached can be described as the result of a phonological process. For this historical example, such a process has two cases. In the case of words beginning with *m*, *r* and *l*, the initial sound of the adjective was fully matched, i.e. **assimilated**, by the prefix *in-*. In the case of words beginning with *p* or *b*, the

assimilation – i.e. the match between the initial sound of the adjective and the final sound of the prefix – was only partial. Phonological processes result in phonetic variants of phonemes which occur in different positions and under different conditions of occurrence.

In general, we will find that pronunciation is highly **variable** and changes a great deal depending on the linguistic context. The amount of contextual alteration of sounds in many varieties of English is considerable, in part because in many English speech contexts, it would be unusual for a speaker to pause very frequently and to clearly distinguish between individual words for the audience. In fact, it is common in English for speakers to **elide** individual words, i.e. to run words together, in casual, non-emphatic speech. This tendency to **elision** has transsegmental effects on speech, as we will see in Chapter 4.

For example, the combination *going + to* may be run together in pronunciation in a way that might be impressionistically written in "pronunciation-spelling" as "gonna" or "gunna". It is very likely that a beginning student would at first interpret this item "gonna"/"gunna" as a single word since the two parts are reduced and run together to make a single auditory unit. Phonologically speaking, we can say that an item like "gunna" forms a **phonological word**, i.e. a combination of sounds spoken as one continuous stream of speech bounded by pauses. An important feature of English is the lack of one-to-one correspondence between a "word", lexically defined, and a "word", phonologically defined.

The need for a special symbol system for representing speech sounds

As the example of *going to* and many others show, in normal English conversation, words are run together and many kinds of contextual processes apply to change the pronunciation of words which would be pronounced in a different way in isolation. It is therefore extremely imprecise to represent English pronunciation in terms of the spelling of words and a poor strategy to try to learn English pronunciation from the written language. The spelling system provides only a rough approximation to the actual pronunciation of lexical items in context. Moreover, as we will see in Chapter 5, English spelling, or **orthography**, does not follow one consistent system of correspondences with pronunciation.

To represent the sounds and the sound patterns of a language in accurate, consistent terms, a special system of symbols and conventions for using these symbols is needed. An unanalyzed, auditory-impressionistic style of transcription, in which the transcriber attempts to write exactly what he or she hears (whether or not it is fully understood) is called **phonetic transcription**. In phonetic transcription, the individual phones are written as alphabetic symbols, in addition to other kinds of symbols or **diacritic** markings, between square brackets, as in [p], [f], [t̪], [š], [ə], [oˑ], etc. Prosody is represented by marks and lines which are written above the segmental transcription, as in:

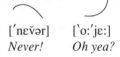

['nɛv̌ər]   [ˋoːˊjɛː]
Never!   *Oh yea?*

As developed by the International Phonetic Association, phonetic transcription is a kind of uniform and universal way of writing based strictly on sound. It is very useful for describing, analyzing and contrasting languages. Since writing systems vary widely in the way of representing the sounds of a language, it is essential to have a common writing system – one that has been abstracted from actual languages – for the description of sounds. Besides teaching you how to represent sounds correctly, transcription also helps you train your ear so that you can pick up more detail from whatever stream of speech you are listening to.

A less detailed form of transcription, indicating only the major categories of sounds in a language and none of the details of pronunciation, is called **phonemic transcription**. Phonemic transcription uses a subset of the symbols for phonetic transcription. When we are transcribing on a general level or wish to represent a sound in a general way without describing the details of its pronunciation, we are transcribing phonemes rather than phones and write the phonemes between slant lines to indicate this. The nature of the English consonant and vowel phonemes and of the transcriptional systems used to represent sounds will be dealt with in detail in this book, beginning in the next chapter.

Introductory activities

1. Views on pronunciation learning and teaching

Compare and contrast your own views on the learning and/or teaching of pronunciation with those of others in terms of the value of pronunciation teaching and the best approach to learning or teaching pronunciation. If you or others you know are currently involved in the learning or teaching of pronunciation or speaking skills more generally, what are the similarities and differences in your experiences?

2. Prestige varieties of English

Which accent(s) of English do you think could be viewed as indicative of social prestige? Do people in different locales recognize different varieties of English as prestigious? Are there any that you think are associated with negative values such as lack of education or low social status? How do you think an accent comes to be associated with social values?

3. Teaching the standard language

What is the purpose of teaching the standard language rather than some other variety? Are there cases where it would be appropriate to teach a combination of the standard language and some other variety or varieties? Can you think of any situations in which it would not be appropriate to focus in instruction on the standard language? Are there any situations in which it is not appropriate to teach the standard language at all?

4. Sociolinguistic variation in pronunciation

Give examples from your own experience of different standards of pronunciation associated with (a)–(g) below.

(a) different countries, regions within one country or neighborhoods within one city
(b) speakers of different ages
(c) speakers who differ in the character of their social networks
(d) male and female speakers
(e) close or distant relationship of the speakers
(f) familiarity to speakers of the topic of conversation
(g) formal vs. informal context or function (e.g. speech in front of an audience vs. casual conversation with friends)

5. Comparison of own and other varieties of English

List some characteristics of the accent of English that you speak and compare these to the characteristics of one or more accents of English other than your own. Practice speaking 2–3 sentences in English with these other accents.

6. Stereotyped phonological features

In research on **stereotyped markers** of English pronunciation, Zuengler (1988) found the American English /r/ to be the most salient feature of an American accent for native speakers of Mexican Spanish. What are some of the other stereotyped markers which might be associated with American English pronunciation? What stereotypes might be applied to other English varieties?

7. Classification of voiced and voiceless sounds

Go through the letters of the alphabet, focusing on the sounds represented by each letter, to decide which of these are voiced and which voiceless. List the two types in two columns, then check your answers with another person.

VOICED SOUNDS	VOICELESS SOUNDS
(vocal folds vibrating)	(vocal folds not vibrating)

8. Sociolinguistic mini-research: pronunciation attitudes

Develop a research project in which you and/or your students will survey members of your community, other teachers or students to determine their views on English pronunciation in the community and/or the world at large. Try to determine which groups of speakers or well-known individuals in the community and/or the world at large are thought to have:

the best pronunciation of English
the worst pronunciation of English

the type of English pronunciation that is easiest to understand
the type of English pronunciation that is hardest to understand

the type of English pronunciation that is the easiest to imitate or learn to speak oneself

the type of English pronunciation that is the hardest to imitate or learn to speak oneself
the most old-fashioned or conservative English pronunciation
the most modern or innovative English pronunciation

the most typical or common English pronunciation
the most atypical or uncommon English pronunciation

the type of English pronunciation that is the most useful to learn to speak
the type of English pronunciation that is the least useful to learn to speak

the type of English pronunciation that is the most useful to learn to understand the type of English pronunciation that is the least useful to learn to understand

To obtain comparable responses and systematic results, it will be useful to develop a set of survey questions in advance. These can then be given to respondents for a written reply or used as a guide in face-to-face questioning of individual respondents. For a more in-depth survey, respondents can be encouraged to give comments which elaborate on their answers by explaining how they interpret "best", "worst", "easiest to understand", etc., and by trying to give reasons for their opinions.

In analyzing the survey results, you should try to group responses of a similar type. For example, different individual speakers whom respondents mention as having the same type of pronunciation ("best", "worst", etc.) can be classified according to characteristics such as their age, socieconomic class, educational level, type of job, geographical or national origin, etc. In this way, it might be possible to find some common characteristics associated with those individuals or social groups mentioned as having one or another type of pronunciation.

In interpreting your results, it will probably be interesting to categorize respondents by their similar characteristics – e.g. same ethnic or national background, same first language background, same socio-economic and/or educational level, same gender group, same age group – and then to compare and contrast the responses of those with similar characteristics to those who are classified in different categories – e.g. graduate vs. non-graduate, male vs. female, older vs. younger people. It is likely that respondents with different social or background characteristics will show different response patterns.

After you have compared the responses of the different groups, consider what they imply about the standards for English that exist among community members, teachers or students in your survey context. For example, do speakers recognize and agree on one variety of English as a prestige norm (the best English)? Is this the same as the variety which is perceived as most useful to learn as a spoken variety? If there is a conflict between the prestige norm and those varieties seen as most useful and easiest to acquire, how is this resolved in daily life or practice? Is there any evidence of a covert norm for English that is different from the overt prestige norm? In other words, do any varieties seem to have covert prestige – e.g. because they are mentioned as most useful or easiest to learn or to understand, while at the same time viewed as the "worst" type of pronunciation by some respondents?

9. Action research: students' awareness of English phonology

Develop an action research project to evaluate and then to expand or improve your students' awareness and understanding of different geographical accents or speaking styles (e.g. casual vs. careful pronunciation) in English. In order to assess your students' awareness and understanding of accents or speaking styles, use taped speech samples to which students respond by means of a cloze or multiple choice exercise, listening comprehension questions, or some other method of checking their recognition and comprehension of the different accents or speaking styles presented. You may then use the same taped material – or other material such as television or video programs – as the basis for exercises to increase the students' recognition and comprehension.

As in all action research, you will want to regularly monitor the effectiveness of the project and, after a certain period of time, retest the students to check their progress, making any necessary adjustments in the schedule of activities. At the end of the project, you will want to do a thorough evaluation of its success and of any difficulties encountered as a guide to future teaching in this area.

10. Action research: introductory teaching ideas

Try one or more of the teaching ideas below in a class, customizing and elaborating the exercise as needed, and then analyze and assess the results. If the results are not as you intended, speculate on the causes of the unintended outcomes. If the teaching idea is not successful, try to analyze the reasons that it did not work well, then make adjustments and try again or select a different one of the teaching ideas to try out. If it is successful, make a note of why it worked well and consider doing a follow-up activity that builds on its positive outcomes.

You may carry out the action research in one or your own classes or comparatively in two different classes. For this purpose, it could be of value to work as a research partner with another teacher, if this can be arranged. If you choose this option, one of you might try out the teaching idea(s) while the other observes and takes notes on the class and then afterwards assists in assessing the results. Or, both teachers might try out the same or different teaching idea(s), either simultaneously or in sequence, comparing the results in the two classes and speculating on the reasons for similarities and differences in experiences.

An advantage of carrying out the research sequentially, first in one class and then in another, is that the second application can build on the experience gained from the first tryout. As the first application of a new teaching idea does not always go smoothly, having a chance to adjust, redesign and retry a teaching idea – or to shift to a different idea and try that out – will maximize the experience gained from the action research.

Introductory teaching ideas

1. Breath control

Work on controlling the expenditure of breath in speaking is a useful introductory activity for students at any level of proficiency since it is breath that drives the whole speech mechanism. Breathing activities can increase the volume of air expended in speaking the second language and improve airflow in whole utterances, resulting in such effects as:

- Utterance of units larger than individual words on one breath, avoiding "choppiness" and enhancing the natural coarticulatory effects of neighboring sounds.
- A louder voice, which adds to overall understandability of speech, lowering of inhibitions and a stronger presentation of self.

  Some students speak their second language in a more timid or softer voice than they normally use in their native language. They are therefore hard to hear, and the difficulty of understanding non-native pronunciation is magnified. Reduced volume in the voice may also give an impression of being shy or lacking confidence, thus possibly further discouraging interaction by native speakers.
- More control over speech rhythm, which makes it easier for native speakers to segment the flow of speech into comprehensible units.
- Stronger productions of individual speech sounds – e.g. more resonant vowels and more carefully articulated consonants.

Activities for increasing the control and volume of breath expended for speech might include the following:

(a) Preliminary breathing exercises to control inhaling and exhaling, e.g. inhaling and exhaling on a count of 5–8 seconds each or in time to music.

  This rhythmic breathing activity can be accompanied, as is often done in exercise classes, by body movements such as bending down during the exhale and coming back up to an erect standing position during the inhale.
(b) Saying a vowel on one breath, beginning softly, then after 10 seconds pushing out all the remaining air from the lungs forcefully while holding the vowel sound.

Since the loudness of the voice will automatically increase when the air is forcefully pushed out of the lungs, this is a memorable demonstration of the relationship of force of articulation to loudness.

(c) Saying a sentence on one breath, progressively increasing its length, as in the following example:
- Meet me tonight.
- Meet me tonight at 7:00 pm.
- Meet me tonight at 7:00 pm under the oak tree.
- Meet me tonight at 7:00 pm under the oak tree behind the house.
- Meet me tonight at 7:00 pm under the oak tree behind the house across from the school.
- Meet me tonight at 7:00 pm under the oak tree behind the house across from the school and don't forget to bring the money!

This activity can also be done as a team line activity in which team members progressively add the additional elements to the basic sentence and in which points are deducted for every pause taken during the utterances.

(d) Uttering a sentence across the room which students on the other side of the room must hear and respond to by performing the requested action, e.g. *The tallest student will walk to the blackboard and pick up a piece of chalk.*

This can be done as a team exercise forming two lines of students across a room facing each other, with individuals from each team taking turns speaking their sentence across the room one by one, beginning with the first person in line on one of the teams. Individual members of the other team or the team as a whole try to decipher the sentence and to perform the requested action. If they succeed, then each team and the individual who spoke the sentence receive the same number of points as there are words in the sentence. If they do not succeed, then no points are awarded. The turn then moves to the first person in line on the opposite team. After everyone on each team has had one or more turns, the scores are tallied to determine which team and which individual are the winners.

Speaking across a room requires a considerable expenditure of breath and is therefore an excellent activity for increasing breath flow and breath control, loudness, clarity and awareness of these features of voice in relation to the comprehensibility of speech.

2. Prosodic awareness

Getting students to focus on the general prosodic characteristics of speech can assist in comprehension and may be of benefit in helping the student to notice how the pronunciation of individual sounds and words are affected by context. Activities to help students at any level of proficiency focus on pitch and rhythm might include having them:

(a) Pronounce a vowel or a one-syllable word several times, beginning on the lowest note possible and increasing the pitch each time so as to end on the highest note possible.
(b) Mimic only the rhythmic or pitch pattern of an utterance (tape-recorded or spoken by the teacher), using a sequence such as [dadadada . . .] or [lalalala . . .] to carry the pitch or rhythmic contour.
(c) Mimic the rhythmic or pitch pattern of an utterance in English vs. another language, using sequences of syllables such as in (b) to carry the pitch or rhythmic contour.
(d) Clap or tap in time to the main beats in a series of phrases or sentences; this activity can be devised so that a basic sentence containing three or four main rhythmic beats is progressively extended by adding endings or words which do not recieve a main beat, starting from the leftmost or the rightmost word in the sentence, as in:
   • KIDS DRINK MILK.
   • The KIDS DRINK MILK.
   • The KIDS want to DRINK MILK.
   • The KIDS want to DRINK some MILK.

   • FRED LEFT HOME.
   • FRED LEFT his HOME.
   • FRED has just LEFT his HOME.
   • Little FRED has just LEFT his HOME.

3. Awareness of language varieties

General work on different accents and speech styles can provide a good starting point for pronunciation lessons designed for intermediate or advanced students. Introducing students to a variety of accents can help them to achieve some important initial goals, such as the following:

• increase flexibility and control of their own performance;
• increase awareness of the range of variation possible in the target language;
• increase knowledge of and, consequently, interest in the target culture and its speakers;

- increase ability to comprehend the pronunciation of words and phrases in context;
- lower inhibitions and resistance to adopting a native-like speaking style in the second language;
- develop a distinctive and comfortable persona when speaking the target language.

Work on accents might include the following activities:

(a) Listening to selections of natural speech (e.g. from the radio or television) by speakers from different regions and trying to identify the region according to the accent.
(b) Comparing and contrasting the features of pronunciation of different native and non-native speakers reading the same passage aloud.
(c) Imitating the accent of speakers from different regions and having other students guess which accent is being portrayed.
(d) Imitating the accent of a famous person who is a native speaker of the target language and having the other students guess who is being portrayed.

 Students can do "research" for this task by watching news broadcasts, television shows or films to practice the accents of the stars of those programs or movies.
(e) Imitating the accent of speakers of the student's native language speaking the target language.
(f) Imitating the accent of speakers of the target language speaking the student's native language.

4. Integration of phonology in a larger context of communication

As an extension or follow-up to the activities in exercise 3 above, students might be asked to roleplay a typical situation in which one of the people imitated might be engaged, carefully selecting the topic of conversation, the gestures, the facial expressions and the movements which might normally accompany the speech of that person. In this way, students will begin to see that pronunciation is an integral part of the larger communicational complex of social and linguistic meaning.

2 Consonants

Characteristics of consonants

The nature of consonants

Consonants are sounds made with closed or nearly closed articulations. As a consequence, they tend to break up the stream up speech, defining a perceptual and articulatory "edge", or **margin**, for a unit (word or syllable in a word) that includes one or more vowels. Complex margins are made of two or more consonants. In English, both initial and final margins may include multiple consonants – up to three initially and up to four finally, as in:

/p/	*pill*	/sp/	*spill*	/pr/	*pram*	/spr/	*spray*
/t/	*till*	/st/	*still*	/tr/	*tram*	/str/	*stray*
/k/	*kill*	/sk/	*skill*	/kr/	*cram*	/skr/	*scray*
/p/	*sap*	/lp/	*whelp*	/rp/	*harp*		
/t/	*sat*	/lt/	*welt*	/rt/	*heart*		
/k/	*sack*	/lk/	*whelk*	/rk/	*hark*		
		/lps/	*whelps*	/rps/	*corpse*		
		/lts/	*welts*	/rts/	*courts*		
		/lks/	*whelks*	/rks/	*corks*		
		/lpt/	*sculpt*	/rst/	*burst*		
		/lpts/	*sculpts*	/rsts/	*bursts*		

The number and complexity of cluster types in English presents an area of difficulty for many non-native speakers.

Place of articulation

The vocal tract is divided into different regions which are used to describe the place of articulation of individual consonants and vowels, i.e. segmental sounds. The terms for the vocal organs and regions used for the production of speech sounds are shown in Figure 2.1. The locations of these organs and regions are shown in Figure 2.2.

Vocal organs and articulatory regions (nouns)	Adjectives
nose	nasal
mouth	oral
lips	labial
teeth	dental
alveoli (*or* alveolar ridge *or* gum ridge)	alveolar
(hard) palate	palatal
velum (*or* soft palate)	velar
pharynx	pharyngeal
uvula	uvular
larynx (*or* vocal folds)	laryngeal
glottis	glottal

Tongue:

apex (or tip)	apical
blade	blade
side	lateral
front	front (laminal)
center	central
back	back
root	root

FIGURE 2.1 Names of vocal organs and articulatory regions

Speech articulations are made primarily in the oral chamber, or **oral tract**, that is, in the area between the epiglottis and the lips. The most forward, or **front**, position in the oral tract is at the lips. The farthest **back** position in the oral tract is at the uvula.

Articulation refers to the movement of one or more vocal organs in the production of speech. Every speech sound is produced by the movement of at least one vocal organ or part of a vocal organ, called the **active articulator**. The articulation of many sounds involves two articulators and their orientation or action in relation to each other. In some cases, two articulators are active. In other cases, one active articulator and one **passive articulator** are involved. The active articulator moves, while the passive articulator is stationary. The tongue, for example, is an active articulator, while the roof of the mouth (**palate**) is a passive articulator. The **place of articulation** is defined by the location of an active articulator functioning alone or in concert with another articulator.

Starting at one end of the vocal tract, **labial** sounds are produced by the action of one or both lips. **Bilabial** sounds involve the lips as two active articulators coming together. There are four bilabial phonemes in English: /m/ (*m*ill), /w/ (*w*ill), /b/ (*b*ill) and /p/ (*p*ill). The first three of these are voiced, the last is voiceless. That is, /m/, /w/ and /b/ are

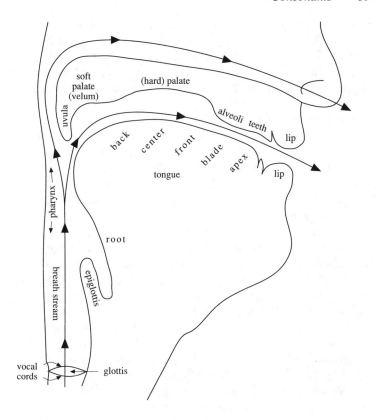

FIGURE 2.2 Diagram of vocal organs and articulatory regions

produced with vocal cord vibration, while /p/ is not. The bottom lip can also function as an active articulator in concert with the stationary top teeth in making **labiodental** sounds. There are two labiodental phonemes in English, /f/ (*f*an) and /v/ (*v*an). /f/ is the voiceless labiodental phoneme; /v/ is the voiced labiodental phoneme.

The tongue is the most important of all articulators in speech because it is the one by which most speech sounds are made. The tongue is divided into different parts for the description of speech sounds. The **apex** or **tip** is the frontmost part of the tongue, and the **blade** is the part of the tongue immediately behind the tip. At the opposite end is the tongue **root**, where it attaches down near the epiglottis. When the tongue is in its resting position, the part of the tongue under the back part of the roof of the mouth is called the **back**, the part under the center is called the **center**, and the part under the front is called the **front**. In a resting position of the tongue, the front part lies under the **pre-palatal** region of the roof of the mouth, while the more forward portion of the tongue blade and tip lie under the **alveoli**, or **gum ridge**, behind the top teeth.

For **interdental** sounds, the tongue is the active articulator. The sounds are made by putting the tongue between the teeth so that the blade is extended just forward of the teeth. The interdental phonemes are /θ/ as in (*th*in) and /ð/ (*th*en). The symbol for the first of these phonemes, which is voiceless, is the Greek letter, **theta**, /θ/. The symbol for the second of these phonemes, which is voiced, is the Germanic letter, **eth**, /ð/. (The theta can be typed by putting a hyphen in the middle of a capital letter *O*. The eth can be typed as a *d* with a hyphen across it.)

Alveolar consonants are those produced with the tip or blade of the tongue in position at the alveolar ridge. English has six alveolar phonemes. The voiced alveolar consonants are: /n/ (*n*ip), /d/ (*d*ip), /z/ (*z*ip) and /l/ (*l*ip). The voiceless alveolar consonants are: /t/ (*t*ip) and /s/ (*s*ip). Alveolar consonants may be pronounced with either the tongue tip or blade. In the latter case, the apex is down at the back of the lower teeth. Try making an /s/ in these two ways. The sound is still recognizable as /s/ no matter which way you make it because the tongue actively articulates on the gum ridge. The difference is only in which part of the tongue is involved, the apex or the blade. In the first case the apex is up behind the teeth, in the second case, the apex is not involved – it is resting as it were, and the blade is the active articulator. This difference between apical and blade articulation for /s/ is the kind of difference which is phonetic, but not phonemic, for English.

The roof of the mouth is referred to as the **palatal** region. The area on the back of the alveoli, as they ascend to the palate, is the **pre-palatal** region. English has five phonemes produced at a pre-palatal place of articulation by the active articulation of the tongue blade touching or nearly touching the region where the alveoli join the front of the palate. Two of these are voiceless. One of the voiceless pre-palatal consonants is symbolized by *s*-**wedge**, i.e. /š/ (ma*sh*). The other voiceless pre-palatal consonant is symbolized by a *c*-wedge, i.e. /č/ (ma*tch*). Of the voiced pre-palatal consonants, one is a relatively rare sound in English, represented by a *z*-wedge, i.e. /ž/(a*z*ure), while the other two are common sounds, represented by *j*-wedge, i.e. /ǰ/ (*judge*), and plain *r*, i.e. /r/ (*r*ed).

The main part of the palate, in the center of the roof of the mouth, is referred to as the **hard palate**, whereas the soft area at the back is called

the **soft palate**, or **velum**. There is only one **palatal** consonant phoneme in English, represented by the letter *j*, i.e. /j/ (*y*ellow). This voiced
consonant is produced with the front of the tongue as the active articulator pushing against the front of the palate (and/or the center of the palate). English has three **velar** consonants: /k/ (*c*ut), /g/ (*g*ut) and /ŋ/
(hu*ng*). The first of these is voiceless and the other two are voiced.
Notice that the last of these, /ŋ/, which is represented by an *n* symbol
which has a left-curving "tail" (its name is **eng**), occurs in English only
in non-initial position.

Front sounds are those produced at the front of the palate or ahead of
this region. Those produced in the center of the palate are referred to as
central sounds. Sounds produced at the **velar** region or farther back are
called **back** sounds. All vowels are produced in the palatal region with
parts of the tongue behind the blade and, as we shall see in the next
chapter, are thus classified as **front**, **central** or **back**.

The farthest back phoneme is produced at the **glottis**. English has one
consonant phoneme which is sometimes classified as **glottal**. This is the
voiceless sound symbolized by /h/ (*h*it), which can be considered to
represent a breath stream coming up through the open glottis. There is
another common glottal sound, called **glottal stop**, which is produced
by bringing the vocal cords tightly together, thereby closing off the
breath stream at the glottis. This sound, which is represented in phonetic transcription by undotted question mark – i.e. [ʔ] – occurs in
English not as a separate phoneme, but as a phonetic variant of other
phonemes.

Sounds produced with active articulation of the tongue can be classified according to the part of the tongue that is involved, i.e. as **apical**,
blade, **front**, **central** or **back**. A precise description of the place of
articulation of these sounds requires noting both the part of the tongue
involved and the part of the oral tract where the tongue is active. For
this kind of precise description, compound words beginning with
apico-, **blade-** and **fronto-** are used. Thus /θ/ and /ð/ are precisely classified as **blade-dental**. Since there is no phonemic distinction in
English based on which one of these parts of the tongue is used to produce any sound and since the part of the tongue used is more or less
determined by the position in the mouth of the passive articulator, we
normally dispense with this type of compound term for describing the
articulation.

On the whole, the uvula can be ignored for English, though for some
other languages, the uvula is used to articulate speech sounds.
For example, varieties of /r/ in French, German and Swedish are

pronounced by moving the uvula in a kind of flapping motion while making a characteristically rounded lip gesture.

Some sounds are produced at two different places of articulation simultaneously. For example, some sounds are produced with an articulation made both at the lips and somewhere farther back in the vocal tract. The place of articulation for such sounds is defined as the place where the strongest, or **primary**, articulation is made. The other articulation is referred to as a **secondary articulation** or a **secondary modification** of the primary articulation. For example, the English /r/, especially in initial position, generally has a secondary modification of lip-rounding.

In cases where both articulations are equally strong, the sound is termed **doubly articulated** and is said to have two primary articulations. No such doubly articulated sounds exist in English, though there are many cases of secondary modifications of primary articulations.

The active articulation of a speech sound may involve vibration of a speech organ such as the uvula or the tip of the tongue, or it may involve the touching of one articulator against another. However, in many cases, the active articulator does not touch anywhere in the mouth. For example, the tongue, instead of actually touching somewhere in the mouth, may just approach a point or area in the mouth, or bunch up near that area or under an area such as the roof of the mouth. The tightening of the muscles that produces touching, vibration or bunching of the tongue to make a bump is called the articulatory **constriction**. The constriction is the type of resistance – an obstruction or movement – in the vocal tract that impinges on the air column coming up from the lungs and which produces a certain sound.

The place of articulation is defined in terms of the location of this constriction. The **manner of articulation** is described in terms of how the constriction is made.

Manner of articulation

The sounds of a language can be classified in different ways. One way of doing this is to define a basic **binary** (two-way) distinction of **voiced** vs. **voiceless**, as was done earlier. Another way is to classify phonemes according to manner of articulation. Figure 2.3 shows a hierarchical classification system of English phonemes according to manner of articulation.

In addition to the voiced/voiceless distinction, the sounds of a language can be divided into **nasal** versus **oral** sounds. English has three nasal phonemes, /m/ (hu*m*), /n/ (Hu*n*), and /ŋ/ (hu*ng*). Within the **oral** category, there are two basic types of sounds, **stops** and **continuants**. Stops are vocal sounds made with a complete obstruction, or stoppage,

Place of articulation	Manner of articulation		
	Nasals		Stops
Bilabial	m	voiced	b
	voiceless	p	
Alveolar	n	voiced	d
	voiceless	t	
Velar	ŋ	voiced	g
		voiceless	k
	Fricatives		Affricates
Labiodental	v	voiced	
	f	voiceless	
Interdental	ð	voiced	
	θ	voiceless	
Alveolar	z	voiced	
	s	voiceless	
Pre-palatal	ž	voiced	ǰ
	š	voiceless	č
	Approximants		
	Central		*Lateral*
Bilabial	w	voiced	
		voiceless	
Alveolar		voiced	l
		voiceless	
Pre-palatal	r	voiced	
		voiceless	
Palatal	j	voiced	
		voiceless	
Glottal		voiced	
	h	voiceless	

FIGURE 2.3 The system of English consonant phonemes

of the airflow coming up from the lungs. Continuants are vocal sounds in which the obstruction of the airflow is only partial, so that the sound can be prolonged for a period of time. For example, /b/ and /p/ are stops, while /v/ and /f/ are continuants. Vowels are one type of continuant, and there are three consonant types of continuant: **fricatives**, **affricates** and **approximants**.

Looking first at the nasals, these consonants are produced in both the nose and the mouth. Nasal sounds are articulated in the mouth, but the air for their production goes out through the nose because the velum, which is the soft muscular area at the top and back of the roof of the mouth, is lowered and lets air go into the nose. Oral sounds are produced with **velic closure**, through a mechanism of raising the velum until it makes a closure at the position high up on the back wall of the pharynx. You can see this closure in Figure 2.4a, contrasted with Figure 2.4b, where the velum is held open for the production of a nasal consonant.

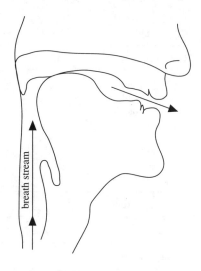

FIGURE 2.4A Position of tongue and velum for production of /g/ and /k/

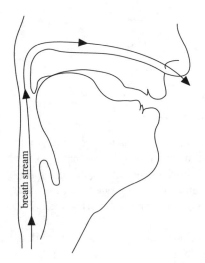

FIGURE 2.4B Position of tongue and velum for production of /ŋ/

All of the nasal phonemes in English are voiced. There are languages that have voiceless nasal consonants, e.g. Burmese. These are produced in exactly the same way as the English nasal consonants but without vibration of the vocal folds.

To achieve the English nasal consonants, there is a stoppage, i.e. a complete closure in which two articulators come completely together, in the oral chamber. For /m/, the closure is made by the two lips coming together; for /n/, it is made by the tip or blade of the tongue touching the alveolar ridge; for /ŋ/, it is made by the back of the tongue touching the velum. Because there is a stoppage of the airflow in the mouth for the production of the nasal consonants, they are sometimes classified as stop consonants. However, from the perspective of the air escaping from the nose, they are continuant sounds, that is, they can be continually pronounced until the speaker's breath is exhausted. Because nasal sounds do not fit neatly into either the category of stop or the category of continuant, we place them in a separate category all of their own.

English has a whole series of oral stops, where the velum is raised so that the air escapes through the mouth rather than through the nose, as shown in Figure 2.4a. The stop consonants, also termed **plosives**, are produced in three steps. First, the speaker brings together two articulators to form a complete closure. Second, this constriction is held for a brief moment, during which time air coming up from the lungs builds up pressure behind the constriction, which completely obstructs its flow out of the mouth. Third, the speaker very rapidly opens the constriction, releasing the air that had built up behind it in a burst or explosion of sound. You may wish to try out these three steps in pronouncing three stop consonants produced at different places of articulation – /p/, /t/ and /k/.

As in many languages, the English stop system is **symmetrical** in that it includes one voiced stop for every voiceless stop produced at the same place of articulation. Two of these, /p/ and /b/, are made at the lips; another pair, /t/ and /d/, are made with the tongue tip or blade at the alveolar ridge; and the third pair, /k/ and /g/, are made with the back of the tongue at the velum. Thus, the position in the oral tract of the three pairs of stops is the same as for the three nasals, i.e. bilabial, alveolar and velar.

In production of fricatives, there is a close approximation, though not a complete stoppage, of the airflow, which results in turbulence, that is, in friction. English includes four pairs of fricatives. Two of the fricative phonemes are produced at a labiodental place of articulation, /f/ and /v/; two are produced at an interdental place, /θ/ and /ð/; one pair is produced at an alveolar place, /s/ and /z/; and another pair is produced at a pre-palatal place, /š/ and /ž/. In English, we have pure fricatives and also affricates, that is, sounds which start out as stops but then open slightly to fricatives, rather than opening all at once to a burst of sound as in plain (unaffricated) stops. There are two affricates in English, both made at a pre-palatal place of articulation, /č/ and /ǰ/. Affricates are classed together with fricatives and stops as **obstruents**, i.e. consonant types which involve an obstruction of the airstream passing through the vocal tract.

The last class of consonant sounds is the approximant. In the production of an approximant sound, one articulator moves close to another, though not so close as to cause a turbulent airflow. The approximant system does not have the symmetry noted in the other consonant systems so far, in that the system is not made up of voiced and voiceless pairs. In general, approximants, like vowels, are voiced sounds.

The /r/ of English is an approximant, that is, a sound in which one articulator is close to another, but not close enough to touch it or to cause friction, as would be the case in a fricative such as /s/. In the production of /r/, the tongue tip or blade is close to, but not touching, the back of the alveolar ridge, and the back of the tongue is raised. /r/ is generally produced with lip protrusion or rounding in English and may have the tongue tip curled back in a **retroflex** position.

For /l/ (*l*ay or de*ll*), another approximant sound, the tongue tip is farther forward than for /r/. Also, the lip position is more spread than for /r/. Another important feature of the approximant /l/ is that it is produced **laterally**, i.e. with some closure between one or both sides of the tongue and the roof of the mouth.

Some speakers produce /l/ by bringing one side of the tongue into contact with the front and one side of the alveolar ridge. When /l/ is produced in this way, air will flow over the tongue body and down over the side of the tongue that is not making the constriction. Others produce this phoneme by arching the body of the tongue up into the palatal region while bending the sides of the tongue down. In this way of pronouncing /l/, air escapes over both sides of the tongue. To find out how you pronounce this sound, put your tongue in position to produce an /l/, then breathe in to see whether one or both sides of the tongue are cooled by the air flowing past.

Two other approximants which occur in English are /j/ (*y*es) and /w/ (*w*ay). The former is a palatal approximant, while the latter is a bilabial approximant. For /j/, a large area of the front of the tongue makes a constriction at the front (and/or center) of the palate. For /w/, the two lips come towards each other – but without touching – in a rounded gesture. /h/ (*h*as and *h*is) is classified as a glottal approximant. It is produced by air rushing through the open glottis and is the only English approximant that is voiceless.

All of the approximants except for /l/ are termed **central approximants** because air passes through the oral tract along the center of the opening at the constriction. /l/ is the only one in which air passes out along the side (or sides) of the articulation; it is therefore called a **lateral approximant**.

In some phonological systems, approximants are classified as **semiconsonants** (especially /l/ and /r/) or **semi-vowels** (especially /j/ and /w/). Consonants are sounds which are typically closed or nearly closed at some point in their articulation. Vowels are sounds that are typically open in their articulation, that is, which have a relatively large **aperture** (opening) of articulation. Figure 2.5 illustrates the increasing aperture of the sounds of English in the order of the oral subgroups from left to right. The relative place of articulation of the sounds is illustrated for each subcategory – nasals, stops, affricates, etc. – from left to right in the diagram. The vertical dimension of the chart for the consonants

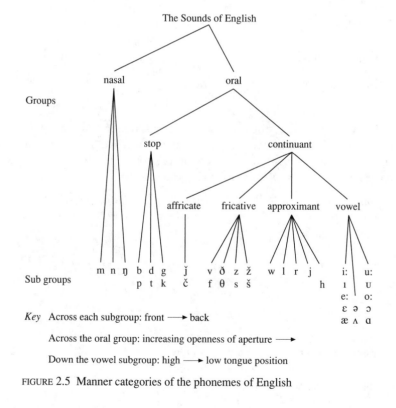

Key Across each subgroup: front ⟶ back

Across the oral group: increasing openness of aperture ⟶

Down the vowel subgroup: high ⟶ low tongue position

FIGURE 2.5 Manner categories of the phonemes of English

indicates pairs of voiced and voiceless sounds produced at the same place of articulation. For the vowels, the vertical dimension indicates tongue height, or degree of jaw opening.

The system of English consonants

English has several categories of consonants. The classification system is based on place of articulation and manner of articulation of the sounds, as shown in Figure 2.3. The environments in which phonemes occur are classified as (1) **initial**, (2) **internal** (medial) and (3) **final**. As each category of consonants is introduced, each phoneme will be shown in any of these three positions in which it occurs.

Nasals

There are three nasal consonants in English:

	INITIAL	INTERNAL	FINAL
/m/ bilabial nasal	*m*ill	di*mm*er	di*m*
		autu*m*nal	
/n/ alveolar nasal	*n*il	di*nn*er	di*n*
		be*n*t	
/ŋ/ velar nasal		si*ng*er	di*ng*
		i*n*k	

The velar nasal is restricted to non-initial position in English, while the other nasal consonants occur in all three positions, initial, medial and final. Within a word, the nasals occur pre-consonantally in clusters preceding obstruents, as in the following examples:

/mp/	*plump*	/nt/	*rent*	/ŋd/	*ringed*
/mt/	*plumped*	/nd/	*rend*	/ŋk/	*rink*
/md/	*plumbed*				
		/nθ/	*tenth*	/ŋz/	*things*
/mz/	*plums*	/ns/	*tense*	/ŋks/	*thinks*
		/nz/	*tens*		
		/nč/	*lunch*		
		/nǰ/	*lunge*		
/mps/	*plumps*	/nts/	*tents*		
/mpt/	*prompt*	/ndz/	*tends*		
		/nθs/	*tenths*		
/mpts/	*prompts*	/nst/	*tensed*		

Stops

The stops in English include phonemes produced at three places of articulation, with a voiced and a voiceless member at each place:

		INITIAL	INTERNAL	FINAL
/b/	voiced bilabial stop	*b*it	ri*bb*ing	lo*b*
		*b*right	o*b*tain	or*b*
/p/	voiceless bilabial stop	*p*it	ri*pp*ing	lo*p*
		*p*lay	clas*p*s	lis*p*
			a*p*titude	
			s*p*in	
/d/	voiced alveolar stop	*d*o	u*dd*er	ba*d*
		*d*rip	gar*d*ner	lan*d*
/t/	voiceless alveolar stop	*t*o	u*tt*er	ba*t*
		*t*ry	vin*t*ner	ben*t*
			las*t*s	
			s*t*ay	
			s*t*ray	
/g/	voiced velar stop	*g*all	ba*gg*ing	tu*g*
		*g*lass	e*gg*nog	mor*gue*
			a*gg*regate	
/k/	voiceless velar stop	*c*all	ba*ck*ing	tu*ck*
		*c*lip	a*ck*nowledge	bun*k*
			as*k*s	
			s*k*ip	
			s*c*ream	

Besides their occurrence with nasals, stop consonants occur in clusters with fricatives and approximants, as well as with each other, as illustrated in the examples below:

/pt/	apt	/bd/	ribbed		
/kt/	act	/gd/	rigged		
/ft/	lift	/vd/	lived		
/ps/	taps	/bz/	tabs		
/ts/	tats	/dz/	dads		
/ks/	tax	/gz/	tags		
/tw/	tweeze	/dw/	dwarf		
/kw/	queasy	/gw/	iguana	/skw/	squeeze

/pr/	pray	/br/	bray	/spr/	spray
/tr/	tray	/dr/	dray	/str/	stray
/kr/	cray	/gr/	gray	/skr/	scray

/pl/	plight	/bl/	blight	/spl/	split
/kl/	clue	/gl/	glue	/skl/	sclera

Fricatives

English has four pairs of voiced and voiceless fricatives:

		INITIAL	INTERNAL	FINAL
/v/	voiced labiodental fricative	*v*at	o*v*er	sto*v*e
			el*v*es	cur*v*e
/f/	voiceless labiodental fricative	*f*at	o*f*fer	stu*ff*
		*f*ly	a*f*ter	gol*f*
			s*ph*ere	
/ð/	voiced interdental fricative	*th*an	ei*th*er	ba*the*
			la*the*s	
/θ/	voiceless interdental fricative	*th*in	e*th*er	ba*th*
			fif*th*s	dep*th*
/z/	voiced alveolar fricative	*z*ip	fu*zz*y	hou*s*e (verb)
			fren*z*y	fur*s*
/s/	voiceless alveolar fricative	*s*ip	fu*ss*y	hou*s*e (noun)
		*s*tamp	a*s*tor	back*s*
/ž/	voiced pre-palatal fricative		fu*s*ion	rou*g*e
			ver*s*ion	
/š/	voiceless pre-palatal fricative	*sh*ip	fi*ss*ion	ru*sh*
		*sh*riek	cen*s*ure	

The voiced pre-palatal fricative is, like the velar nasal, restricted to non-initial position in English.

The alveolar and pre-palatal fricatives are often distinguished from the other fricatives by being labeled **sibilants**. (Sometimes, the alveolar and pre-palatal fricatives are further distinguished as **sibilants** and **shibilants**, respectively.) In addition to the difference in tongue position, the alveolar and pre-palatal sibilants are distinguished in many speakers' articulation by a difference in lip shape. By this secondary modification, the alveolar sibilants tend to have a slightly spread lip shape, whereas the pre-palatal sibilants tend to have a slightly protruded or rounded lip shape. In addition, the alveolar sibilants have a special status in English as compared to the other fricatives because they occur in the grammatical forms of the third person singular present tense of verbs, and of the possessives and plurals of nouns.

In addition to the cluster types illustrated above, fricatives occur in combinations with each other and with approximants, as in:

/θs/	*baths*	/fs/	*laughs*	/sf/	*sphere*
/θz/	*bathes*	/vz/	*graves*		
/θw/	*thwart*	/sl/	*slit*		
/sw/	*swan*	/šr/	*shrimp*		
/rs/	*hearse*	/rč/	*lurch*		
/rz/	*hers*	/rǰ/	*urge*		
/ls/	*false*	/lč/	*mulch*		
/lz/	*falls*	/lǰ/	*bulge*		
/rθ/	*earth*	/lθ/	*wealth*	/lf/	*elf*
/rð/	*worthy*			/lv/	*selves*

Affricates

English has only two affricate phonemes, one voiced and the other voiceless:

		INITIAL	INTERNAL	FINAL
/ǰ/	voiced pre-palatal affricate	*j*ug	le*dg*er	e*dge*
/č/	voiceless pre-palatal affricate	*ch*ug	le*tch*er	e*tch*

The stop and fricative portions of each affricate are coarticulated and form a **homorganic** affricate, that is, one in which the place of articulation of the stop and fricative portions is the same (which is slightly farther back than the usual position for /t/ and /d/, closer to the position of /š/ and /ž/). Non-homorganic affricates occur in some languages, such as Greek.

The combinations of affricates with nasals and stops, which are the only possible cluster types (within a single syllable), have already been illustrated.

Approximants

English has five approximant phonemes:

		INITIAL	INTERNAL	FINAL
/w/	voiced (central) bilabial approximant	*w*oo	to*w*er	
		s*w*an	for*w*ard	
/l/	voiced (alveolar) lateral approximant	*l*ard	co*l*or	ga*l*
			c*l*ap	hur*l*
			s*l*im	
/r/	voiced (central) pre-palatal approximant	*r*ue	to*rr*id	to*r*e
			p*r*y	
/j/	voiced (central) palatal approximant	*y*ard	pla*y*er	
			m*u*te	
/h/	voiceless (central) glottal approximant	*h*ard	a*h*ead	

The alveolar and pre-palatal approximants are sometimes called **liquids**. /w/ and /j/ are sometimes called **glides**. All of the approximant sounds characteristically involve a raised position of the back of the tongue as a secondary articulation.

In addition to the cluster types illustrated above in which approximants occur, combinations of /r/ and /l/ are also possible, as in *girl* and *curl*. In addition to these clusters, English includes a set of words spelled *mu* or *mew*, *pu* or *pew*, *hu* or *hew* which have a /j/ following the initial consonant before /u:/, as in:

/mj/	*music, mute, mews*
/pj/	*pure, putrid, pews*
/hj/	*humid, hue, hew*

Positional variation

It is a common process in languages for the articulatory gestures that produce one sound to anticipate the articulatory gestures used to produce the following sound. In other cases, a phoneme assimilates a feature of a preceding, rather than a following, sound, though such **regressive assimilation** is far less common in English than the progressive type that results from anticipatory coarticulation. The different types of positional effects on consonants can be classified as durational effects, place effects, manner effects, and strenghtening and weakening effects.

Durational effects

General context effects

Consonants are generally prolonged before a pause and shortened before another phoneme. When a consonant follows another consonant in a cluster, it is shorter than when it follows a vowel. Consonants are also shorter in long words than in short words. The general principle is that as more context is added following a phoneme – and this holds for vowels as well – its relative share of the utterance is reduced. Consonants are also shorter in weak positions and in rapid utterances than in strong, emphatic pronunciation. As a general principle, rapid speech weakens the articulation of individual phonemes, while a slow rate or dramatic speaking style strengthens them.

Voice onset time

The difference between voiced and voiceless stops is essentially one of duration and timing of the closure and its release relative to the start of vocal cord vibration. This timing feature of stops is referred to as "**voice onset time** (VOT)." In the production of voiced stops, vocal fold vibration begins during the period of oral closure for the stop. Another way of saying this is that there is a **voicing lead** in relation to the oral closure period for the production of the stop. In other words, the period of voicing overlaps the period of oral closure for the voiced stop.

If a vowel follows the voiced stop – e.g. in words such as *be*, *do* or *go* – we can say that the voicing period of the vowel overlaps the voicing period of the preceding voiced stop. In other words, there is no gap between the voicing of the stop /b/, /d/ or /g/ and the voicing of the following vowel; the vibration of the vocal folds is continuous from the voiced stop through the voicing of the following vowel. This is another example of the continuous and overlapping nature of speech sounds.

In contrast to the case of voiced stops, a voiceless stop followed by a vowel has a period of **voicing lag** just after its production. In the production of a voiceless stop, the vocal folds do not vibrate at all throughout the period of oral closure. In addition, the vocal folds remain slack and open for a period of time before the vocal fold vibration of a following vowel begins. During this period, air may be released through the open glottis as a concomitant of the opening of the oral closure. This release of air is called **aspiration**.

Native speakers of languages such as Japanese, Spanish and French – which have a very brief voicing lag between a voiceless stop and a following vowel – must learn to lengthen this lag period in producing the voiceless aspirated stops of English. In contrast, native speakers of languages such as Thai and Korean, in which a very long voicing lag occurs for certain voiceless aspirated stops, must learn to shorten the period of voicing lag during which aspiration of voiceless stops occurs, if they are to achieve the correct duration of aspiration for the English voiceless stops.

Place effects

The place of articulation of a consonant may be altered somewhat from its reference position, or target position, by the place of articulation of a following consonant or vowel. Coarticulatory effects on consonants include a tendency for the place of articulation to assimilate to or toward that of neighboring sounds, particularly those which follow the consonant. Place effects include general place assimilation, forward movement (**fronting**) and backward movement (**backing**) of the place of articulation, tongue-**raising** and tongue-**lowering** under the influence of neighboring sounds.

Place assimilation of nasals

Nasals generally assimilate to the place of the following phoneme, as in:

    in bed [ɪmbɛd]   *incur* [ɪŋkʰər]

Fronting (dentalization) of alveolars

A common environmental effect is the fronting of alveolar consonants, particularly /t/, /d/ and /n/, before the interdental fricatives /θ/ and /ð/. This type of fronting is termed **dentalization**. Dentalization is indicated by a special diacritic under the consonant, e.g. [t̪]. Using a dynamic style of description, we can say that this dentalization is another instance of fronting under the influence of a following sound. It is therefore an instance of anticipatory coarticulation. The dentalization process in English results in such forms as the following:

    tenth   [tʰɛn̪θ]
    sit there   [sɪt̪̚ðeːr]
    width   [wɪd̪ð] or [wɪt̪θ]

Fronting and raising (palatalization) of velars

Velar stops are fronted before a front vowel. This fronting can be indicated by a left-pointing raised arrow to the right of the consonant symbol, as in:

    kid   [kˑɪd]   *gear*   [gˑiːr]

Because this coarticulatory effect moves velars to a palatal place of articulation, it can be referred to as **palatalization**.

    As part of the palatalization effect, the tongue is often raised to produce a [j]-segment which provides the release of the /k/ or the /g/ and transitions to the following vowel. This transitional sound is represented by a raised *j* to the right of the consonant symbol, as in the examples below:

| *Ken* | [kʲɛn] | *gill* | [gʲɪl] |
| *cat* | [kʲætˀ] | *get* | [gʲɛtˀ] |

Backing (palatalization) of alveolars

Just as velar consonants can be influenced to move to a more forward place of articulation by a following front vowel, so can alveolar consonants be backed under the influence of a following back vowel. Such backing generally moves alveolar consonants to a (pre-)palatal position, where it is still possible to articulate with the tongue tip. The backing of consonants can be indicated by a right-pointing arrow beside the consonant symbol, as in:

tick-tock   [tʰɪkˀtʰ→ɑkˀ]

Backing (velarization) of /l/

In the most common production of /l/ in **pre-vocalic** position (i.e. preceding a vowel), the so-called **light** variant, the tip of the tongue is in position at the alveolar ridge. For many speakers, /l/ has a **velarized** positional variant, especially following a vowel (i.e. in **post-vocalic** position). This **dark** variant, which is produced with a high back tongue position, is symbolized by a wavy line across the *l* symbol, i.e. [ɫ], as in:

bell	[bɛɫ]
ball	[bɑɫ]
bald	[bɑɫd]

Manner effects

In addition to assimilation of place of articulation, it is common for consonants to assimilate the manner of articulation of neighbouring sounds. Through this process, consonants can become denasalized, affricated, stopped, flapped or more open in their articulation. In addition, the secondary attributes of consonants can be altered by the nature of the neighbouring sounds to become devoiced, lip-rounded or lip-spread.

Denasalization

Under the influence of a following non-nasal consonant, a nasal may lose its nasal characteristic, i.e. be produced with a raised velum, so that air escapes out of the mouth instead of the nose. When this happens, the nasal is said to undergo a process of **denasalization**, whereby, for example, *hand* and *had* become homophonous.

Affrication

In clusters where a nasal precedes a sibilant, a homorganic stop may arise as a transition between the nasal and the oral consonant (see Release features, p. 57), as in:

rinse [rɪnts]
lens [lɛndz]

When this happens, the cluster following the nasal becomes affricated. Initial /s/ is sometimes affricated by producing it with a preceding alveolar stop segment, as in:

so [ˈsoː]

Affrication also sometimes occurs in place of aspiration in the release of the voiceless alveolar stop in initial or final position, as in:

tan [tˢæn] instead of [tʰæn]   *it* [ɪtˢ] instead of [ɪtʰ]

Stopping of sibilants

Before a weak syllable with /n/, a sibilant may be closed to form a stop, as in:

business [bɪdnɪs]   *cousin* [kʰʌdɪn]   *isn't* [ɪdn̩t˺]

Devoicing of final obstruents

In final position, voiced obstruents in English tend to be fully or partially **devoiced**. In other words, they lose vocal fold vibration throughout their articulation or in the final stage of their articulation. In the latter case, the sound starts out voiced and ends up voiceless.

Partial devoicing of final obstruents is common in English. Full devoicing of final obstruents is common in several non-standard varieties. Hence, a non-native speaker of English who fully devoices final obstruents, i.e. who pronounces final voiced obstruents as identical to their voiceless counterparts, may be perceived as adopting a non-standard pronunciation of English.

Devoicing is a common but not absolute effect in English, either in terms of its frequency or degree. It can therefore not be correctly described as a **categorical** process applying 100% of the time but must be described as a **variable** process applying to some extent sometimes under some conditions. It is possible to investigate the frequency and the conditions under which different English speakers devoice final obstruents to varying degrees and then to describe the phenomenon in precise terms.

This (partial) devoicing is presented by a hollow dot under the sound, as in these examples:

beg	[bɛg̊]
raid	[reɪd̥]
hoods	[hʊd̥z̥]
judge	[d̥ʌd̥ʒ̊]

In **perseverative coarticulation**, some aspect of the production of a sound is carried over into the production of a later sound, causing a **progressive** type of ("left-to-right") **assimilation**. Such assimilations are not very common in English, where the regressive type, resulting from anticipatory ("right-to-left") coarticulation, is much more usual. Nevertheless, in one common perserverative effect, both /r/ and /l/ may be partially or fully devoiced when they occur in a cluster with a voiceless obstruent, as in:

ploy	[pʰl̥ɔɪ]		*trip*	[tʰr̥ɪp˺]
clip	[kʰl̥ɪp˺]		*stripe*	[str̥aɪp˺]
slip	[sl̥ɪp˺]		*shrink*	[sr̥ɪŋk˺]
thread	[θr̥ɛd]		*pray*	[pʰr̥eɪ]
			cringe	[kʰr̥ɪnd̥ʒ]

Release features

It is usual in English for the air behind the closure of a voiceless stop to be released all at once in a burst of aspiration. When this occurs, the release of the stop is indicated by a raised *h*. In some languages, a more gradual release is usual, with the air **leaking** rather than **bursting** out. In such cases, the **release feature** of the consonant is indicated by a raised symbol to the right of the stop symbol indicating the type of release.

In general, release features and other types of secondary modifications of a sound are indicated by a raised letter written to the right and smaller than the primary sound. For example, if the air leaks out gradually between the teeth with the tongue tip in alveolar position, the release is written as a raised *s*. Such gradual releases of the air behind a stop closure also occur occasionally in English in final position as non-significant variants of the burst release. Typically, however, the air bursts out all at once, as shown in the following examples:

ship#	[šɪp^{h}]	(where # = word boundary or silence)
bit#	[bɪt^{h}]	
hick#	[hɪk^{h}]	

In English, a voiced stop generally has no release in final position. By convention, the lack of release of a voiced stop is not indicated in transcription for English by any special diacritic marking. Voiced stops – and other voiced consonants – may occasionally be released with a slight vowel sound, especially in emphatic speech. This vocalic release is indicated by a raised schwa. Examples of transcriptions for voiced stops are shown below:

	UNEMPHATIC	EMPHATIC
bud	[bʌd]	[bʌd^{ə}]
band	[bænd]	[bænd^{ə}]
fig	[fɪg]	[fɪg^{ə}]
buzz	[bʌz]	[bʌz^{ə}]
badge	[bæǰ]	[bæǰ^{ə}]

When transcribing speech phonetically, the release feature of a stop consonant should be indicated. When transcribing phonemically, however, this detail of sound is insignificant. This is because a phonemic transcription indicates only the meaningful distinctions for the language being transcribed.

In initial position, English voiceless stops are generally strongly aspirated. This aspiration is lost in the position following /s/, in the consonant clusters *sp* [sp], *spr* [spr], *spl* [spl]; *st* [st] *str* [str]; *sk/sc* [sk] and *skr/scr* [skr]. In final position, English speakers often do not release a voiceless stop at all, unless they are trying to pronounce the final word in an emphatic or a formal way. We indicate the lack of release by a raised ($^{\urcorner}$) (right-angle bracket) to the right of the consonant symbol, as shown in the final consonants of the words below:

pep	[p^{h}ɛp$^{\urcorner}$]
kit	[k^{h}ɪt$^{\urcorner}$]
tack	[t^{h}æk$^{\urcorner}$]

Non-native speakers may have trouble hearing the difference between unreleased final /p/, /t/ and /k/, though this can be learned by repeating words that contain the final unreleased stop for contrastive auditory discrimination practice, as in *pap*, *pat*, *pack*. For perception of the difference between an unreleased final voiceless stop and its voiced counterpart, the difference in length of the preceding vowel can be an important cue. Thus, the vowel in *pub* is noticeably longer than the vowel in *pup*. The same relationship holds for the pairs *kid/kit* and *tag/tack*.

Sometimes a final stop, especially if unreleased, is preceded by a glottal stop, indicated by [ʔ] as in:

pep	[pʰɛʔp̚]
kit	[kʰɪʔt̚]
tack	[tʰæʔk̚]

This glottal stop can be heard as a kind of catch or tightening of the diaphragm as the oral closure for the stop is being made.

The flap variant of alveolar stops

A medial /t/ or /d/ preceding a weak (unstressed or unaccented) syllable may be pronounced as a **flap** sound in which the tip of the tongue rapidly flaps against the alveolar ridge in passing to the place of articulation of the succeeding sound. The flap sound is indicated by the symbol [ɾ], called "fish-hook r". Examples in which the medial consonant should be transcribed as a flap [ɾ] for many English speakers are the following:

later	[leːɾər]	*ladle*	[leːɾəl]
latter	[læɾər]	*kettle*	[kʰɛɾəl]
ladder	[læɾər]	*saddle*	[sæɾəl]

In medial position, then, an alveolar flap [ɾ] can substitute for an unflapped /d/ or an aspirated /t/. In this position, we say that unflapped /d/ and aspirated /t/ **alternate** (vary) with the flap pronunciation, depending on certain factors such as the background of the speaker, the level of formality of speech, the rate (speed) of speech and the nature of the following sounds. The flap variant of /t/ and /d/ is particularly common before *-er* and *-le*.

Some English speakers pronounce /t/ in an aspirated way in medial position before *er* in *later* and *latter*. English speakers may also aspirate /t/ before an unaccented syllable where /n/ follows a vowel, as in *mountain*, *button*, *sentence*, *kitten*, *mitten*, etc. However, in many varieties of English, a **(pre-)glottalized**, unreleased /t/ occurs in this position, i.e. preceding a weak syllable with /n/. In such cases, the vowel following the glottal stop drops out completely, leaving what is referred to as a **syllabic** /n/. A syllabic consonant is a continuant which alone makes up a whole syllable. The syllabic /n/ is represented by *n* with a short vertical line under it, i.e. [n̩]. Examples of the two pronunciations of these words are as shown below. As illustrated in the examples of the first column, vowels are often weakened in unaccented syllables, changing to schwa.

sentence	[sɛntʰəns]	or	[sɛnʔt˺n̩s]
kitten	[kʰɪtʰən]	or	[kʰɪʔt˺n̩]
mitten	[mɪtʰən]	or	[mɪʔt˺n̩]

Like /n/, /l/ can be syllabic, symbolized by [l̩]. This [l̩] occurs in a weak syllable without a vowel, as in the following examples:

| *table* | [tʰeɪbəl] | or | [tʰeɪbl̩] |
| *bottle* | [bɑrəl] | or | [bɑrl̩] |

In the symbolization used here, the difference between [əl] and [l̩] or between [ən] and [n̩] is largely a difference in length. Hence, we would expect the variants with schwa, [əl] and [ən], to occur more frequently in slower and more emphatic speech than the variants with syllabic [l̩] or [n̩].

Lip-rounding and lip-spreading

Under the influence of a following rounded or spread vowel, a preceding consonant may take on a spread or rounded lip position in anticipation of the vowel:

| *tick* | spread /t/ |
| *took* | rounded /t/ |

Strengthening and weakening

When consonants are affected by environmental influences, they are generally either strengthened or weakened in their articulation. Consonants are weakened by loss of distinctive features of their articulation and by opening of aperture. Consonants are strengthened in their articulation when they gain a distinctive feature or have their articulation sharpened or closed by the influence of a neighboring sound.

Addition or loss of distinctive feature

Denasalization loses a distinctive feature of a nasal consonant – its nasality – and causes it to be assimilated to a neighboring non-nasal manner of articulation. Likewise, when nasals assimilate to the place of articulation of the following sound, a feature of difference – distinctive place – is lost. On the other hand, when lip-rounding or lip-spreading is added to a consonant, a distinguishing property is gained.

Closing or opening of aperture

When a fricative becomes a stop, as in the examples discussed above of *business*, etc., this can be said to strengthen the consonant by closing its articulation. Similarly, when a sibilant is affricated by addition of a preceding stop segment, this can be seen as a strengthening of articulation, as it closes articulation at the start of the phoneme, thus sharpening its phonetic edge. On the other hand, when a stop is affricated by addition of a following sibilant segment, this can be seen as a weakening effect, in that the sibilant opens the articulation of the stop somewhat. Intervocalic (i.e. in position between vowels) flapping is a weakening of the consonant articulation in being a less closed and a less stable articulation than a stop. In extreme cases of adjustment, the comparatively open position of a vowel may cause the articulation of neighboring consonants to openᷠ, e.g. from stop to fricative, or from fricative to approximant, particularly when a consonant is flanked by two vowels, as in:

   ready [rɛzi], [rɛji]   *leizure* [liːjər]

In such cases, a vocalic manner of articulation of neighboring sounds adjusts the articulation of the consonant to a more open manner category.

Regional and social variation

Besides the type of **linguistic contextual effect** illustrated above, sounds may vary in their articulation according to some **regional or social contextual effects**. Regional and social effects fall into two categories, variation in the consonant system and variation in an individual consonant or consonant class.

Systemic variation

There are three basic styles of articulation of English apical consonants: apical non-retroflex, apical retroflex and non-apical (blade) articulation. Since the tip of the tongue naturally lies near the front of the mouth, people who have highly apical speech generally also have relatively front articulation of all sounds, unless the tongue tip is curled back and held in a retroflex position. If so, then this moves the tongue tip sounds back a little. Try pronouncing the following sentence with the tongue tip up and curling slightly backwards into the pre-palatal region to get a retroflex articulation:

Timmy sucks tiny suckers in town.

It is normal to pronounce this sentence so that all of the alveolar consonants have an apical, non-retroflex tongue position. Try pronouncing the sentence in this usual way, contrasting it with the retroflex style of pronunciation. Now pronounce the sentence with the tongue tip as far forward as you can, in the dental region. Notice how this tongue position gives a different voice quality to the sentence as a whole. In this fronted, dentalized style of pronunciation the sounds are much clearer or sharper than in the former case, where the curled back tongue position causes a muffling or dulling of sound. Notice also that the general dental or retroflex articulatory posture which is maintained throughout speech affects not only overall voice quality but also the pronunciation of individual sounds – /s/, for example.

The retroflex style of pronunciation is the norm for Indian English. A dentalized style of pronunciation is common in Irish English. A generally fronted and apical style of pronunciation is found among some female speaker groups, while a generally back style is found among some male speaker groups, as discussed in Chapter 4 under the heading of Voice Quality. In the fronted style, the relatively front tongue position causes fronting of alveolar consonants to a dental position and velar consonants to a more palatal position. In the backed style, alveolar consonants may be produced with the tongue tip in a retroflex position or with the tongue blade used to articulate the sounds at a pre-palatal position. In this back style of articulation velar phonemes might be produced with a constriction in the pharynx, giving those phonemes a very deep and throaty quality.

In addition to these general systemic tendencies, the New Englishes often reflect the primary community language(s) in some aspects of their consonant systems. This holds true for the retroflex feature of Indian English. It is also true of the English spoken in Kenya, where prenasalization of voiced stops and devoicing of voiced obstruents mirrors the pattern of the languages which are native to the region, yielding such forms as:

> [mband] *bad*   [hand] *had*
> *bible*, *drive* and *give* with voiceless obstruents (Kanyoro 1991: 409)

Other systemic tendencies that may affect consonant articulation in African varieties of English are raising and lowering of the larynx to produce stops which have a kind of click release (**ejectives**) or which are produced as **implosives**, with an in-flowing (**ingressive**) airstream, rather than the usual out-flowing (**egressive**) airstream. In addition, timing differences related to the VOT of the vernacular language(s) may alter the nature of the voiced/voiceless distinction, so that, for example, in some varieties of English, the voiceless stops are produced with a greater or lesser voicing lag (hence with more or less aspiration) and the voiced stops with greater or lesser voicing lead.

Variation in individual consonants

Nasals

Stopping of velar nasal

In New York City, the velar nasal in medial or final position is sometimes closed by a stop, namely, [g], as in:

sing [sɪŋg]   singer [sɪŋgər]

Addition of a voiced velar stop to a velar nasal occurs in final position in many parts of England such as Liverpool, the Bristol-Severnside area and the West Midlands (Russ 1984: 41). It is also a feature of some varieties of English as spoken in Sydney, Australia (Horvath 1985: ch. 7).

-ing

The pronunciation of the grammatical morpheme *-ing* varies in many English varieties between an articulation ending with a final alveolar nasal [n] and one ending with a final velar nasal [ŋ], depending on speech style and other social variables. Generally speaking, the alveolar nasal occurs in informal conversational contexts and in the speech of younger speakers. For example, Woods (1991: 139) reports the pattern shown in Figure 2.6 for various social groups in Ottawa, indicating that speakers classified as lower-upper class make the greatest use of the velar nasal in *-ing*.

Stops

Affrication or frication of stops

/t/ is often released via a sibilant in Leeds (Russ 1984: 50), producing an affricated pronunciation. Affrication of /t/ can be noted in other regions of England, and in Hong Kong any voiceless stop in final position may have an affricated release. In Liverpool, fricatives are often substituted for final voiceless stops, i.e. a voiceless bilabial fricative [ɸ] for /p/, [s] for /t/, and a voiceless palatal fricative [x] for /k/ (Russ 1984: 46).

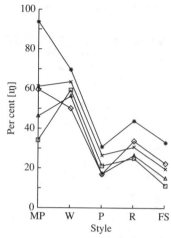

Class key: □ working; △ lower middle; x middle; ◇ upper middle;
　　　　* lower upper
Style key: MP – minimal pairs, W – word list, P – pictures, R – reading,
　　　　FS – free speech
Source: Woods 1991; 139

FIGURE 2.6 Percentage frequency of [ɪŋ] by social class

Glottalization

Some American and British speakers replace final /t/ by glottal stop in some words, i.e. they form a glottal stop by tightly closing the glottis but do not make an oral closure. An example is the expression *Right!* [raɪʔ] spoken as a form of assent or agreement. In some dialects of British English (e.g. Cockney), medial /t/ is replaced by glottal stop in words such as *bottom, kettle*. Intervocalic stops may be not only pre-glottalized, as in final position, but also **post-glottalized** in some varieties such as Hong Kong English and the variety spoken in Tyneside in England, e.g. [sɪtʔi] *city*, [hapʔi] *happy* (Russ 1984: 48).

Loss of /t/ after /n/

/t/ in combination with a preceding /n/ is variably lost, e.g. in *winter* and *twenty*, in American English, Canadian English and British English. The alveolar stop is most commonly lost in free speech style, though females retain /t/ more than males in all speech styles (Woods 1991: 137).

Opening of stop clusters with /r/

In Hawaiian English, /dr/, /tr/ and /str/ are opened to [ǰr], [čr] and /ščr/, respectively, as in:

drive [ǰraiv]   *trip* [čr̥ɪp˥]   *street* [ščr̥iːt˥]

Fricatives

Voicing of voiceless fricatives
Voicing of voiceless fricatives occurs in the southwestern dialects of England in the initial sounds of words such as *five, seven, thimble* and *sure* (Russ 1984: 36).

Stopping of interdentals
In several parts of the United States – e.g. rural parts of the South, some inner-city neighborhoods in New York and Philadelphia, and Hawaii – a local variant of the interdental fricatives occurs. In words such as *think, three, month* and *bath*, the variant is [t̪]; in words such as *this, that, the* and *bathe*, the variant is [d̪]. These dental variants also occur in Liverpool and other areas of Britain, in many indigenous varieties of English such as those existing in Africa and the Caribbean, as well as in many learner varieties spoken by non-native speakers. The recurrence of these variants in so many different areas may mean that the [t̪] and [d̪] pronunciations are in some sense simpler, or less marked, phoneti- cally speaking, than are the interdental pronunciations of the phonemes /θ/ and /ð/.

Another possible explanation for the widespread occurrence of dental variants of the /θ/ and /ð/ phonemes is that this pronunciation exempli- fies what might be termed a **distributed prestige** phonetic variant – that is, a marker of local solidarity whose prestige has been distributed across many parts of the English-speaking world. The spread of a local variant through conscious adoption or other means is a potential inter- mediate step on the way to becoming a generalized variant. The more widely distributed a variant becomes across individual speech com- munities, the more likely it is to accrue generalized prestige and so to affect the basic, or standard, system of English consonant phonemes.

/f/ for /θ/
Several varieties of English, such as Cockney (Wells 1982: 330) Hong Kong English (Bolton and Kwok 1990) and those studied by Horvath (1985: ch. 7) in Sydney, Australia, substitute [f] for /θ/ pre-vocalically, as in *think* and *thing*.

Coalescence of alveolar and pre-palatal fricative
Non-Bantu speakers in East Africa (Hancock and Angogo 1984: 313) and Kenyan English speakers (Kanyoro 1991: 408) substitute [s] for /š/

in *sugar*. The same tendency can be found in Filipino English and Hong Kong English.

Palatalization of obstruents before /u:/

In some varieties of English – generally not American varieties – the alveolar nasals, stops and fricatives are articulated with an intervening palatal glide [j] before /u:/ in words spelled with *nu* or *new*, *du* or *dew*, *tu* or *tew* and *su*, such as the following:

nude [nu:d], [nju:d]	*new, knew* [nu:], [nju:]
dune [du:n], [dju:n], [ǰu:n]	*due, dew* [du:], [dju:], [ǰu:]
tune [tu:n], [tju:wn]	*Tewkesbury* [tu:ksbɛri:], [ču:ksbɛri:]
stupid [stu:pɪd], [stju:pɪd],	[sču:pɪd] *stew* [stu:], [stju:]
suit [su:t˺], [sju:t˺]	*sue* (verb) [su:], [sju:]

Trudgill (1974) documents [n], [s] and [d] rather than [nj], [sj] and [dj] in *new*, *suit* and *dune*, particularly among working class speakers, in Norwich. Woods (1991: 141) shows the palatalized pronunciation to be most common for lower-upper class speakers in Ottawa (see Figure 2.7).

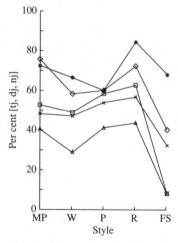

Class key: □ working; △ lower middle; x middle; ◇ upper middle;
             * lower upper
Style key: MP – minimal pairs, W – word list, P – pictures, R – reading,
             FS – free speech
Source: Woods 1991; 141

FIGURE 2.7 Percentage frequency of [tj, dj, nj] by social class

Approximants

Voiceless /w/

Voiceless /w/ is retained in the far north of England, Southern Appalachia and Canada, as in *wheel* and *white* (Russ 1984: 44). In Ottawa, it is again the lower-upper class who have the greatest occurrence of this variant, symbolized as [hw], as shown in Figure 2.8.

Post-vocalic /r/

Varieties of English can be distinguished as to whether they are **rhotic** ("r-ful") or **non-rhotic** ("r-less") in post-vocalic position. Whereas RP and its offshoots in England and elsewhere – e.g. in Australia and New Zealand – are non-rhotic, many of the other varieties of English spoken in England and America are rhotic. The New Englishes are generally non-rhotic. In rhotic varieties, combinations spelled with a vowel + /r/ are pronounced with a definite /r/ sound or "/r/-coloring". The pronunciation of the non-rhotic varieties show [ə] or a plain vowel, sometimes lengthened, where other varieties will have these vowels followed by /r/ or /r/-coloring, indicated by an r-tail on the vowel, as in:

they're   [θeːə] [θɛəʳ] [θeːər]   *car*   [kʰɑː] [kʰɑr]

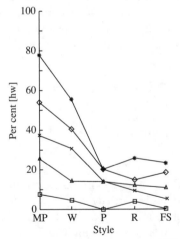

Class key: □ working; △ lower middle; x middle; ◇ upper middle;
              * lower upper
Style key: MP – minimal pairs, W – word list, P – pictures, R – reading,
             FS – free speech
Source: Woods 1991; 143

FIGURE 2.8 Percentage frequency of [hw] by social class

Some varieties show a pattern of variation in use or non-use of /r/ following a vowel, as Labov (1972) found for different speech styles in New York City and as can be noted for different social classes in Boston and in London. The varieties spoken in Texas show patterned variation in degree of retroflexion of /r/ (Harris 1969). A strongly retroflexed /r/ is most characteristic of American Southern and Southwestern speech, whereas a moderately retroflexed /r/ or non-retroflexed (**bunched-**tongue) /r/ is probably the most common American pronunciation of this phoneme. A study of the variation in post-vocalic /r/ in Scotland revealed "a neat pattern of sex differentiation which operates without exception" (Romaine 1978: 148), with males in all age groups having a stronger /r/ than females. A recent study (Li, Lim and Wong forthcoming) found a pattern of variation in post-vocalic /r/ for Chinese bilingual speakers of Hong Kong English that can be described as a blend of the patterns for American and British speakers living in the same community.

Post-consonantal /r/

While the most common pronunciation for English /r/ is an approximant sound in which the tongue does not move, for emphatic or formal pronunciation, especially in RP or Scottish English, /r/ may be pronounced as a **trill**, represented as [rr]. In a trill, the tongue tip vibrates back and forth, usually at the alveolar ridge. This trilled pronunciation is rare in most varieties of English but does occasionally occur in clusters with a stop, as in:

	NON-TRILLED	TRILLED
drone	[dro:n]	[drro:n]
train	[tʰre:n]	[tʰrre:n]
strewn	[stru:n]	[strru:n]

Pre-consonantal /r/

As an example of progressive assimilatory effects in English, a retroflex tongue tip position for /r/ may sometimes be carried over to the production of a following stop, e.g. the final /n/ in *burn* or the final /d/ in *bird*. Since /r/, /n/ and /d/ are all apical sounds, it is not a difficult matter to maintain the tongue tip in a retroflex position for the articulation of all of these consonants following a retroflex /r/. The tendency to do so appears to be most pronounced for speakers who have a strong degree of retroflexion of /r/ – e.g. those from Texas or the Southern Appalachians in the US. Retroflexion is indicated by a closed dot under the sound or by a backwards comma under the sound, symbolizing the backwards curling of the apex of the tongue, as in some people's pronunciations of the following words:

burn	[bəɾn̩]	or	[bəɻn̩]
bird	[bəɾd]	or	[bəɻd̩]

Fricated /r/

In Northumberland, Durham and Scotland, words ending in /r/ may be pronounced as ending in a uvular fricative preceded by a back rounded vowel, as in *fire, chair, flowers, hear, pears, hare, bird, word* (Russ 1984: 44). In Northumberland, initial /r/ is also pronounced as a uvular fricative – the Northumbrian burr – in words like *rat* and *red* (Russ 1984: 43–44).

Vocalization of /l/

In some varieties, pronunciations of /l/ have evolved in which there is no involvement of the forward part of the tongue. Sometimes, only the secondary modification of the /l/ – i.e. the raised position of the back of the tongue – remains in some contexts. It is common for sounds to be modified or to change historically in this way, i.e. so that a secondary modification of a sound becomes the primary place of articulation of that sound over time.

For example, Londoners, American Blacks and Hongkongers may substitute a back vowel [ou] for /l/ in the positions where velar /l/ occurs for other speakers. For these speakers, *help* is [hɛoup˥] and *sell* is [sɛou]. The process of **vocalization** of /l/, in which the consonantal phoneme changes to a vowel, is particularly common in pre-consonantal position. In this position, it is also possible for /l/ to drop out completely, as in the pronunciation of *help* as [hɛp˥] or *self* as [sɛf] by some American Black and Southern speakers. A possibly related phenomenon is the intrusive [l] in Bristol, e.g. in [əˈmɛrəkəl] *America*, [ivəl] *Eva* (as in *evil*). In the view of Russ (1984: 47): "This 'Bristol *l*' is a widespread but highly stigmatized feature and may result from the vocalization of final [l] in *bill, tool, nibble* and *single*".

Uvular /l/

The /l/ phoneme has evolved in a somewhat different way in the speech of some Americans, assuming an even backer position of articulation to become a uvular flap /l/, symbolized [ʟ]. This pronunciation of /l/ can be heard in the speech of well-educated male speakers in the Northeastern part of the United States and Canada. It seems most common in **post-consonantal** position, as in *glean* [gʟiːn] or *play* [pʟeɪ], but occurs as well in pre-vocalic initial position, as in *lean* [ʟi:n] or *lay* [ʟeɪ]. Since the uvula is the farthest back position in the mouth where a sound can be articulated, it can be hypothesized that the articulation of /l/ at a uvular position is the result of moving the articulation of /l/, which is normally pronounced farther forward in the mouth, to a back position. Notice that at this extreme back position, /l/ is no longer a lateral and the tongue is no longer involved as the active articulator.

Non-syllabic /n/ and /l/

In some varieties of English, e.g. the varieties spoken in Hawaii and in the Philippines, the syllabic variants of /n/ and /l/ are rare, and an unstressed syllable containing these phonemes will be produced with a schwa vowel instead, as in *button* [ən] and *table* [əl].

Loss or addition of /h/

In Cockney, initial *h* is dropped (Russ 1984: 49). The tendency to drop initial /h/ is being picked up by the younger generation of immigrant Sikh children in England as well (Russ 1984: 50). In Norwich, Trudgill (1974) has documented cases of intrusive [h] in words beginning with a vowel.

Consonants activities

1. Consonant transcription errors

Find the errors in the following broad (phonemic) transcriptions of the consonants and consonant clusters in each word. Correct errors to the right of any incorrect transcriptions. Put a check mark next to all correct transcriptions.

cook	/c/ /k/
think	/th/ /nk/
runway	/r/ /n/ /w/
visual	/v/ /z/ /w/ /l/
noon	/n/ /n/
pack	/p/ /k/
stop	/st/ /p/
capture	/k/ /p/ /sh/ /r/
inkstands	/nk/ /st/ /ŋdz/
screwball	/škr/ /w/ /b/ /ll/
dodge	/d/ /dz/

watch	/w/ /ts/
crimewave	/kr/ /m/ /w/ /v/
Cheryl	/ch/ /r/ /l/
Japan	/j/ /p/ /ṇ/
rung	/r/ /ng/
box	/b/ /x/

2. Consonant phoneme examples

The following is a list of common English words which each begin and end with one of the consonant phonemes of English. Write the phonemic symbols for the initial and final consonants in each word. Then find at least two other examples of each of the consonant phonemes.

	INITIAL CONSONANT	OTHER EXAMPLES	FINAL CONSONANT	OTHER EXAMPLES
(1) *big*				
(2) *miss*				
(3) *quit*				
(4) *thing*				
(5) *church*				
(6) *red*				
(7) *shock*				
(8) *will*				
(9) *judge*				
(10) *zip*				
(11) *them*				
(12) *garage*				
(13) *hash*				
(14) *switch*				
(15) *five*				

3. Most difficult English consonants

What are some of the consonants of English that may be difficult for most non-native speakers to pronounce? Why?

Give examples from a specific language with which you are familiar of problems that native speakers of that language experience in learning to pronounce English consonants. Try to give reasons for their difficulties.

4. Consonant comparison

Compare your speech to that of another person you know who speaks a different variety of English. Compare your speech to that of the other person in terms of each of the categories shown below to find the points of similarity and difference. You may wish to compare tape recordings of yourself and the other person reading the same word list, sentences or reading passage. Or, you may tape record yourself and the other person speaking on the same topic for a brief period.

	OWN SPEECH	OTHER'S SPEECH
Medial stops		
Final stops		
Interdental fricatives		
Final /r/		

5. Consonant chart for other language

Find or make a consonant chart for another language with which you are familiar, using the format of one of the figures in this chapter, a format designed by someone else or your own original variation on one of these formats. Then summarize the differences between the consonant system of English and that language in each of the manner categories.

6. Denasalization

Why does a cold cause /m/ to be denasalized, with [b] substituting for /m/?

7. A phonological rule for *-ed* and *-(e)s* endings

Generate a list of regular verbs that take *-ed* in the past tense. Build your list to get the maximum amount of variety in the final phoneme of the uninflected form of the verb. Then add *-ed* to each of the regular verbs and consider the pattern of pronunciation. You will find three different pronunciations of the past tense ending, depending on the preceding consonant.

After you have determined what the three possible pronunciations of *-ed* are, group each of the verbs of your list into three columns according to which of the three pronunciations of the past tense ending it takes. Then try to figure out what the general phonological rule is that determines the pronunciation of the past tense ending.

Do the same thing for *-(e)s* endings for noun plurals and the third person singular present tense. The same rule applies in both cases, based on pronunciation of the final consonant of the base noun or verb. There are again three possible pronunciations, and the rule is similar (but not identical) to that for the pronunciation of the past tense. Now, try to generalize by combining the two rules just developed.

8. Sociolinguistic mini-research: pronunciation of English post-vocalic /r/

Develop a research project in which you and/or your students will tape record members of your community, other teachers or students to discover the pattern among the speakers of rhotic and non-rhotic pronunciation of orthographic *r* in post-vocalic position.

To gather your tape-recorded data in a systematic and comparable manner, you can ask subjects to read a number of words containing *r* in post-vocalic position after a variety of vowels. These words may appear in a word list, in sentences or in a reading passage containing all of the words. To elicit a more natural type of performance, you might also ask subjects to use the words given in a word list to make up their own sentences. A more elaborate design for the research would be to have subjects perform two or more tasks and then compare their pronunciation under different task conditions.

First, you will need to compile or devise the words, sentences and/or readings you wish to use as your material. If you start from a word list, you may need to spend time making up sentences and/or a reading passage to use all of the words in a different task. If you start from a reading passage, you will need to extract all of the words to make sentences or a word list (if you also plan to have subjects read the words in a list and/or in sentences).

Then you will need to decide on your subjects. You may wish to have two or more different types of subjects so that you may compare their pattern of pronunciation of post-vocalic *r*. If possible, tape record or informally listen to potential subjects in advance to determine whether they might show an interesting, variable pattern for post-vocalic *r*.

The next step is to gather your data by tape recording each individual subject performing the tasks you have set for them or by having the subjects do this themselves (e.g. in a language lab or at home).

To analyze the data, first classify your subjects' productions as:

(1)   vowel + [r]
(2)   vowel + [r]-coloring
(3)   vowel only; no [r]

Then you may compare and contrast the responses to individual tasks or words for speakers with similar and different characteristics, or compare/contrast the overall pattern of responses for different tasks or words. This can be done in two ways. One is to tabulate the frequency of each of the responses (1–3) for each group, task or word. The other is to compute an **index score**, which is calculated the same way as an average, or mean, score, and then multiplied by 100. For example, imagine that you had 12 male and 12 female respondents and you wanted to compare their index scores for a word list reading task involving 30 words, based on the following frequency of response ($30 \times 12 = 360$ is the total number of responses for each group):

	MALES (n=12)	FEMALES (n=12)
(1) vowel + [r]	48/360	36/360
(2) vowel + [r]-coloring	106/360	71/360
(3) vowel only; no [r]	206/360	253/360

The index score is calculated by multiplying the number of responses in each category by the index (1–3) for that category, then summing the total and dividing by the number of items, which is 360. In our example:

MALES		FEMALES	
$1 \times 48 =$	48	$1 \times 36 =$	36
$2 \times 106 =$	212	$2 \times 71 =$	142
$3 \times 206 =$	318	$3 \times 253 =$	759
	578		937
$570/360 =$	1.61	$937/360 =$	2.60

In this hypothetical example, the male subjects, with $1.61 \times 100 = 161$, have a lower index score than the female subjects, with an index score of $2.60 \times 100 = 260$. Thus, the female subjects on average have less rhotic pronunciation than the males. Index scores, in which a group of pronunciation variants are represented in a numerical range, as illustrated here, are a simple way to compare the pronunciation profiles of different groups of speakers.

9. Action research: students' perception and production of a consonant contrast

Develop an action research project to evaluate and remediate your students' production and perception of a consonant contrast (e.g. interdental fricatives vs. alveolar stops or voiced vs. voiceless stops). Your evaluation should incorporate (1) a listening measure such as a cloze exercise or identification of minimal pairs (e.g. *thin/tin* and *then/den* or *pit/bit*, *tot/dot*, *cot/got*) and (2) a speaking measure such as imitation of minimal pairs or words spoken in context.

First, decide on a set of words to test. It is recommended to include a minimum of 3 test words for each member of the consonant contrast. Next, decide how to present the test items, e.g. in commonly confused pairs, in individual sentence contexts, in a reading passage, etc. Then decide what the students will be asked to do, e.g to discriminate minimal pairs by marking the correct answer choice on a list of minimal pairs, to complete a cloze or listening comprehension exercise, to read aloud, to imitate or repeat after a speaker on tape, etc.

Code the data by marking students' responses as correct or incorrect and/or by transcribing the students' productions. Base your remediation program on your evaluation of the students' most serious problems in perception and/or production, and continuously monitor your instruction for its effectiveness, adjusting as needed.

10. Action research: teaching ideas for consonants

Try one or more of the teaching ideas below in a class, customizing and elaborating the exercise as needed, and then analyze and assess the results, both positive and negative, intended and unintended. As before (see exercise 10 in Chapter 1), you may carry out the action research in one or your own classes or comparatively in two different classes, with or without a research partner working on the same or a different lesson simultaneously or sequentially.

Whichever format you choose for your action research, you should regularly monitor effectiveness and make adjustments as necessary to maintain student motivation and to achieve the desired results. Upon completion, you should also evaluate the degree to which you achieved what you set out to achieve, as well as any unexpected results or difficulties encountered, in order to develop a deeper understanding of yourself as a teacher, your students, teaching techniques, the area of language addressed, and the interaction of these factors in producing an effective lesson.

Teaching ideas for consonants

1. A sequence of activities for students who have trouble with the voiced/voiceless stop contrast (e.g. Arabic and Spanish)

A. *Presentation*

VOICELESS	VOICED
/p/ /t/ /k/	/b/ /d/ /g/
– Vibration of vocal cords	+ Vibration of vocal cords

No vibration can be felt when Adam's Apple is touched with finger tips or when hands are put over ears when whispering [hahaha] [papapa] [tatata] [kakaka].

Feel vibration of larynx of self or another using finger tips at Adam's Apple or with hands over ears when saying [aaaa] [bababa] [dadada] [gagaga].

Initial
Aspirated (breathy): a puff of air accompanies release of the stop.

Initial
Unaspirated: No puff of air accompanies the release of the stop.

Demonstrate and then let students try, using key syllables [pa pe pi po pu].
(1) Blow out burning match or candle with puff of air.
(2) Blow strip of paper with puff of air so that it moves.
(3) Blow off the paper wrapper of a drinking straw with puff of air.
Write key syllables on board with raised *h*, written in a different color, to symbolize puff of air written in a different color.

Contrast with [ba be bi bo bu]. Then let students try.
(1) Match or candle will not blow out.
(2) Strip of paper will not move.
(3) Straw wrapper will not blow off.

Final
Unreleased (unexploded): The closure of the stop is not opened at the end of the word.

Final
Unreleased or released with a slight schwa sound for emphasis.

The preceding vowel is short.

The preceding vowel is long.

Demonstrate and then let students try using key syllables [ap at ak] [ep et ek] [ip it ik] [op ot ok] [up ut uk].

Contrast with [ab ad ag]; [eb ed eg] [ib id ig] [ob od og] [ub ud ug]. Then let students try.

B. *Repetition practice: minimal pairs*

Students repeat the minimal pairs of voiceless and voiced syllables [pa/ba] [ta/da] [ka/ga] etc. [ap/ab] [at/ad] [ak/ag] etc. after the teacher, first in chorus and then individually.

C. *Discrimination practice: minimal pairs*

Students guess which sound of the minimal pair syllables the teacher pronounces by holding up one finger if the sound is voiceless, two if the sound is voiced. Then individual students come in front of the class to "play teacher" in the same activity.

D. *Individual practice on final stops*

For students who have trouble pronouncing the final stops, individual work with the teacher using a tape recorder can be helpful – possibly with other students watching. For the voiceless stops, the student makes a tape recording of each of the nonsense words below, imitating the teacher's model. The teacher models exaggerated pronunciation of the word, pronouncing the stop with a long period of closure and heavy aspiration. The student repeats after the teacher until s/he achieves a good imitation, then records the exaggerated production of that word. The same procedure is followed for each of the nonsense words.

'bepu 'bopa 'bopu 'bati 'boti 'buti 'bika 'beka 'buka

The teacher then plays back the recording of each nonsense word, stopping the tape before the burst of aspiration, drawing the learner's attention to the fact that the stop is – to that point – unreleased. If a tape player with variable speed control is available, a slight decrease in tape speed is useful for drawing attention to the closure period of the stop and for cutting off the consonant articulation at just the right point.

This procedure is a graphic demonstration of the fact that in final position – i.e. if the following vowel is removed – the typical English stop is produced without a release. The stop is literally cut off before its release. The student practices producing the stop in this "cut-off style" of articulation, generally with a new awareness that leads to improved pronunciation.

The same basic procedure can be used to demonstrate and practice final voiced stops, starting with exaggerated productions of the nonsense syllables below, which are modeled by the teacher and then recorded by the student. When replaying the recording, the teacher should stop the tape just at the period of closure of the stop, but before the second vowel begins.

'bibi 'boba 'bobu 'bidi 'bodo 'budu 'bego 'bagi 'bugu

E. *Pronunciation challenge: mini tongue twisters*

Students repeat simplified tongue twisters in chorus, then individually.

Peter Piper picked a pepper.
Tiny Tim took his time.
Ken can't cook Cajun cauliflower.

F. *Work for student pairs, part I: minimal pair discrimination*

Using the same minimal pair syllables and format as in exercise C above, students work in pairs to guess whether the voiceless or the voiced item in a pair is being pronounced, holding up one or two fingers. Each student takes a turn with all of the syllables before giving the turn to the other student.

As a follow-up and to prepare the students for the next two exercises, students can do the above activity with the minimal pairs below:

pat/bat   time/dime   pack/back   back/bag

G. *Work for student pairs, part II: contextual discrimination*

Pairs of students practice the dialogues below until they feel satisfied that they are making the correct distinctions. They may also present these dialogues, or others they make up themselves, to other student pairs for Feedback.

(1)   *pat/bat*
    S1: I want to _____ that kitten.
    S2: Go ahead and _____ it.

    S1: I want to _____ that ball.
    S2: Go ahead and _____ it.

(2)   *time/dime*
    S1: I can't see the clock. Do you have the _____?
    S2: Yes, the _____ is . . .
        No, I don't have the _____.

    S1: I need to make a call. Do you have a _____?
    S2: Yes, here's a _____.
        No, I'm sorry, but I don't have a _____.

H. *Work for student pairs, part III: communicative practice*

Props needed: a backpack, a pack of chewing gum, a paper bag.

Pairs of students work with the props in a guessing game. One student closes his/her eyes during the game (or can be blindfolded, or seated with his/her back turned to the other student) while the other student places the pack of gum some place in relation to the backpack and the bag. The first student then tries to guess the location of the pack of gum in relation to the backpack and the bag by asking questions about spatial location such as *in, beside, under, between,* etc. An example is given below for Student B as the one who guesses. After 2–3 rounds of play, students can reverse roles.

STUDENT A: Where's the gum?
No, the gum is not in the bag.
Yes, the gum is in the backpack.
No, the bag is not in the backpack.
Yes, the backpack is in the bag.
Yes, the gum is in the backpack,
and the backpack is in the bag.

STUDENT B: Is the gum in the bag?
Is the gum in the backpack?
Is the bag in the backpack?
Is the backpack in the bag?
So the gum is in the backpack,
and the backpack is in the bag?

2. A sequence of activities for working on the interdentals

A. *TPR pronunciation exercise*

To put students in touch with the interdental place of articulation in the context of other places of articulation.

Warm-up
(1) With your pencil, touch your nose,
 top lip,
 bottom lip,
 top teeth,
 bottom teeth.
(2) Put your finger between your teeth and touch your tongue.
(3) Open your mouth wide.
 Breathe out.
 Stop.
 Now close your mouth.

Tongue calisthenics
(1) Put your tongue tip up,
 down,
 up,
 down.
(2) Curl your tongue tip back.
(3) Stick your tongue out and wag it side to side.
(4) Put your tongue tip up and sing "la-la-la-la".

Say a word
 (1) Touch your nose with the side of your pencil, so the pencil tip is pointing up and the other end is pointing to the floor.
 (2) Stick your tongue out between your teeth and touch the pencil with it.
 (3) Keep your tongue there.
 (4) Now blow out a lot of air.
 (5) Keep blowing.
 (6) Say "th" three times.
 (7) Curl your tongue tip back quickly and put it up.
 (8) Say "n" and keep saying it.
 (9) Say "th"
       "n"
       "th"
       "n".
(10) Make the sound "i" between "th" and "n".
(11) Say "thin" four times slowly.
(12) Say "thin" four times quickly.
      That's all for now!

B. *Odd one out*

To give students a simple and creative environment for practicing the pronunciation of the interdentals in a communicative activity.

Teacher modeling
The teacher has several different groups of three or more items, at least one of which is different from the others within one group. These items may be classroom objects such as pens, home objects such as buttons, or pictures (e.g. of animals or people) taken from magazines or drawn for the purpose of the exercise. The teacher lines the items up in a row in view of the students and asks questions for individual or choral response, such as:

"Which one is different?"
"Which one has [a certain property]?" (e.g. "Which one is red?"
"Which one is made of plastic?" "Which one is metal?")

These questions are intended to elicit the ordinal numbers, particularly *third, fourth, fifth*, etc., all of which end in a voiceless interdental fricative, in answers such as the following:

"The third one is."
"The sixth [object] is red."
"The fourth [object] is made of plastic."

Any correct answer that includes an ordinal number correctly pronounced can be accepted.

Pair practice
Students carry out the same activity in pairs, using items or pictures given to them by the teacher, brought in from home, or self-made (e.g. drawings).

Extension
The same idea can be developed for a whole-class or small group format using a "Concentration"-type card game, in which a deck of cards is lined up in four horizontal rows. The object of the game is to match as many pairs of cards as possible. One student takes the role of turning over the cards while other individual students or teams play against each other to make guesses about which cards will match, asking for a certain card in a certain row to be turned over. For example, the student asks, "Please turn over the fifth card in the third row. Now, please turn over the fourth card in the fourth row. They are both sixes. It's a match!"

C. *TH word game*

To practice the pronunciation of the interdentals in the context of developing vocabulary skills.

Directions
This game has three players. The first player will have words which the seçond player will try to guess. The second player is given only the first two letters of each word, and s/he has to ask questions to try to discover what the other letters of the word are and where they occur in the word. Every time the answer to a questions is "no", the scorekeeper, who is the third player, crosses out a number, beginning with 10. The second player's score at the end of the game is the highest number between 10 and 0 which has not been crossed out.

The game is played as follows: Moving from left to right across the blank spaces in the word, the second player tries to guess the next letter by asking, "Is the third (fourth, fifth, etc.) letter a "b" ("c", "d", etc.)?" The second player may ask about any one of the blank spaces s/he wishes, in any order, and also about any letter of the alphabet.

The first player answers using one of the following responses:

"No, and no other letter is, either."
"No, but the _____ letter is."
"Yes, but no other letter is."
"Yes, and the _____ letter is, too."

The scorekeeper monitors the questions and answers of both of the other players. If the second player asks an incorrect type of question (e.g. one without an ordinal number or one which does not have a *yes* or *no* answer), s/he loses a point. If the first player answers incorrectly, i.e. falsely or with anything other than one of the indicated responses, the second player gains a bonus point to be added to the final score. All players receive the instructions and the handout below. Only the first player and the scorekeeper receive the answers to the exercise. On subsequent plays, students can make up their own words.

SCORE

(1) D I __ __ __ __ __ __ __ __ __ __ __   0 1 2 3 4 5 6 7 8 9 10
    1 2 3 4 5 6 7 8 9 10 11 12   Bonus points:

(2) D E __ __ __ __ __ __ __ __ __ __ __ __   0 1 2 3 4 5 6 7 8 9 10
    1 2 3 4 5 6 7 8 9 10 11 12 13   Bonus points:

(3) C O __ __ __ __ __ __ __ __ __ __   0 1 2 3 4 5 6 7 8 9 10
    1 2 3 4 5 6 7 8 9 10 11 12   Bonus points:

(4) D I __ __ __ __ __ __ __ __ __ __ __   0 1 2 3 4 5 6 7 8 9 10
    1 2 3 4 5 6 7 8 9 10 11 12   Bonus points:

(Answers are provided at the end of the Teaching Ideas section.)

3. A sequence of activities for working on the /p/–/f/ contrast (e.g. with Korean students)

A. *Awareness*

Is it true that Koreans prefer to eat pork with a fork?

B. *Pronunciation tips*

/p/ 1. Put your two lips together so they are tightly closed.
    2. Build up some air pressure behind your closed lips.
    3. Open the closure suddenly, so that the air bursts out.

/f/ 1. Loosely bite your bottom lip with your top front teeth.
    2. Continuously blow out plenty of air between your top teeth and bottom lip.

C. *Mechanical practice: words to practice alone or with a partner*

pig   park   pork   picnic   plenty   party   plastic
pepper   people   pink   April   paper   pretty   plums
plump   purple   potatoes   pickled   playing   punch

fat   figs   feet   fifty   fork   fantastic   fresh
fillets   flavorful   flipping   fifteen   forty   fried
French   frisbees   famished   families   afternoon   fish

D. *Contextualization: sentences to practice alone or with a partner*

Forty families went to the party.
They played with four plastic frisbees.

Modified tongue twisters:
Peter picked a peck of peppers.
Forty families fought the fire.

E. *Structured, creative (meaningful and communicative) practice for small groups: picnic in the park*

Groups of 3–4 students each make up a story based on the phrases below. Each group writes down its story and then presents it to the class.

a picnic in the park
a pretty April afternoon
fifteen famished people
families playing
flipping frisbees
a pack of paper plates
fifty plastic forks
pink party punch
pickled pigs' feet
flavorful pork
fresh fish fillets
plenty of pepper
French fried potatoes
forty fat figs
plump purple plums

F. *Real practice for pairs: personal survey*

Student pairs ask and answer the questions below. As a follow-up, tallies can be made in groups or whole-class format for additional practice.

(1) Do you eat pork with a fork?
(2) Do you like French fried potatoes?
(3) Which do you like better, plums, figs, or neither?
(4) Which color do you like better, pink or purple?
(5) Do you know a park where we can go on a picnic?
(6) How many people in your family?

G. *Real practice for whole class: planning a picnic or a party*

The whole class plans a party in the classroom or a picnic in a local park, possibly with family members invited.

4. A sequence of activities for working on the /w/, /v/, /f/, /h/ contrast
    (e.g. for Japense students)

A. *Awareness*

When a Japanese student says "manfood", what does s/he mean?

(1) food made for humans (cf. *dogfood*)
(2) the condition of being a man (*manhood*)
(3) part of a conditional statement about a man (*man would*)
(4) part of a relative clause statement about a man (*man who'd*)
(5) any or all of the above

B. *Pronunciation tips*

/f/ 1. Bite your bottom lip with your top front teeth.
     2. Continuously blow out plenty of air between your top teeth
        and bottom lip.

/v/ 1. Bite your bottom lip with your top front teeth.
     2. Continuously blow out plenty of air between your top teeth
        and bottom lip, while adding voice.

/w/ 1. Push out your lips and make them round.
     2. Leave a very small hole inside the circle of your lips.
     3. Blow out some air and add voice.

/h/ 1. Relax your lips and open them.
     2. Put the tip of your tongue down.
     3. Blow out plenty of air.

C. *Incorporation: questions on pronunciation*

(1) For which sound(s) are the lips round?
(2) For which sound(s) do we need to use the teeth?
(3) For which sound(s) is the mouth most open?
(4) For which sound(s) is the mouth most closed?
(5) For which sound(s) can you feel your Adam's Apple vibrate?

D. *Mechanical practice: words to practice alone or with a partner*

veal	veer				vow	vee				vat	
feel	fear	fill	flew	fall		fee	fight		feed	fat	food
we'll	we're	will	whew	wall	wow	we	white	wood	we'd		wooed
heel	hear	hill	hue	hall	how	he	height	hood	he'd	hat	who'd

E. *Pair matching exercise for /w/, /v/, /f/ and /h/, Partner A*

Directions

Working with Partner B, pronounce each of the underlined words below. Your partner will underline the word that s/he thinks you pronounced on his/her paper. After each of your turns, your partner will have a turn to pronounce a word for you to guess. After you have finished all of the items, check your answers. If you have any questions about the pronunciation of the words, ask your teacher or a classmate. You will go first with item 1. Then it is Partner B's turn.

(1) <u>foam</u> home	(4) fit hit wit	(7) <u>weather</u> feather heather	(10) we he vee fee
(2) foal hole	(5) fat <u>vat</u> hat	(8) who'd wooed food	(11) veal feel he'll <u>we'll</u>
(3) wood <u>hood</u>	(6) hoe foe woe	(9) view hue <u>few</u>	(12) we're hear fear veer

Pair matching exercise for /w/, /v/, /f/ and /h/, Partner B

Directions

Working with Partner A, pronounce each of the underlined words below. Your partner will underline the word that s/he thinks you pronounced on his/her paper. After each of your turns, your partner will have a turn to pronounce a word for you to guess. After you have finished all of the items, check your answers. If you have any questions about the pronunciation of the words, ask your teacher or a classmate. Your partner will go first with item 1. Then it will be your turn with item 2.

(1)	foam	(4)	fit	(7)	weather	(10)	we
	home		hit		feather		he
			<u>wit</u>		heather		<u>vee</u>
							fee
(2)	<u>foal</u>	(5)	fat	(8)	<u>who'd</u>	(11)	veal
	hole		vat		wooed		feel
			hat		food		he'll
							we'll
(3)	wood	(6)	<u>hoe</u>	(9)	view	(12)	we're
	hood		foe		hue		hear
			woe		few		<u>fear</u>
							veer

F. *Other words to practice alone or with a partner*

/f/	in the middle:	*coffee*	*often*
/v/	in the middle:	*ever*	*oven*
/w/	in the middle:	*shower*	*firewood*
/h/	in the middle:	*ahead*	*childhood*

G. *Contextualized practice: sentences to practice alone or with a partner*

(1) We don't drink coffee often.
(2) She hasn't ever been without an oven.
(3) He'll take a shower after he brings in the firewood.
(4) Go ahead and tell us about your childhood.

H. *Creative pair or small group work, structured*

Student pairs or small groups make up a story in the format below, each one using words for the blanks which all begin with one of the sounds /w/, /v/, /f/ or /h/. Thus, one pair or group fills in the blanks in the story with words beginning only with /w/, while another pair uses only words beginning with /v/, etc. Pairs or groups can read their stories aloud to the class, lead the class in choral reading, or exchange their stories with other pairs/groups to read.

There once was a _____ named _____, who
        animal/occupation   *name 1*
lived in _____ and drove a _____. Now
        place   *vehicle*
_____ loved to eat _____ and to drink
    name 1   *food 1*
_____, but never ate _____ and never
    beverage 1   *food 2*
drank _____. When there was spare time, _____
        beverage 2   *name 1*
liked to _____ or to _____ with a friend
            verb 1   *verb 2*
named _____. One day, something terrible happened.
        name 2
_____ _____ _____. After that,
    name 2   *verb 3-past*   *name 1*
_____ and _____ drifted apart, as most
    name 1   *name 2*
friends eventually do.

I. *Communicative pair practice*

Student pairs make up questions using as many of the words in exercises D and E as possible. Then one pair asks its questions of another
pair, each student taking turns asking and answering the questions.
When all the questions of the first pair have been answered, the second
pair asks its questions of the first pair.

Sample questions

"Do you have a white hat?"
"How do you feel about this school?"
"Were you ever in a fight?"

Answers to TH word game

(1) D I S S A T I S F I E D
     ─ ─ ─ ─ ─ ─ ─ ─ ─ ── ── ──
     1 2 3 4 5 6 7 8 9 10 11 12

(2) D E V E L O P M E N T A L
     ─ ─ ─ ─ ─ ─ ─ ─ ─ ─ ── ── ──
     1 2 3 4 5 6 7 8 9 10 11 12 13

(3) C O R P O R A T I O N S
     ─ ─ ─ ─ ─ ─ ─ ─ ─ ── ── ──
     1 2 3 4 5 6 7 8 9 10 11 12

(4)   D I S C R I M I N A T E
       1 2 3 4 5 6 7 8 9 10 11 12

3 Vowels

Characteristics of vowels

The nature of vowels

Vowels can be distinguished definitionally from consonants as having a relatively open aperture of articulation. All vowels are more open in aperture than all consonants. In general, when we speak of vowels, we are referring to voiced vowels. It is possible to produce vowels in a voiceless way, i.e. without vocal fold vibration, as in whispering a word that contains a vowel. However, since the vowel phonemes of most languages are voiced, voiceless vowels are considered to be highly marked, and when people speak of vowels, they generally mean the unmarked, i.e. voiced, type. Therefore, unless explicitly stated otherwise, all references to vowels below are to voiced vowels.

The class of **sonorant** sounds, which includes voiced vowels, nasal consonants and voiced approximants, is opposed to the class of obstruent sounds (stops, fricatives and affricates). Of all the sonorants, vowels have the greatest **sonority**. The sonority of a sound is its inherent loudness, or strength. Vowels are inherently louder than consonants because the energy used in producing them escapes out of the vocal tract with relatively little of it being dissipated by obstructions along the way. The perception of loudness is a consequence of the amount of energy which exits the vocal tract and reaches the ear of the listener.

The sonority of vowels makes it easy to prolong them, as in singing. Because vowels are inherently louder than consonants and can be prolonged, they form the core, or **nucleus**, of most syllables in most languages. As a consequence of the inherent difference between vowels and consonants, the two types of segments convey different types of information in speech. In the words of Werker and Polka (1993):

> As continuants, vowels are articulated more slowly, have more prominent and long-lasting acoustic cues, and can be used to provide more prosodic information than consonants. Thus vowels carry information about stress, speaker identity and emotional tone. In

comparison, consonants convey less prosodic information, but play a central role in signaling differences in lexical meaning. (p. 89)

The role of consonants in expressing lexical meaning is a consequence of their defining an articulatory and perceptual margin for a syllable or word.

Phonetic properties of vowels

All vowels are produced with a primary articulation made by the front, center or back of the tongue and located at the front, center or back of the palate. Thus, the tip and blade of the tongue are not involved in the (primary) articulatory constrictions of vowels, nor are other vocal regions or structures. All vowels are produced in the oral tract, though they may be modified by a secondary feature of nasalization when they occur before a nasal consonant (as described in the section on Manner effects in the present chapter).

Vowels are traditionally classified according to tongue position as:

(a) front, central or back; and
(b) high, mid-high, mid, mid-low or low.

The front-to-back dimension, when combined with a specification of tongue height, uniquely identifies the articulatory position of all vowels. There is a natural association of tongue height and the amount of opening of the jaw in the production of vowels. Thus, high vowels are produced with a nearly closed mouth, mid vowels with the jaw half open, and low vowels with a wide jaw angle and a large vertical mouth opening.

Additionally, a secondary modification at the lips is usually part of the articulation of front and back vowels in English. Front vowels generally have a **spread** lip gesture and back vowels characteristically have a **rounded** lip gesture, while central vowels have a **neutral** lip gesture (i.e. neither spread nor rounded). Figure 3.1 shows the positions of the tongue, jaw and lips for most of the vowel phonemes of English. For each vowel position, a representative word in Figure 3.2 shows the approximate position of each of the vowels within the vocal tract.

The names of the vowel symbols are given below:

i:	lower case *i* with long mark		u:	lower case *u* with long mark
ɪ	small capital *i*		ʊ	small capital *u*
e:	lower case *e* with long mark	ə schwa	o:	lower case *o* with long mark
ɛ	epsilon	ʌ inverted *v*	ɔ	open *o*
æ	ash		ɑ	script *a*

LIPS	Spread	Neutral	Rounded	JAW
High	/iː/		/u:/	Close
Mid-high	/ɪ/		/ʊ/	
Mid	/e:/	/ə/	/o:/	
Mid-low	/ɛ/	/ʌ/	/ɔ/	
Low	/æ/		/ɑ/	Open
TONGUE	Front	Central	Back	

FIGURE 3.1 Tongue, jaw and lip positions for some English vowels

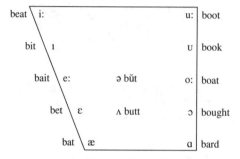

FIGURE 3.2 Position of some English vowels in the vocal tract

When jaw opening is combined with lip gesture, individual vowels can be identified rather accurately by the shape of the lips and the opening between them, as lip-readers are well aware. To convince yourself that this is true, watch another person silently "pronouncing" the basic vowels shown in Figure 3.2, going first down each column, with increasing jaw opening, then across each row from front to back, changing from spread to rounded lips.

The English vowels of Figure 3.1 include five **front vowels**, two **central vowels** and five **back vowels**. Front vowels involve a tongue constriction made with the front of the tongue at the front of the hard palate. Figure 3.3a shows the tongue position for the front vowel of the word *beat*. Central vowels involve a tongue constriction made with the center of the tongue at the center of the palate. Back vowels involve a constriction made with the back of the tongue at the back of the palate, i.e. the velar region. Figure 3.3b shows the tongue position for the back vowel of the word *boot*.

Because the jaw opening for high vowels is slight, their natural pronunciation is relatively quick as compared to vowels produced with greater jaw opening, which takes longer to achieve. They are thus

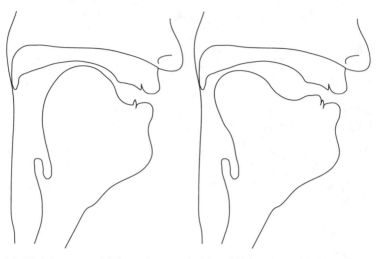

(a) High front vowel /iː/ (e.g. *beat*)   (b) High back vowel /uː/ (e.g. *boot*)

FIGURE 3.3 Contrasting tongue positions for high vowels

inherently short vowels, though they can be prolonged, if desired, for as long as breath holds out. Low vowels are the most sonorant of vowels. Because the opening of the jaw for low vowels takes some time to achieve, these vowels have inherent length, i.e. they are naturally longer than other vowels.

Vowels produced at the most extreme positions – i.e. with the most exaggerated tongue and lip gestures and in the most front and most back positions – are said to have a **colorful** auditory quality (Donegan 1978), while those produced at less extreme positions are said to be **colorless** or "dull" in auditory quality. As you move from more extreme, or **peripheral**, vowel positions to less extreme positions, the auditory color of vowels diminishes. The most colorful vowel is /iː/, which is produced at a very high and front position within the mouth, as shown in Figure 3.2. The least colorful vowel, produced at mid central position – i.e. between front and back, high and low – is /ə/.

Monophthongs and diphthongs

The English vowel system includes both **monophthongs** and **diphthongs**. In the production of monophthongs, the tongue remains in a relatively unchanging position throughout articulation. In the production of diphthongs, in contrast, the tongue moves from one position to another. The two articulations of a diphthong can be described as **nucleus** plus **glide**. The nucleus is that part of the diphthong which is sustained the longest. The glide can be thought of as a more **transient** sound which provides a transition into (i.e. preceding) or out of (i.e. following) the nucleus.

We can think of monophthongs as relatively homogeneous and pure as compared to diphthongs, which are comparatively heterogeneous mixtures of two different vowel sounds. Of course, as in all connected speech, the movement of the tongue either to or from the articulatory position of a neighboring sound may cause the tongue position for a vowel to be altered somewhat in context. Commonly, in connected speech, monophthongs become less homogeneous and diphthongs become less heterogeneous (i.e. more homogeneous). In other words, in connected speech the differences between monophthongs and diphthongs are **neutralized** to some extent under the influence of neighboring sounds.

The vowel system for English includes more vowels than shown in Figure 3.1. Missing from Figure 3.1 are three diphthong phonemes. Three of these diphthongs glide both up and either forward (/aɪ/, /ɔɪ/) or backward (/aʊ/). Note that in /aɪ/ and /aʊ/, the symbol for the nucleus is not script *a* but lower case *a*. /a/ is a low vowel at approximately the same height as /ɑ/ but produced at a more forward position. As compared to /æ/, /a/ is somewhat lower and less front.

In the three diphthongs /aɪ/, /ɔɪ/ and /aʊ/, the nucleus is considered to be the first vowel sound, and the glide is considered to be the second part, since the first vowel sound is longer. Since the position of each of the diphthongs changes dramatically during their production, their articulatory place is usually represented by arrows showing their starting and ending position, as in Figure 3.4, which also indicates their tongue positions relative to the other vowel phonemes.

The system of English vowels

Full and reduced vowels

Vowels can be divided into **full** (or **strong**) and **reduced** (or **weak**) vowels. Full vowels are those which occur in positions of strength or focus in words and longer utterances, e.g. in stressed (strong) syllables or in **monosyllabic** (one-syllable) words spoken in isolation from any context. Reduced vowels occur in non-focal, weak positions in words or longer utterances.

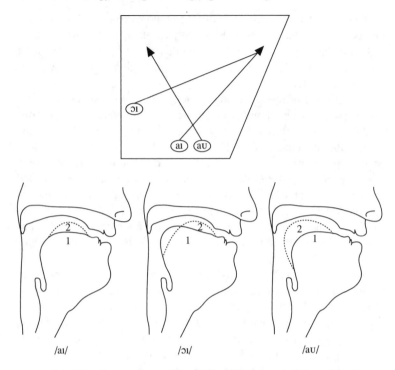

FIGURE 3.4 Changing tongue positions of the diphthongs /aɪ/, /ɔɪ/ and /aʊ/

As individual words increase in length, the number of weak syllables – and therefore the number of reduced vowels – will often increase. In slow, careful speech, people tend to articulate vowels fully, whereas in rapid, casual speech, the incidence of reduced vowels increases. In fact, experimental evidence has demonstrated that in rapid speech, all vowels tend toward the middle of the vowel space, towards the position of schwa, which can be considered the **neutral** vowel position for English. The tendency to weaken vowels towards schwa in conversational English seems to be a difficult aspect of English to learn for most non-native speakers, possibly in part because of an over-reliance on spelling as a guide to pronunciation.

English contains both monosyllabic and **polysyllabic** (multi-syllable) words. Every word spoken in isolation contains at least one stressed (or accented) syllable. For monosyllables spoken in isolation, the only syllable is stressed. For polysyllables, only certain syllables are stressed, with the exact location of the stresses depending on the history of the individual word.

In words of two or more syllables, one syllable will receive the main stress, and the other syllables will either receive a lesser degree of stress or be unstressed (unaccented). Only the stressed syllables will be pronounced with full vowels. The unstressed syllables will be pronounced with reduced vowels. By convention, the phonemic symbol for a reduced vowel is /ə/ (schwa). Examples of full and reduced vowels in morphologically related words are shown in Figure 3.5.

There are many possibilities in English for the location of stressed and unstressed syllables, and for the corresponding full and reduced vowels. The nature of vowels as full or reduced within individual lexical items of more than one syllable is (relatively) fixed, though there is some individual, social and regional variation in the location of the

Full vowel	Reduced vowel
city	citify
history	historical
implicit	implication
beautician	beautify
able	ability
explain	explanation
reference	refer
necessary	necessitate
application	apply
Japanese	Japan
product	production
conduct (noun)	conduct (verb)
confront	confrontation
production	product
super	superlative
capsule	encapsulate
full	artful
full	fulfilment
photograph	photography
promo (slang)	promotion
geology	geological
economy	economical
computerize	computerization
mechanize	mechanization

FIGURE 3.5 Full and reduced vowels in morphologically related words

main stress in individual words and the degree to which vowels not under the main stress are reduced. For example, *abdomen* may be pronounced either /ˈæbdoːmən/ or /əbˈdoːmən/, and *controversy* may be pronounced /ˈkɑntrəvərsiː/ or /kənˈtrɔvərsiː/. This type of variation will not be dealt with in this chapter but is saved for the discussion of stress in Chapter 4.

Stress is related to vowel quality not only at the lexical level, but also at the level of longer utterances. As will be discussed in more detail in Chapter 4, in the context of whole utterances, individual words or phrases may have their stress reduced as a way to informationally background them – and to foreground other linguistic elements. Certain categories of words tend to be reduced because they are generally not the focus of information in utterances, while other categories of words tend to be pronounced more fully because they are more typically the focus of information in utterances.

The words which often receive reduced pronunciations are termed **function words**. The class of function words includes auxiliaries (forms of *have*, *do* and *be* used to make compound tenses), prepositions, conjunctions, articles and pronouns (personal, possessive and demonstrative). The words which tend to be pronounced more fully are often termed **content words**. These include the major grammatical categories, i.e. nouns, verbs, adjectives and adverbs. Figure 3.6 illustrates full and reduced pronunciations of function words.

It is important to realize that these are only general guidelines indicating which words are likely to be reduced or fully pronounced in context. In general, the speaker always has the option of emphasizing a particular word or not, depending on his or her exact intention.

The short conversation below illustrates reduced and full pronunciations of the vowel of the word *can*. It would be quite typical for the utterance of (a) to include a reduced pronunciation of the vowel of *can*, i.e. /ə/, since this word is not in an informationally focal position within the utterance. In contrast, the vowel of *can't* in (b) and of *can* in (c) will be unreduced /æ/ because these words are strongly accented as a result of the informational focus on their meaning in these two utterances.

(a) Marty: You can do it if you really want to.
(b) Pat: No, I can't.
(c) Marty: Yes, you can!

Likewise, some adverbs may be weakened in context. Compare (a) below, where *just* is an adjective, with (b) and (c), where *just* is used as an adverb.

Word	Full form	Reduced form	Sample context for reduced form
a	/eː/	[ə]	a girl [ə'gəɬ]
the	/ði:/	[ðə]	the girl [ðə'gəɬ]
that	/ðæt/	[ðəʔt˺]	You said that you would. ['jə'sɛd̥ðəʔt˺jə'wʊd]
you	/ju:/	[jə]	What do you want: ['wəjə'wɑ:nt˺]
his	/hɪz/	[ɪz]	Here's his seat. ['hirzɪz'si:ʔt˺]
to	/tu:/	[tʰə]	To go, please. [tʰə'gou'pʰl̥i:z̥]
at	/æt/	[ət˺]	at 5:00 [ət˺'faɪvə'kʰlɑ'k˺]
as	/æz/	[əz]	as soon as I can [əz'su:nəzaɪ'kʰæ:n]
and	/ænd/	[ɛnd], [ɛn], [m̩], [n̩], [ŋ̍]	girls and guys ['gəɬzn̩'gaɪz]
do	/du:/	[də], [d]	Do you want to go? [djə'wɑnə'go:]
has	/hæz/	[həz], [əz], [z], [s]	He has made it. [iəz'meɪɾɪʔt˺]
have	/hæv/	[həv], [əv], [v]	We have arrived. ['wi:əvə'raɪvd]
can	/kæn/	[kʰən], [kʰn], [kʰŋ̍]	You can go. ['ju:kʰŋ̍'gou]
would	/wʊd/	[wəd], [əd], [d]	She would like some ['ši:əd'laɪʔksəm]

FIGURE 3.6 Full and reduced forms of function words in context

(a) He's a just man.
(b) He's just a man.
(c) He's just arrived.

Notice that in (a), the vowel of *just* will not be reduced – i.e. it will be /ʌ/ – whereas (b) and (c) may both be pronounced with that same full vowel or a reduced vowel – /ə/ – depending on whether or not the speaker wants to emphasize the meaning of the word *just*.

The predictable variation in pronunciation of vowels based on whether or not a syllable is unstressed is only one type of regular **alternation**, i.e. predictable phonological modification, in vowel pronunciations in English. Other types of alternations in morphologically related words, as illustrated in the word pairs of Figure 3.7 (and as taken up again in Chapter 5), are common. Notice that in these cases, a full diphthong or long monophthong in one word alternates with a short monophthong in another morphologically related form of the word. In some cases, the spelling of the word varies with the varying pronunciation. In other cases, the spelling is constant across the alternation, i.e. it does not vary according to pronunciation. As we will see in Chapter 5, there is a strong tendency in English for orthography to correspond to morphology rather than to phonology. This morphological consistency, which implies phonological inconsistency, is often a source of difficulty in pronunciation for literate non-native speakers.

/iː/	/ɛ/
serene	serenity
dream	drempt

/eː/	/æ/
explain	explanatory
inflame	inflamatory

/uː/	/ɑ/
school	scholar
knew	knowledge

/oː/	/ɑ/
telephone	telephonic
neurosis	neurotic

/aɪ/	/ɪ/
line	lineage
rise	risen

/aʊ/	/ʌ/
south	southern
pronounce	pronunciation

FIGURE 3.7 Alternations involving full vowels in morphologically related words

Tense and lax vowels

A main part of the English vowel system is usefully described in terms of contrasting pairs of vowels, as follows:

FRONT		BACK	
iː	high ⟩ HIGH	uː	high ⟩ HIGH
ɪ	low	ʊ	low
eː	high ⟩ MID	oː	high ⟩ MID
ɛ	low	ɔ	low

In English, the front and back vowels in the high to mid-low range occur in pairs. These pairs are made up of (1) a higher and longer member and (2) a lower and shorter member. In each pair, the lower member has a somewhat more open jaw and lip position than the higher member.

Note that although the higher member in each pair is a vowel which is inherently shorter than the lower member, this inherent shortness is overridden in normal English pronunciation. That is, in English, the higher member of each pair is pronounced with greater duration than the lower member. For example, Giegerich (1992: 234) shows durations for British English of /iː/ that are 60–90% longer then /ɪ/ (depending on what follows), and Lindsey (1990: 114) shows values in RP for the higher member of each of these pairs which are 50–85% longer then the lower member of the pair. Though the length difference is less pronounced in some varieties – for example, the higher member of each pair is given by Lindsey (1990: 114) as generally only about 30–35% longer than the lower member in American English – the length difference is consistent enough that the higher phoneme in each of these pairs is represented with a long mark.

It is possible to view the lower and shorter vowel in each pair as a more open or relaxed version of the higher and longer vowel with which it is paired. The contrast between such pairs is sometimes characterized as a difference between **lax** and **tense** vowels (though some would argue that /ɔ/ is more accurately classified as tense than lax). This characterization may have particular value for teaching the English vowels, to help students separate the vowels of English into the correct system of oppositions.

For convenience, the distinction between tense and lax can also be extended to the other vowels in the system, with the diphthong phonemes /aɪ/, /aʊ/ and /ɔɪ/ classified as tense and /ə/ and /ʌ/ classified as lax. Because they are produced at relatively extreme positions within the vowel space, requiring considerable effort in production, /æ/ and /ɑ/ are also sometimes considered tense – as opposed to /a/, which is considered lax. (However, for short–long vowel distinctions as discussed in Chapter 5, /æ/ and /ɑ/ must both be considered short, or lax).

Positional variation

Like consonants, vowels initiate contextual effects on neighboring sounds and are also subject to contextual effects in which they may partially assimilate a feature or features of neighboring sounds with which they coarticulate. Vowels may be lengthened, shortened, raised, lowered, fronted, backed, complexified, simplified or lost in certain phonological contexts. They may also precipitate various changes in the consonants with which they coarticulate. The positional effects involving vowels can be subsumed, as in the case of consonants, under the categories of durational effects, place effects, manner effects and strengthening and weakening effects of various sorts.

Durational effects

A given vowel is longer in certain contexts than others, in the following order:

before: Voiced obstruents > pause > nasals > voiceless obstruents

Giegerich (1992: 234), for example, gives the following values (in centiseconds) for /iː/ and /ɪ/ in a "typical RP speaker":

before:	Voiced fricative	Voiced stop	Pause	Nasal	Voiceless fricative	Voiceless stop
/iː/	36.0	28.5	28.0	19.5	13.0	12.3
/ɪ/	18.6	14.7	–	11.0	8.3	7.3

A phonetic transcription for vowels before voiced obstruents, pause or nasals will often indicate this length, using a colon, as in *buzz* ['bʌːz], *want* ['wɑːntˀ], *Come!* ['kʰʌːm]

A tendency for complementarity in length of the consonant and vowel in syllables made up of Vowel + Consonant (VC) – and to a lesser extent in CV syllables – has been found for English. According to this tendency, a durationally long consonant is preceded (or followed) by a short vowel, and a durationally short consonant is preceded (or followed) by a short vowel. Thus, voiceless stops, which are generally longer than voiced stops because of aspiration (in CV position) and pre-glottalization (in VC position), occur next to short vowels, and voiced stops occur next to long vowels.

Given identical context, vowels are longer in stressed than unstressed syllables and in monosyllables than polysyllables. As the number of syllables increases, the length of vowels decreases. The shortest vowels are found in rapidly articulated, long and unbroken stretches of speech. Not only the longest, but also the most heterogeneous, vowels occur – all else being equal – in slow speech.

Place effects

When there is a long distance between the place of articulation of a vowel and a neighboring consonant, the spatial gap between the two phonemes is often minimized in one of two ways:

(1) a transitional glide develops to bridge the gap; or
(2) the place of the vowel and/or the consonant is shifted to a less extreme position.

A large articulatory gap occurs between:

- a front vowel and
  a consonant with a back (velar) tongue position;
- a back vowel and
  a consonant with a front (alveolar or interdental) tongue position;

- a vowel produced with a low tongue position and
  a consonant produced with a high or front tongue position, or a more
  closed jaw position;
- a vowel produced with a high tongue position and
  a consonant produced with a low position of all or part of the tongue.

In addition to becoming more similar in articulation, neighboring phonemes may also become more similar in terms of perception.

High-to-low dimension

Fronting and raising with velar stops and nasals

A common contextual effect is raising of non-high front vowels next to
velar stops and preceding nasals. In cases where a vowel is raised from
its "normal" reference position, a slight degree of raising is indicated by
an up-pointing, v-shaped arrow placed to the right of the phonetic symbol. In more extreme cases of raising, e.g. in some varieties of British
English, Irish English and American English, the vowel may actually
shift upwards to the tongue position of a higher vowel phoneme. After
velar stops, the coarticulation of the stop with a front vowel often produces a palatalized glide [j] between the consonant and the vowel.
Examples of these raising and palatalization effects are:

> *and* [æ^nd] or [ɛnd]
> *pen* [pʰɛ^n], [pʰen] or [pʰɪn]
> *get* [gɛ^t˺], [gʲet˺] or [gʲɪt˺]
> *kit* [kʰɪ^t˺] or [kʲɪ^t˺]
> *bag* [bæ^g] or [bɛg]

Raising and lowering before /l/ and /r/

In some varieties of English, the lax vowels of words spelled with *-ill*
and *-ell* are raised under the influence of the high tongue position of the
consonant, especially when produced as the "light" /l/ variant with
raised tongue tip. Examples are:

> *pill*   [pʰɪ^l]
> *silly* [sɪ^lɨ]
> *sell*   [sɛ^l]

On the other hand, a "dark" /l/ may cause lowering of the tongue
position of a preceding vowel, as may /r/. In such cases, a down-point-
ing arrow following a vowel symbol indicates a slight degree of lowering. Sometimes, the vowel lowers enough so that a different vowel

symbol should be selected. Often, a slight vocalic glide transition develops in the position before the liquid, with or without the lowering effect. Examples of contextual effects in this position are as follows:

peel	[pʰiːˇl] or [pʰɪəl]		*poor*	[pʰuːˇr] or [pʰuər]
feel	[fiːˇl] or [fɪəl]		*tour*	[tʰuːˇr] or [tʰuər]
sail	[seːˇl] or [sɛəl]		*door*	[doːˇr] or [dɔər]

Note that the raising of lax vowels and the lowering of tense ones before /l/ tend to neutralize the distinction between neighboring tense and lax vowels and to make words such as the following homophonous in some varieties:

peel/pill	e.g.	[pʰɪːˇəl]
feel/fill	e.g.	[fiːˇəl]
sail/sell	e.g.	[seːˇəl]

Front-to-back dimension

Peripheral and non-peripheral articulation

In emphatic speech, front and back vowels may be produced at very peripheral positions, i.e. the most front and back places of articulation. In non-emphatic, casual speech, on the other hand, it is common for the most peripheral vowels to be produced in a less peripheral location of the vowel space. The more relaxed articulation becomes, the more the vowels tend to collapse inward, towards the position of schwa, as illustrated in Figure 3.8.

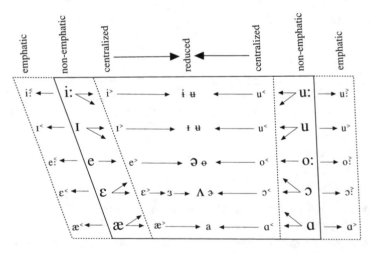

FIGURE 3.8 Contrast of positions of vowels in morphologically related words

The barred phones ("barred i", "barred ɪ", "barred u" and "barred ʊ")
are the central counterparts of the non-barred phones with the same lip
shapes. Besides being positional variants of vowel phonemes, the
barred phones also occur in some regional and social variants (see
below).

Backing before back consonants
Before back consonants, including velar stops, velar nasal, "dark" /l/,
and back-raised or retroflexed /r/, backing of non-back vowels is likely
to occur, symbolized with a back-pointing arrow, as in:

beg	[bɛ⁾g]
big	[bɪ⁾g]
bell	[bɛ⁾ɫ]
beer	[bi:⁾r]

In addition, before a strongly retroflexed /r/, the preceding vowel may
be both backed and retroflexed, as in:

bar [bɑ⁾ɽ]   *beard* [bɨ:⁾ɽd] or [bɨːɽd]

In the combination /ər/, the weak vowel is usually retroflexed under the
influence of a strongly retroflexed /r/.

Fronting before front consonants
Under the influence of a following consonant that has a relatively front
tongue position, a back vowel may be fronted somewhat, symbolized
by a front-pointing arrow, as in:

tooth	[tʰu:⁽θ]
lost	[lɔ⁽stʰ]

Manner effects

Nasalization

Nasalization of vowels preceding nasal consonants is a common
phenomenon in English, occurring almost categorically in many varieties, as the articulation of the nasal consonant is anticipated in the
lowering of the velum during the production of the vowel. Nasalization
is represented by ~ over the vowel, as in:

am [æ̃m]   *gone* [gɔ̃n]   *king* [kʰĩ:ŋ]

Devoicing

Vowels may be (partially) devoiced when they occur flanked by voice-less stops, as in:

sit [s ɪt˺]   *kiss* [kʰɪs]   *hip* [h ɪp˺]

Strengthening and weakening

Complexification by strong articulation

In the context of slow, emphatic speech, vowels are strongly articulated and strengthened by lengthening and gliding. In such cases, mono-phthongs may become diphthongal, as a long nucleus breaks into more than one vowel sound.

Any effect which makes a vowel longer or more complex strengthens it, since the nature of vowels is to be prolonged. Any effect which lowers a vowel is also a strengthening effect, as low vowels are more sonorant than high vowels. Finally, effects involving fronting and back-ing which make vowels more peripheral can also be considered as strengthening their articulation as well as their perceptual characteristics.

Simplification by weak articulation

Conversely, rapid and unemphatic articulation produces short, homoge-neous vowels which coarticulate maximally with surrounding conso-nants. Changes which close the articulation of vowels make them more like consonants and so represent weakening effects. Effects which move vowels to a more central position are also weakenings, as vowels become less colorful the farther they are away from the extremities of the vowel space.

Under such conditions of weakening, vowels undergo simplification and loss, as well as monophthongization and centralization. As we will see in more detail in Chapter 4, the conditions that weaken articulation destress speech, making individual segments less distinctive and result-ing in loss of segments from the stream of speech.

A main effect of destressing is to centralize vowels, as mentioned above. Destressing also means considerable overlapping in the planning and execution of syllables and the segments that comprise them. Under conditions of maximum coarticulation, individual segments achieve compromise positions between the articulatory place of each neighbor-ing sound. Accordingly, at a relatively rapid rate of articulation in which speech is destressed, consonants tend to open a bit, and vowels tend to close a bit in their articulation.

Regional and social variation

Systemic variation

Type 1 and Type 2 vowel systems

The varieties of English fall into two large groups (for a similar insight, see Giegerich 1992: chs. 3, 4):

> *Type 1 vowel system* The vowels, particularly the tense ones, tend to be diphthongal. The distinction between tense and lax vowels is one between very diphthongized and slightly diphthongized vowels or between diphthongs and monophthongs. In Type 1 vowel systems, unstressed vowels tend to be produced at a central position within the mid–high to mid–low range.

> *Type 2 vowel system* The vowels tend to be monophthongal, with the tense ones generally being longer than the lax ones. Tense and lax vowels differ in either quantity or quality, although in some varieties the distinction is not maintained, and the tense and lax vowel in each pair have merged to one phoneme, generally closer to the position of the higher member. In Type 2 vowel systems, reduced vowels may not occur, and /a/ may substitute for /ə/ as well as for /æ/ and /ɑ/.

For Type 1 vowel systems, the vowel space is most symmetrically modeled by a trapezoid (Figure 3.9a), which corresponds roughly to the shape of the area of the mouth at and under the palatal region that is used for producing the English vowel sounds. For Type 2 vowel systems, where there is only one low vowel, a triangle is a better model of the vowel space (Figure 3.9b).

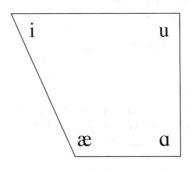
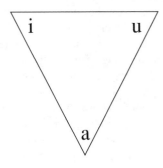

(a) type 1 vowel space: trapezoid   (b) type 2 vowel space: triangle

FIGURE 3.9 Two models of phonetic space corresponding to the two types of vowel systems

The Type 1 vowel system is essentially a **color-based** one, in that distinctions between neighboring vowels are made in terms of vowel color. Pairs of tense and lax vowels can be characterized as a more colorful one – i.e. the more diphthongal one – and a less colorful one – i.e. the more monophthongal one. The Type 1 vowel system is therefore based primarily on distinctions in quality involving the type and degree of diphthongization. Length distinctions between vowels are secondary in the sense that the length of the tense vowels is a consequence of their more heterogeneous nature.

In the Type 2 vowel system, the distinction between neighboring vowels is more in terms of quantity, or length, and degree of opening of the jaw, or tongue height. Such a system, where quantity and height distinctions predominate, can be termed **sonority-based**.

In systems which have diphthongal vowels, these are generally either **upgliding** – i.e. towards a higher position – or **ingliding** – i.e. towards a more central position. Some examples of upgliding and ingliding pronunciations are given below.

	UPGLIDING	INGLIDING
/i:/	$[i^{v_i}]$, $[i^j]$	$[i^ə]$
/e:/	$[e^{\underline{I}}]$	$[e^ə]$
/u:/	$[u^{v_u}]$, $[u^w]$	$[u^ə]$
/o:/	$[o^{ʊ}]$	$[o^ə]$

While no variety perfectly represents either type, most of the "Old Englishes" such as British, American, Canadian, Australian and New Zealand – with Scottish and Irish varieties being notable exceptions – tend towards Type 1. In contrast, most of the "New Englishes" such as many African, Caribbean, Pacific and Asian varieties tend towards the Type 2 vowel system. As the Type 2 system is simpler than the Type 1, it may be the preferred vowel system for a community which adopts English as a communicational resource in addition to another (or other) primary language(s) of the community.

The Type 2 system, being phonetically less complex than the Type 1, is presumably easier to acquire and so may be the most learnable vowel system for those communities which have recently acquired English as an additional language. Moreover, while the phonetically more complex Type 1 system is well-suited to defining complex *variation* within or between groups, the simpler Type 2 system is suited to defining in-group or inter-group *similarities*. A Type 2 English vowel system may also be favored to the extent that it mirrors the type of vowel system of other primary community languages in locales where English is a recent arrival on the language scene.

As an additional reason for the prevalance of Type 2 systems among the New Englishes, the Type 1 system is generally that of the older English-speaking nations and is therefore associated with "outsider" connotations which community members where English has been recently imported may choose not to adopt. This shows that the difference between two vowel systems, like other linguistic differences, can take on a social value which helps to delimit groups of speakers. As another example of this, the observations of Labov (1972: 303–4) and Hindle (1978) that women in the US produce vowels at more peripheral positions than men is evidence of a possible tendency on the part of females to have more "colorful" vowel systems than men. Generalizing on these observations, it could be speculated that women tend more to Type 1 vowel systems and men to Type 2. The reason might have to do with a tendency among women to define difference or distinctiveness by means of language, or it might relate to natural physiological differences in phonetic perception and production between men and women.

The following data from the 1930s on the vowels of Black and White speakers from three East Coast states in the US (Maryland, Virginia and North Carolina) further illustrates the differential tendencies of groups of speakers towards either a Type 1 or a Type 2 vowel system in some of the front and back vowels, as well as specific tendencies for individual vowels:

Table 3.1. Percentages of Monophthongal, Upgliding and Ingliding
Pronunciations of Five Stressed Vowels (Dorrill 1986: 150)

			Monophthongal	Upgliding	Ingliding
/i:/	Black	(N = 93)	83% (N = 77)	12% (N = 11)	5% (N = 5)
	White	(N = 88)	36% (N = 32)	52% (N = 46)	11% (N = 10)
/u:/	Black	(N = 106)	79% (N = 84)	16% (N = 17)	5% (N = 5)
	White	(N = 118)	58% (N = 68)	37% (N = 44)	5% (N = 6)
/e:/	Black	(N = 145)	56% (N = 81)	29% (N = 42)	15% (N = 22)
	White	(N = 147)	17% (N = 25)	71% (N = 104)	12% (N = 18)
/o:/	Black	(N = 139)	71% (N = 99)	14% (N = 19)	15% (N = 21)
	White	(N = 135)	36% (N = 49)	58% (N = 78)	6% (N = 8)
/ɔ/	Black	(N = 98)	61% (N = 59)	21% (N = 21)	18% (N = 18)
	White	(N = 98)	52% (N = 51)	31% (N = 30)	17% (N = 17)

At the time this data was gathered, it would appear that the vowel system of Black American speakers tended more strongly towards the

Type 2 system than that of White Americans, who had a larger percentage of diphthongal vowels, particularly upgliding ones.

Some Type 1 systems

On the whole, American English tends towards a Type 1 system, as does British English. Below are shown some common realizations of the vowel phonemes in British and American English (based on Lindsey 1990; Trudgill and Hannah 1985: chs. 2, 3; Wells 1982: v. 2, ch. 4):

/iː/	bead, beat [iᵛⁱ], [iʲ], [iː]
	beer, pier [iː], [ɪə]
/ɪ/	bid [ɪ]
/eː/	bayed, bait [eɪ], [eʲ]
	bear, pare [eɪ], [eː] [ɛə], [ɛ]
/ɛ/	bed, bet [ɛ]
/æ/	bad, bat [æ], [a]
/ə/	rabbit, butter [ə]
	burr, bird [ə], [əː]
/ʌ/	bud, butt, butter [ʌ]
/uː/	booed, boot [uᵛ], [uʷ], [uː]
	boor, poor [uː], [ʊə]
/ʊ/	book, bull [ʊ], [ʊˤ]
/oː/	bode, boat [oʊ], [oʷ], [ʌʊ]
/ɔ/	bought, paw [ɔ], [ɔː]
	bore, pore [ɔ], [ɔː], [ɔə]
/ɑ/	balm, bard, body [a], [aː], [ɑ], [ɑː]
/aɪ/	buy, blind, blight [aɪ], [ʌɪ]
	fire [aɪ], [aɪə]
/ɔɪ/	boy, coin [ɔɪ], [oɪ], [ʌɪ]
/aʊ/	bound, now [aʊ], [æʊ], [ɑʊ], [ʌʊ]
	sour [aʊ], [aʊə]

For both rhotic and non-rhotic varieties, the phonetic variants before /r/ may be monophthongal or diphthongal – or triphthongal in the case of [aɪə] and [aʊə]. For the rhotic varieties, they tend to be monophthongal and for the non-rhotic, diphthongal (or triphthongal) as /r/ is realized as [ə].

Australian varieties of English, which range from a type near RP to a "broader" Australian Type 1 system, have the following common realizations of the phonemes (based on Horvath 1985: ch. 6; Mitchell and Delbridge 1965: ch. V; Trudgill and Hannah 1985: ch. 2; Wells 1982: v. 3, ch. 8):

/iː/	bead, beat [ʌɪ], [iᵛɪ̞]
	beer, pier [ɪə], [iː]
/ɪ/	bid [ɪˆ]
/eː/	bayed, bait [ʌɪ], [aɪ]
	bear, pare [eː], [eə]
/ɛ/	bed, bet [e], [ɛˆ]
/æ/	bad, bat [ɛ] [æˆ]
/ə/	rabb*i*t, butt*e*r [ə]
	burr, bird [ə], [əː]
/ʌ/	bud, butt, b*u*tter [ʌ]
/uː/	booed, boot [əʉ] [uᵛʉ]
	boor, poor [ɔə], [ɔː], [ʊə]
/ʊ/	book, bull [ʊ]
/oː/	bode, boat [ʌu], [ʌu], [aʉ]
/ɔ/	bought, paw [ɔː], [oː]
	bore, pore [ɔː], [ɔə]
/ɑ/	balm, bard, b*o*dy [aː], [ɑː]
/aɪ/	buy, blind, blight [aɪ], [ɑɪ], [ɑə]
	fire [aɪə], [ɑɪə]
/ɔɪ/	boy, coin [ɔɪ], [oɪ]
/aʊ/	bound, now [æʊ], [æʉ], [æo], [ɛo], [aʊ]
	sour [æʊə]

New Zealand English is similar to Australian English, but has [ɨ] as the realization of /ɪ/ and [ʉː] or [ɨː] as the realization of /uː/. Before /l/, [ʊ] is centralized as well, so that *will* and *wool* may both be pronounced [ɨ]. There is also a tendency in New Zealand English for /iː/ and /eː/ to merge before /r/, so that both *bear* and *beer* are pronounced [beˆː], [beˆə] or [bɪə] (Trudgill and Hannah 1985: 19; Wells 1982: 608). South African English has similar features to New Zealand English, though the vowel of *house* tends to [aə] or even to a monophthongal, low and fairly front vowel (Lass 1990; Trudgill and Hannah 1985: 25–6).

Some Type 2 systems

Scottish English tends towards a Type 2 system with differences in vowel quality for tense and lax vowels as follows:

MONOPHTHONGS			DIPHTHONGS	
i		u	æ	*sighed*
ɪ		(ʊ)	ʌi	*side*
e	ə	o	ʌu	*house*
ɛ		ɔ	ɔe	*boy*
(æ)	a	(ɑ)		

For many speakers of Scottish English, the only vowel phonemes are those shown outside parentheses. For such speakers, /a/ substitutes for /æ/ and /ɑ/, so that *bad* and *bard* have the same vowel, and /ʊ/ has merged with /u/, so that *pool* and *pull* have the same vowel. The vowels shown in parentheses are additional contrasts which may be realized in middle class speech (Macafee 1983: 34).

Northern Irish English shares many features with Scottish English (Trudgill and Hannah 1985: 90), though /e:/ is often diphthongal, [ei] or [ɛə], except when not closed by a consonant, as in *bay*, [bɛ:]. In addition, the vowel of *house* generally glides to a central position, being realized in Northern Irish English by such variants as [æʉ] or [ɑʉ] (Trudgill and Hannah 1985: 90). Southern Irish English is a Type 2 system with long/short vowel contrasts for the tense/lax pairs, centralization of the high back phoneme, a rounded variant of /ʌ/, and [a] as the usual phonetic realization of words with /æ/ in other varieties:

MONOPHTHONGS			DIPHTHONGS	
i:		ʉ:	ʌɪ	*buy*
ɪ		ʊ	ʌʉ	*house*
e:	ə	o:	ɔɪ	*boy*
ɛ		ɔ˂ ɔ:		
	a	ɑ:		

(adapted from Trudgill and Hannah 1985: 92)

As another Type 2 example, in Jamaican English, vowels generally occur in tense and lax pairs of monophthongs which vary in length and quality, with the approximate positions shown in the following diagram:

i:	*fleece*	u:	*goose*
ɪ	*kit*	ʊ	*foot*
e:	*face* (or [iɛ])	o:	*goat* (or [uɔ])
ɛ	*dress*	ɔ:	*cloth* (or [a:])
	a *trap*	a: *bath*	

(Wells 1982: 576)

In Indian English, the tense vowels tend to be monophthongal, and a length distinction may not be consistently maintained (Bansal 1990: 224; Wells 1982: 626). In addition, the phonological process operative in some other varieties such as American and British English which results in longer vowels before voiced than voiceless consonants does not apply in Indian English. For some speakers of Indian English, certain phonemic distinctions are lost and the vowel system is reduced, as /ɛ/ merges with /æ/ or /e:/ (Bansal 1990: 223).

In the West African English vernacular, a quality distinction is maintained for the tense and lax vowels at mid and mid–low height, whereas in the East African English vernacular, the distinction between tense and lax vowels is not maintained:

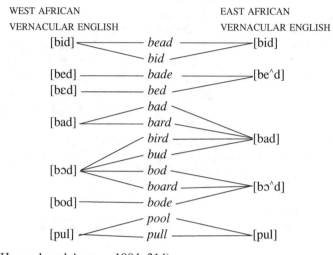

WEST AFRICAN VERNACULAR ENGLISH   EAST AFRICAN VERNACULAR ENGLISH

(Hancock and Angogo 1984: 314)

Variation in individual vowels

Front vowels

The non-low front vowels may be centralized, as in the case of /ɪ/ in New Zealand English and South African English, as well as lowered or raised in some varieties. Thus, for example, /i:/ is lowered to [ɛɪ] and [e:] in *eat*, *speak* in the Midland region of England (Russ 1984: 41), while in the Birmingham area of the West Midlands, these words may be pronounced with [ɜɪ] for /i:/ (Russ 1984: 47).

In Northern England /e:/ is monophthongal [ɛ] in *make* (Russ 1984: 45), while in Cockney /e:/ is [æɪ] (Russ 1984: 49). In the interior of the American Southeast, /ɛ/ is often raised to the position of /ɪ/ before /n/. In the American Southeast, the front vowels tend to converge on the position of [ɪ] following an initial alveolar or velar stop, as in *Timmy*, *gater*, *kettle* and *Daddy* (Pennington 1982: 178).

The low front vowel typically undergoes raising and/or backing in some contexts in all varieties. In New Zealand, /æ/ merges with /ɛ/ before /l/ in words like *Ellen/Alan* (Bayard 1991). /æ/ is [ɛ] or [eɪ] in Cockney (Russ 1984: 49) and for the Northern rim urban areas of the Eastern and Mid-Western United States, it is often produced at the position of [ɛ] or higher (Labov, Yaeger and Steiner 1972). While American speakers will usually pronounce the vowel of *after*, *bath*, *half*, *last* and *class* as the low front vowel [æ] or a higher front vowel, many Bostonians (LaFerriere 1977), Canadians (Esling and Warkentyne 1993) and British speakers have a low central [a] or low back [ɑ] vowel in these words. The Midland and northern dialects of England have [a] for both RP [æ] (in words such as *apple* and *cat*) and RP [ɑ:] (in words such as *chaff* and *last*), although there is considerable variation. In addition, Russ (1984: 41) reports a higher back vowel, [ɔ], for /æ/ in *man* in the West Midland dialect area of England.

To give an idea of the range of variation possible in a given community, the following realizations of the group of short-a words can be found in inner-city Belfast, Northern Ireland:

[ɛ]	*bag, bang*
[æ]	*back, flash*
[a], [aᶜ]	*back, bag, flash, chap, hat, can't, can, ant, aunt, dance*
ɑ	*grass, bad, man, pal, hand, can*
ɔ	*bad, man, can, hand*

(Milroy 1991: 78)

Through systematic investigation of the variation in this group of words, it can be shown that in Belfast, a somewhat different pattern of usage exists for three different neighborhoods in formal vs. casual speech style and for male and female as well as older and younger speakers. Based on an index score in which the higher values indicate backing, Milroy and Milroy (1978: 28) note the patterns shown in Figure 3.10 in three areas of Belfast – Ballymacarrett (B), Hammer (H) and Clonard (C).

Using an indexing scale ranging from 1 = [æ] to 5 = [ɑ], Romaine (1985: 175) documents the range of values shown in Tables 3.2 and 3.3 for short-a in Edinburgh in different phonological environments. As these index scores show, a following voiceless consonant is more likely to co-occur with front variants than a following voiced one, and most front variants of /æ/ occur before nasals. Romaine (1985: 177) also notes the pattern shown in Table 3.4 of co-variation of age and sex in her Edinburgh short-a data. From this data, it would appear that in Edinburgh, males above the age of 6 tend to use backer variants of short-a than females.

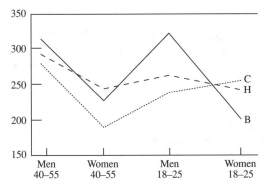

Source Milroy and Milroy 1978: 28

FIGURE 3.10 Backing of /a/ in the three communities

Table 3.2 The effect of voicing on values of short-a (Romaine 1985: 175)

Environment	Total tokens	Index score
voiced consonants	1144/362	316
voiceless consonants	2648/1096	242

Table 3.3 The effect of following consonant type (manner of articulation) on values of short-a (Romaine 1985: 175)

Higher values of short-a

Consonant type	Index score
/l/	273
stops	262
fricatives	256
nasals	210

Table 3.4 The co-variation of short-a with age and sex (Romaine 1985: 177)

10-year-olds		8-year-olds		6-year olds			All ages	
Males	Females	Males	Females	Males	Females		Males	Females
246	224	271	260	227	228		248	240
236		264		227				

Central vowels

Phonetically /ə/ is the most common weak vowel in English and may substitute for any other vowel in an a weak (unstressed) syllable. [ə] in unstressed syllables is particularly common in some varieties, such as Australian English, New Zealand English and Irish English, while other varieties may show more use of [ɨ] in words such as:

ac*i*d	velv*e*t	certific*a*te
stup*i*d	leafl*e*t	priv*a*te
orig*i*n	spotl*e*ss	
fug*i*tive	wit*e*ss	
antic*i*pate	busin*e*ss	

Both [i] and [ɨ] are common phonetic variants for the unstressed vowel of *-ing*, as in *running* and *stopping*, and for final *-y*, as in *city*, *Daddy* and *ruddy*. In all these words, full [i] or [ɪ] may also occur.

In Liverpool as well as in the North of England, /ʌ/ is realized as [ʊ] or [ə]: [mʊd], [məd] *mud*. (Russ 1984: 45, 49–50). Both *bird* and *bed* are pronounced with a front vowel, [bɛːd], in Liverpool (Russ 1984: 46). For rhotic and non-rhotic speakers, *bird* may be pronounced with [ə] or a somewhat lower vowel, [ʌ] or [ɜ], which is somewhat fronter than [ʌ], i.e. between the position of [ɛ] and [ʌ].

Back vowels

A collapsing of /uː/ and /ʊ/ in some or all words is a common phenomenon in English around the world. Thus, in the set *suit/soot/root*, some English speakers have the same vowel for all three words; others have the high back vowel /uː/ only for *suit* and the mid–high back vowel /ʊ/ for *soot* and *root*. In the set *roof/hoof/hooves*, both the high back vowel /uː/ and mid–high back vowel /ʊ/ are common in this group of words, depending on the speaker's geographical or sociolinguistic background.

Unrounding accompanying centralization or fronting of the high and mid–high back vowels is common in many varieties. In the interior of the American Southeast, the back vowels /uː/, /ʊ/ and /oː/ are generally centralized, as in *school*, *good* and *pole* (Pennington 1982: 179–80). For some /ʊ/ words – e.g. *pull*, *pudding*, *took*, *look* – [ʌ] is a common variant around the world. This variant occurs in the three neighborhoods of Belfast studied by Milroy and Milroy (1978: 26), where they found men in the 18–25-year-old age category to have a high percentage of [ʌ] for /ʊ/ in all neighborhoods, thus showing "the covert prestige of a vernacular variant amongst young males throughout the city (despite strict territorial segregation)". In Scottish English, as Romaine (1984: 79, n. 13) remarks: "*Boot* and *school* have unrounded front variants close to [ɨ]; other words (e.g., *pull* and *push*) may have unrounded centralized variants; still others (e.g., *shoe* and *lose*) occur only as rounded vowels". /uː/ as in *goose* and *moon* is [iə] in Northern England (Russ 1984: 41) and [ɜʊ] in the Birmingham area of the West Midlands (Russ 1984: 47).

As Russ (1984: 49) notes, "Cockney has a contrast between [ɔː] *paws* and [oː] *pause* which is absent in RP". In New Zealand, /oː/ and /ɔ/ are often both pronounced [ɑʊ] before /l/, as in *doll* and *dole* (Bayard 1991: 172). /oː/ is [əʊ] in *cold* and *old*; [ɛə] for southern parts of the Midlands (Russ 1984: 42); and [æʉ] for Cockney (Russ 1984: 49). /oː/ and /ɔ/ occur as [uə] in the North of England in *no, more, folk, roar, so, doors* (Russ 1984: 45). /oː/ is pronounced in *road* as [əʊ] in RP, but as [u] or [ʊ] in working class speech in Norwich (Trudgill 1974). Midland and northern dialects of England have [uə] in *coal, foal, coat*, which are [ɔɪ] in the Midland dialect (Russ 1984: p. 41).

Many speakers have the low back vowel only in a few words, e.g. those spelled *ar*, as in *bar, bard, darling*. According to Russ (1984): "Tyneside has two long *a* phonemes, a back [ɑː] in words spelled with *ar* (e.g., *farm*), and a front [aː] in words with *al* (e.g., *walk*)" (p. 48). The /ɑ/ in *fox* and *dog* is [œ] in parts of Northumberland and Durham, in the North of England (Russ 1984: 44). The vowel of *not* and *nought* tends for Mid-Western Americans and Californians to be the low central vowel [a]. In the set, *Astin/Austin/Osterize*, the initial vowel of the first word of this group is commonly a low front vowel [æ] for American speakers but may be low central [a] or low back [ɑ] for speakers in different parts of the British Isles. The vowel of the initial syllable of *Austin* and *Osterize* is generally back, either low [ɑ] or mid–low [ɔ], though for some speakers one or both of these words may have a low central vowel, i.e. [a].

/aɪ/, /ɔɪ/ and /aʊ/

The English diphthong /aɪ/ likewise shows variation depending on regional and stylistic factors. In some northern dialects of British English, in the West Midlands and among Cockney speakers in London, this diphthong is pronounced with a back vowel in the nucleus, as [ɔɪ] or /ɑɪ/ (Russ 1984: 47, 49). In these regions, pairs of words such as *boy* and *buy*, *Toyland* and *Thailand*, may become homophonous. In South Philadelphia and in parts of New York City, /aɪ/ is often pronounced [ʌɪ]. Both the [ɔɪ] and [ʌɪ] pronunciations of /aɪ/ can be considered local variants which occur most commonly in the casual speech of those with the strongest local orientation and least commonly in the careful speech of those with the weakest local orientation.

Milroy and Milroy (1978) examined the pronunciation of /aɪ/ in the three neighborhoods of Belfast in three speech styles: casual style (CS), formal style (FS) and word list style (WL). They found three different pronunciations of this vowel, which they assigned the following index scores:

[əɪ] = 0
[ɛɪ] = 1
[eɪ] = 2

Based on these index scores, they documented the patterns of variation shown in Figures 3.11, 3.12 and 3.13 in the three neighborhoods. From this pattern of variation, it would appear that in Belfast, "in all three communities casual style is distinguished from more monitored styles by marked fronting and raising" (Milroy and Milroy 1978: 32). Thus, whereas the centralized variant of /aɪ/ may be a vernacular variant in other dialect areas, it would appear to be the most generalized variant in Belfast.

In the North of England, /aɪ/ is sometimes realized as a monophthongal [i] in *blind* (Russ 1984: 41). In the American Southeast, there is also a variable tendency for monophthongization of /aɪ/ towards [æ] or a

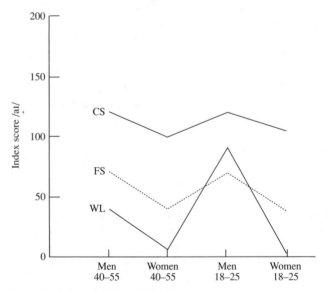

Source Milroy and Milroy 1978: 32

FIGURE 3.11 Clonard – all styles /aɪ/

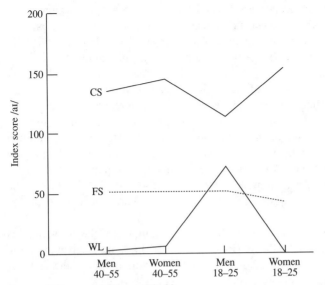

Source Milroy and Milroy 1978: 33

FIGURE 3.12 Hammer – all styles /aɪ/

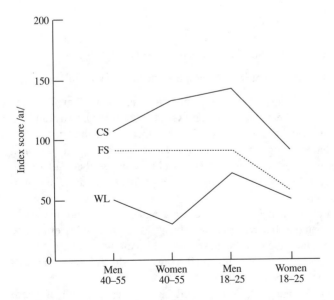

Source Milroy and Milroy 1978: 33

FIGURE 3.13 Ballymacarrett – all styles /aɪ/

somewhat lower and very fronted [a<]. In the Southeast region of the US, the monophthongal pronunciation of /aɪ/ in words such as *nice*, *rice*, *my*, *I* and *eye* is a marker of Southern pronunciation which is stigmatized for many people, both Southerners and non-Southerners.

For many speakers, /aʊ/ begins at low front position, rather than low central. In some parts of the English-speaking world, historical /aʊ/ has lost its gliding element and has become a monophthong, merging with /æ/. This tendency has been noted above for South African English and can also be observed in the Northeast of the US – for example, in South Philadelphia, where *mouth* and *math* may be pronounced with the same vowel, [æ]. In Cockney, /aʊ/ is [æə], while in Northern England, /aʊ/ is [u] in *house*, *pound* and *cow* (Russ 1984: 41, 45, 49). [u] is also the most common variant of /aʊ/ in Canada in words such as *about* and *house*.

/ɔɪ/ is [ɛɪ], [aɪ] and [ɑɪ] in different communities of the northern parts of the English Midlands (Russ 1984: 42). In some English speaking communities, /ɔɪ/ is a closer variant, [oɪ], while in others, the first element of the diphthong is centralized, yielding [ʌɪ].

Vowels activities

1. Identification of reduced and variable vowels

Consider the passage below and complete the tasks which follow:

> Ann was teaching in a private school in Asia. It was her first time overseas, and she wanted to go and visit her Aunt Pat in Australia. At first, she thought she wouldn't be able to manage the trip, as she didn't have enough money for the airfare. Luckily, she had just enough mileage coupons that she could exchange them all for an economy class ticket. She planned to go to Australia during her summer holiday.
>
> Unfortunately, her employer did not agree to her plan and asked her to postpone her trip to a less busy time, preferably some time after the fall holidays in the new year. Poor Ann was so disappointed that she considered not going at all. However, she eventually decided to go to her aunt's in February.
>
> So on February 10, Ann packed her big suitcase full of warm clothing and took off for ten days in Sydney. You can imagine her amazement when she arrived there. It was February and the temperature

was over 30 degrees Centigrade (over 90 degrees Fahrenheit)! Naturally, Ann was delighted, and her Aunt Pat was happy to lend her niece a bathing suit and some summer clothes. So Ann had a great time and went home in the dead of winter with a sun tan.

(a) Circle the vowels in the monosyllables in the passage to which a native speaker will generally give a reduced pronunciation in reading it aloud.

(b) Circle the vowels in the polysyllables that are generally reduced to a mid or high central vowel when read aloud by a native speaker.

(c) Underline the vowels in the class of "short-a" words in the passage. Of the underlined vowels, put a star under those that are likely to undergo raising in some varieties of English. Put a dot under any which you think may be backed to a low back [ɑ] in British RP accents.

2. Difficult vowels for non-native speakers of English

What are some of the vowels of English that may be difficult for most non-native speakers to pronounce? Why?

3. Difficult vowels for native speakers of English

What are some of the vowels of other languages that are often difficult for English speakers to pronounce? Why?

4. Vowel chart of other language

Chart the vowel system of another language or variety and describe the similarities and differences between that vowel system and your own variety of English.

5. Comprehensibility of non-native speaker's vowels/consonants

Which is harder to understand, a non-native speaker:

(a) who only approximates the correct articulation of the vowels of the target language but who has accurate pronunciation of consonants; or

(b) whose vowels are accurately produced but who does not achieve the target place or manner of articulation for certain consonants?

Which non-native speaker, (a) or (b), would you consider to have the most accented, or non-native, speech?

Which do you think is more common?

What implications do the answers given have for teaching?

6. Tying the teaching of vowels to orthography

What are the advantages and disadvantages of teaching the pronunciation of vowels in relation to orthography?

7. Contrastive teaching of vowels

Do you think it is valuable to explicitly teach the contrast of the vowels in English vs. the native language? If so, how might you go about teaching this contrast?

8. Sociolinguistic mini-research: pronunciation of English short-a words

Develop a research project in which you and/or your students will tape record members of your community, other teachers or students to discover similarities and differences in pronunciation of the following group of 15 short-a words: *class, bath, path, pass, gas, bad, sad, mad, plan, can, can't, hand, planet, language, daddy.*

To gather the tape-recorded data, you may have subjects read the short-a words in a list, in sentences or in a reading passage containing all of the words. A more elaborate design for the research would be to have subjects perform two or more of these tasks, possibly coupled with some kind of "free" production such as using short-a words in sentences which they create on the spot, and then to compare their pronunciation under different task conditions.

As for the project on post-vocalic *r* in Chapter 2, you will want to try to select your subjects to obtain an interesting pattern of variation.

To analyze the data, first classify your subjects' productions as:

(1)   mid front vowel   [e:]/[ɛ]
(2)   low front vowel   [æ]
(3)   low central vowel [a]
(4)   low back vowel   [ɑ]

Then you may compare and contrast the responses on individual words for speakers with similar and different characteristics or compare/contrast the overall pattern of responses for different subgroups of your respondents by tabulating the frequency of each of the responses (1–4) or by computing an index score for each group. For example, assuming 12 male and 12 female respondents with the following frequency of response:

			FEMALES (n = 12)	MALES (n = 12)
(1)	mid front vowel	[e:]/[ɛ]	58	43
(2)	low front vowel	[æ]	96	87
(3)	low central vowel	[a]	14	31
(4)	low back vowel	[ɑ]	12	19
		TOTAL	180	180

As before, the index score is calculated by multiplying the number of responses in each category by the index (1–4) for that category, summing the total and dividing by the number of items, which is $15 \times 12 = 180$ each for males and females, then multiplying the final result by 100. In our example:

FEMALES	MALES
$1 \times 58 = 58$	$1 \times 43 = 43$
$2 \times 96 = 192$	$2 \times 87 = 174$
$3 \times 14 = 42$	$3 \times 31 = 93$
$4 \times 12 = 48$	$4 \times 19 = 76$
TOTAL $340 / 180 = 1.89$	$386 / 180 = 2.14$
$1.89 \times 100 = 189$	$2.14 \times 100 = 214$

In this hypothetical example, the female subjects, with 189, have a lower index score than the male subjects, with an index score of 214. Thus, the females subjects on average have a fronter and higher pronunciation of the short-a words than the males.

9. Action research: students' perception and production of vowels

Develop an action research project to evaluate and remediate your students' production and perception of full and reduced vowels using (1) a listening measure such as a cloze exercise or identification of minimal pairs (e.g. *pin/pen*, *object*, noun and verb) and (2) a speaking measure such as imitation of minimal pairs or words spoken in context. First, decide on a set of words to test. It is recommended to include a minimum of 3 test words for each English vowel phoneme. Next, decide on how to present the test items, e.g. in commonly confused pairs such as tense/lax vowel pairs or noun/verb combinations with shifting stress, in individual sentence contexts, in a reading passage, etc. Then decide on what the students will be asked to do, e.g. to discriminate minimal pairs by marking the correct answer choice on a list of minimal pairs, to complete a cloze or listening comprehension exercise, to read aloud, to imitate or repeat after a speaker on tape, etc.

Code the data by marking students' responses as correct or incorrect and/or by transcribing the students' productions. Base your remediation program on an evaluation of the students' most serious problems in perception and/or production. Continually monitor the remediation program for its effectiveness and adjust periodically as needed.

10. Action research: teaching ideas for vowels

Try one or more of the teaching ideas below in a class, customizing and elaborating the exercise as needed, and then analyze and assess the results, following the procedures outlined for action research in previous chapters (exercises 9 and 10, Chapters 1 and 2). In designing your project, you will need to decide whether to carry out the research:

• in one or two classes;
• with or without a research partner;
• in your own class(es) and/or in someone else's;
• by trying out lessons simultaneously or sequentially.

Once you have designed your project, you will need to attend to its ongoing implementation and evaluation by:

• monitoring the effectiveness of instruction;
• making any necessary changes in curriculum or teaching approach;
• retrospectively assessing the teaching process and effects of instruction.

Teaching ideas for vowels

1. A sequence of activities for differentiating tense and lax vowels

These activities are appropriate for beginners and non-beginners.

A. *Modelling of tense and lax pairs*

The teacher models the tense and lax pairs of non-back vowels using a rubber band. For the tense member of each pair, the rubber band is stretched while the teacher pronounces the vowel. For the lax member of the pair, the rubber band is relaxed.

The teacher then models the tense member of pairs such as those listed below with clenched fists while saying "tense", the lax member with hands open saying "relaxed".

Example of tense/lax pairs

NON-BACK	BACK	MIXED
eat/it	pool/pull	bite/bot
beat/bit	fool/full	night/not
seat/sit	Luke/look	ride/rod
read/rid	nuke/nook	high/ha
aid/Ed	boat/bought	toyed/Todd
raid/red	coat/caught	joy/jaw
laid/led	low/law	foil/fall
bait/bet	so/saw	soy/saw
gad/god		gout/got
bat/bot		bout/bot
hat/hot		outer/otter
sack/sock		spout/spot

B. *Pair practice*

(1) Student pairs practice tense/lax non-back vowel pairs using a rubber band to model the difference in pronunciation. They then practice all of the pairs using the tense and relaxed hand motions to model the sounds simultaneous to their pronunciation.

(2) Students make lists of words for each pair of tense and lax vowels. Pairs or groups can be timed to see which can come up with the longest lists in 2–3 minutes. Points can be deducted for words placed in the wrong list. For example:

/iː/	/ɪ/
seen	pit
bean	hit
lean	hid
green	rid
lead	lid
read	lick

etc.

(3) Other pair and small group activities can be devised in the same formats as those shown in Teaching Ideas for Consonants, but using tense/lax vowel pairs such as those above as the basis for the activities.

C. *Vowel bingo*

Make up a bingo board in which each square contains a minimal pair including a tense and lax vowel contrast. To get ready for the bingo game, students circle one or the other word in each box. The teacher then acts as a "caller" who calls out one of the words in each box. If the word that the student has previously circled is the one called, the student places an "x" over this box. When a student has an "x" in every box, s/he says "bingo." This student wins a point if the circled words match the words on the caller's list. Individual students may act as callers to the rest of the class, or pairs or small groups may be formed to continue the game. Thus, the game can be repeated many times without boredom for additional practice.

In subsequent rounds of play, students receive a fresh bingo board. Thus, the teacher will want to make multiple copies of the bingo board. It is also possible to develop a set of multi-use differing bingo boards, each of which has only *one* word (the tense or lax member of a minimal pair) in each box. In this case, the teacher may want to use cardboard to make the boards and to laminate them so that they will last through many rounds of play by students. If the boards are to be reused, some kind of game piece is needed to place on individual squares instead of writing "x".

Variation

A 3 × 3 tic-tac-toe (or noughts and crosses) board, where players win by matching three of the caller's words in a straight line, can be constructed in the same way.

2. A sequence of activities for noticing lip shapes

All of these activities can be used with intermediate or advanced learners. Many of them can also be used or adapted for beginners.

A. *Awareness of lip shapes*

The teacher models the different lip shapes of the vowels using nonsense syllables.

- For some sounds of English the lips are open and neutral or loose, e.g. *uh*.
- For some sounds of English the lips are wide open, e.g. *ah*.
- For some sounds of English the lips are rounded and protruded, e.g. *oh*.

beat	bite	pool
bit	bat	pull
bait	but	boat
bet	bout	bought
hat	gut	soy
hot	got	so

beat	bite	pool
bit	bat	pull
bait	but	boat
bet	bout	bought
hat	gut	soy
hot	got	so

FIGURE 3.14 Bingo board templates

- For some sounds of English the lips are strongly rounded and protruded, e.g. *ooh*.
- For some sounds of English the lips are spread, e.g. *eek*.

B. *Contrastive modeling of lip shapes*

Teacher models spread and rounded pairs of vowels or consonants as follows:

SPREAD	*A*l	t*ea*	*l*ed	*v*ine	*s*ee
ROUNDED	*a*ll	t*oo*	*r*ed	*w*ine	*sh*e

C. *Non-contrastive modeling of individual lip shapes*

Students work in pairs to group the words listed below into columns according to the lip shapes of the underlined portions as the teacher dictates the words. Students list the words under the headings 'spread lips', 'rounded lips' and 'neutral lips'.

fem*i*nine	mar*i*ne	m*oo*n	h*oo*d
*r*un	sist*er*	*ea*gle	c*u*p
*w*ait	g*o*	p*i*ll	p*aw*
*s*ick	*v*alley	n*o*t	s*a*t
w*o*n	*e*dge	*sh*ell	*l*ick

SPREAD LIPS   ROUNDED LIPS   NEUTRAL LIPS

D. *Silent dictation*

(1) Teacher modeling
     The teacher dictates the words in B above in random order, using "silent dictation", i.e. mouthing the words silently without pronouncing them. Students write down the words and then check their answers. The same exercise is then repeated for the words in C above.

(2) Pair work
     As a follow-up, students silently dictate to each other the words in list B and then list C.

(3) Small group work
     Students are organized into groups of 4 or more. In each group, half of the students act as "Dictators" and the other half as "Scribes". The Dictators use silent dictation to mouth the words in the lists below while the Scribes write down what they think they hear. The roles of Dictators and Scribes can be alternated, so that the members of Group 1 are Dictators for word lists A and C, while the members of Group 2 are Dictators for lists B and D. Only the Dictators should be allowed to see the word list that they are dictating. After all the words in a list have been silently dictated, Scribes compare their answers with each other and with the correct answers.

NOTE: Homonyms of the word dictated or other words with the same place of articulation will look the same in "silent dictation".

Silent dictation word lists

LIST A	LIST B	LIST C	LIST D
one	twice	queen	add
send	win	why	go
after	father	mother	bought
all	rat	zip	kill
for	see	red	ear
there	play	few	oil
rung	three	drag	flavor
weaver	flip	lick	this
flag	owl	tree	men
stay	river	mud	sand

(The teacher can make individual word lists by cutting the list page into four strips.)

E. *Meaningful pair or small group exercise*

Students divide into pairs or small groups. Using a dictionary, each pair/group looks up the definitions of the following words.

thwart	splice	sphinx	sclerosis
thrombosis	splay	sphincter	sclaffer

Non-contrastive modeling and repetition. When they are sure they understand the meaning of the words, each pair/group makes up a context of 1–2 sentences using each of the words correctly without defining it. These sentences can be the basis of a game in which individual pairs/groups become teams. First, one pair or team should be selected to play the role of "Judges". All other pairs/groups become "Contestants". For each word in the list above, one member of each pair/group will read their sentences aloud. The reader's productions will be judged based on pronunciation, grammar and context. The Judges make individual decisions which are averaged to give a point award for each turn. The maximum number of points for each turn is 10. Points may be deducted in any of the categories depending on whether the words are correctly pronounced, whether the sentences contain any grammatical errors, and whether the contexts are good contexts for illustrating the usage of the words.

4 Prosody

The components of prosody

Prosody is a term which refers to the **transsegmental** or **supra-segmental** aspects of speech, that is, to those aspects of pronunciation which span more than one segment or which are the property of **stretches** of speech rather than individual sounds. Conservatively, prosody refers to the patterns in individual words of **stress**, of **pitch** and of **tone**, as well as the **rhythmic** and **intonational patterns** of longer utterances.

In a more liberal definition, the topic of prosody or suprasegmental phonology includes **voice setting**, or **voice quality**, and a variety of contextual effects, specifically, those **fluent speech phenomena** which involve **phonological fluency** (Pennington 1989) as opposed to other types of fluency (such as lexical or rhetorical fluency).

The marking of prosodic units

Stress at the level of syllables and words

In general, the different aspects of stress can be described in relation to the syllable. In English, every word is made up of one or more syllables, consisting of one vowel alone or a vowel with 1–3 preceding and/or 1–4 following consonants. The range of syllable types in English can be abbreviated as follows:

(C) (C) (C) V (C) (C) (C) (C)

Here are examples of words illustrating the different possible compositions of syllables in English:

I	V
in	VC
ink	VCC
inks	VCCC

p i	CV
p i n	CVC
p i n t	CVCC
p i n t s	CVCCC
p r o m	CCVC
p r o m s	CCVCC
p r o m p t	CCVCCC
p r o m p t s	CCVCCCC
s p l i t	CCCVC
s p l i n t	CCCVCC
s p l i n t s	CCCVCCC

All of the sounds of a syllable are planned together and pronounced together as an unbroken unit. For this reason, the length of a syllable remains fairly constant, no matter how many phonemes it includes. The longest part of a syllable is its vowel. The vowel is longest when not surrounded by any additional consonants. With every consonant added before or after the vowel, the vowel shortens a bit to compensate for the added elements of the syllable.

Stress is the amount of effort or energy expended in producing a syllable. For the hearer, stress is manifested as perceptual **prominence**, or strength. In other words, a stressed syllable seems more prominent or stronger than the other syllables in its environment: it stands out.

SPEAKER'S PERSPECTIVE ON STRESS	HEARER'S PERSPECTIVE ON STRESS
Amount of effort expended	Degree of perceptual prominence

When a speaker places a stress – or what is also called an **accent** – on a syllable, it becomes **accentuated** for the listener. It is understood that when we say **stressed**, we are referring to a syllable whose degree of stress is strong in comparison to other syllables in the surrounding context. In opposition to these **stressed** (or **accented**) syllables are **weakly stressed** syllables, referred to as **unstressed** or **destressed** (or **unaccented**).

Stress is a cover-term for three prosodic features, any of which may result when extra effort is expended in producing a syllable and any of which may give an impression of perceptual prominence. These are **duration**, or length; **intensity**, or loudness; and **pitch**, or fundamental frequency. In English, all three of these factors – duration, intensity and pitch – are associated with prominence. Accordingly, the English stressed syllable – especially its vocalic nucleus – tends to have a greater degree of length, loudness and pitch associated with it. It therefore tends to be much longer, much louder, and either much higher or much lower in pitch – i.e. to be the locus of a dramatic pitch change in comparison to the surrounding context – than the unstressed syllable.

A one-syllable word in English is generally designated as stressed when the word is pronounced in isolation, though it may become unstressed in context. As we saw in Chapter 3 (see, e.g. Figure 3.6), this weakening effect of context is particularly common for one-syllable function words such as articles and short prepositions. The basic stress pattern of one-syllable words such as *dad* and *at* can be represented as a **unary foot**, i.e. a one-syllable structure. In two-syllable words such as *daddy* and *attack*, the stress pattern is said to comprise a **binary foot**, that is, a connected sequence of two syllables, one of which is stronger than the other. In English, both left-oriented (stressed–unstressed) and right-oriented (unstressed–stressed) binary stress feet are common. (In poetry, the left-oriented, stress-initial type, as in *daddy*, is called a **trochee**, or **trochaic foot**, and the right-oriented, stress-final type, as in *attack*, is called an **iamb**, or **iambic foot**.)

While unoriented (unstressed–unstressed) feet are not possible, English does allow for two-syllable words in which both syllables are stressed. These are so-called "compound words", as in *signpost* and *eggshell*. If we compare the second syllable of these words to the first syllable of a word such as *attack*, we can hear a difference in the degree of stress. At a finer level of analysis, the second syllable of compound words can be represented as of a somewhat lesser degree of stress than the first syllable, so that the first syllable of *signpost* and *eggshell* is said to receive a strong degree of stress, and the second syllable a medium degree of stress.

In words of more than two syllables, it is often necessary to recognize three degrees of stress: strong (or **primary**), medium (or **tertiary**) and weak (or **quaternary**) stress. For example, in the word *politics*, the stress pattern of the syllables is strong–weak–medium; in *mechanistic*, the stress pattern of the syllables is medium–weak–strong–medium. These patterns can be represented as a sequence of two feet in each word. In the case of *politics*, the first foot is binary and the second unary. In the case of *mechanistic*, both feet are binary.

The pattern in *mechanistic* is a typical pattern for four-syllable words in English: a sequence of two pairs of syllables such that:

(a) in each pair, the strongest syllable is first; and
(b) in the word as a whole, the most prominent stressed syllable is in the rightmost pair.

These two properties, (a) and (b), which define the stress pattern of this four-syllable word, can be represented visually by bracketing the stress patterns of the syllables into pairs, making two left-oriented prosodic feet, as follows:

(medium–weak) + (strong–medium)
   me   cha   nis   tic

There is disagreement among linguists about exactly how many levels of stress are needed to describe English and other languages. For careful transcription, four or more levels can probably be distinguished. In the system shown in Figure 4.1, six levels of stress are indicated for transcribing stress in native and non-native speech. Note that in this book the stress mark is placed at the beginning of the syllable, rather than over the vowel, as is sometimes done.

To the levels already discussed have been added an emphatic/contrastive level that is higher than primary stress. This level of stress can be thought of as "double-primary". A level below quaternary (weak) stress has been added, termed a **demi-beat**. This level of stress is so low that the syllable almost (or in some cases, actually) disappears. Examples are the British RP pronunciation of words such as *auditory*, *lavatory*, *sedentary* and *momentary*, where the third syllable is lost or almost lost. In non-native speech, a demi-beat stress may indicate the speaker's unsuccessful attempt to achieve normal weak (quaternary) stress. In such a case, the speaker has "overshot" the target stress value by making the value of weak stress too low. For example, the one-syllable word *please* and the two-syllable word *police* may be nearly indistinguishable when the latter is pronounced by Japanese speaker as:

ˇpoˈlice

Stress level		Symbols		Examples
	Emphatic/Contrastive	″	1+	(command to dog): ″Sit! Not ″there. Sit ″here.
HIGH	Primary	′	1	(roll call): ′Ann? ′Here. ′Greg? ′Here. ′Wallace?
	Secondary	^		′White^House ′clam^shell
MEDIUM	Tertiary	`	3	`green ′door `might ′go
	Quaternary	ˇ	4	ˇap′ply ˇthe ′boy ′faˇther ′read ˇit
WEAKEST	Demi-beat	˅	4–	`saˇtis′facˇto ˇry ˅pa′trol ˅sup ′posed

FIGURE 4.1 Levels of stress

The stress level termed "secondary" is sometimes used to indicate the degree of stress in the second element of compound nouns or the first element in some hyphenated words, as in:

ˈlightˆhouse   ˈhouseˆkeeˇper   ˆself-ˈstarˇter   ˆauˋto-ˈreˇguˋlaˇting

Notice how stress can differentiate between two meanings of an expression, as in the following pair (from Chomsky and Halle 1968):

ˈlight   ˈhouseˆkeeˇper   'a person who does light housekeeping'
ˈlightˋhouse   ˆkeeˇper   'a person who takes care of a lighthouse'

Regional and social variation in word stress

In words of more than one syllable, stress is generally fixed on a particular syllable, as in the following examples:

FIRST	THIRD	FIFTH
ˈconstitute	constiˈtution	constitutionˈality
ˈorigin	constiˈtutional	
	constiˈtutionally	SIXTH
SECOND		multidimensionˈality
conˈstituent	FOURTH	
conˈstituency	originˈality	
oˈriginal	originˈation	
oˈriginally	dimensionˈality	
oˈriginate	multidiˈmensional	
diˈmension		
diˈmensional		

There is, however, considerable variation across speakers and varieties in the placement of word stress. In many varieties of English, the placement of stress in some individual words and sets of words is not entirely fixed. In other cases, different varieties fix stress on a different syllable in individual words or sets of words.

For example, stress may be regularized on either the first or the second syllable in noun/verb pairs such as ˈpermit/perˈmit and ˈconduct/conˈduct, as reported by Bansal (1990: 227) for Indian English. In some varieties, the stress shifts which are common in other varieties when a word stem occurs in construction with different affixes are not part of the system. Rather, the stress pattern of the stem of the word is maintained in some or all of its derived forms. For example, the stress shift in the last word of the following lexical set does not occur in all varieties of English:

de'mocracy
de'mocratize
demo'cratic

In the non-stress-shifting varieties, *democratic* would follow the pattern of *democracy* in retaining stress on the second syllable.

In such cases, the highly variable placement of English stress becomes more regular and predictable, thereby simplifying the stress system and making it easier to learn within that variety. However, as suggested in Chapter 1, such changes as introduce regularity at a local level at the same time often represent added complexity at a more generalized level of English norms, as each local variety may regularize English patterns in a different direction (e.g by fixing stress on a different syllable). Moreover, these local innovations may act as the locus or starting point for locally induced changes that diversify and complexify the phonological system.

For example, a shift of final to initial stress occurs in the British English pronunciation of originally French words such as *ballet*, *debris* and *chauffeur*; in American English, these loanwords are all pronounced with the main stress on the final syllable, as in the original French, whereas in *magazine* and *cigarette*, the main stress varies between initial and final position. Across varieties of English, a primary stress can be found on either the first or the second syllable of *address*, *adult*, *affluence*, *inquiry*, *laboratory* and *orchestra*. Both American and Irish English are examples of varieties that have variable first- or second-syllable word stress in these lexical items. Additionally, Irish English speakers alternate first and last syllable stress in words ending in -*ate* (e.g. *concentrate* and *educate*) and -*ize* (e.g. *recognize* and *specialize*) (Wells 1982: 436), whereas speakers of West Indian English (Wells 1982: 572), West African English (Trudgill and Hannah 1985: 103), Indian English (Bansal 1990: 227), Hong Kong English, Malaysian English and Singaporean English (Platt 1984: 395) show a regular pattern of final stress in words ending in -*ate*, -*ize* and -*ism* (e.g. *criticize*, *criticism*). In Kenya, initial stress has become final in *execute*, *demonstrate*, *argument*, and in the nouns *convict*, *present* and *progress* (Kanyoro 1991: 408), and in Hong Kong English, stress has shifted from the initial syllable to later in the word in *foot'ball*, *popu'lated* and *usual'ly* (Platt 1984: 409).

The pattern of non-initial stress on words of more than one syllable seems relatively widespread in varieties of English around the world, with second-syllable stress being a particularly common pattern. In Guyanese English, a large set of two-syllable words which refer to everyday objects – e.g. *orange, cotton, water, paper, finger, window, pillow* – receive second-syllable (final) stress (Holder 1972). The pattern of second-syllable stress extends to other cases as well, since Guyanese speakers stress some three-syllable words on the second syllable – e.g. *manager, bicycle, passenger, calendar* (Holder 1972). In Singaporean English, many words of more than one syllable have primary stress placed on the second syllable, including *advantageous, character, colleague, economic, faculty*, and some compound words such as *doorkey* (Wells 1982: 646). In Indian English, stress has shifted in many initially stressed words to the second syllable – e.g. *necessary, suitable, minister, character, atmosphere*; Indian English shows evidence of an opposite trend as well, that is, of stress shifting from second to first syllable – e.g. *about, mistake, defence, events, degree, hotel, percent* (Bansal 1990: 227; Wells 1982: 631).

In some varieties of English, stress patterns are replaced by patterns of **tones**, or pitch contours, on individual words. This effect may be heard, for example, in the discourse of some speakers of Hong Kong English. As another example, according to Lawton (1984): "Relative pitch functions in Jamaican English over utterances the way stress functions in standard English" (p. 266). Because of the substratum of African languages underlying Jamaican English, the latter variety shows some tendency to use tonal contrast, i.e. differences in pitch, to replace stress contrasts in words of two or more syllables (Lawton 1984: 257–258). A common pattern in Jamaican English is for "[t]wo-syllable and three-syllable words [to] have rising pitch on final syllables" (Lawton 1984: 267). There is also some evidence in Jamaican English of pitch substituting for other kinds of phonological contrasts in some lexical items: "For example, [kjãa] *can't* or *can* is distinguished by a tonal contrast in which the form for *can* carries a high, level tone and the form for *can't* carries a high, falling tone" (Lawton 1984: 257).

As the foregoing discussion makes clear, varieties of English may differ in their stress patterns according to any of the following three characteristics:

(1) the placement of stress on one or another specific syllable;
(2) the stability or variability of stress placement within a particular word or set of words;
(3) the parameter or combination of parameters by which stress is manifested.

Stress in larger contexts

In English, there tends to be a regular alternation of strong and weak syllables such that a stressed syllable generally recurs every 2–3 syllables, except in very rapid speech, where stress tends to diminish. This alternation of strongly and weakly stressed syllables makes up the **rhythm** of the typical English word or longer utterance. The rhythmic basis of most varieties of English is therefore **stress-timing**, meaning that the timing of utterances is based on the number of stressed syllables, which tend to be evenly spaced, with the unstressed syllables squeezed in between.

The pressure to maintain stress-timing and alternating rhythm is so strong for most varieties of English that the stress of words may shift in context, particularly from a left-oriented, stress-initial foot, to a right-oriented, stress-final foot. This commonly happens when numbers occur in context, as in the following illustrative sentences and conversations:

The 'date was 'fifteen 'ten.
The 'time is 'ten fif'teen.

Pat: Is she 'eighteen 'yet?
Marty: Yeah. She's 'just turned eigh'teen.
Pat: You say she's 'eighteen years 'old?
Marty: Right. Like I 'said: eigh'teen.

Marty: He 'studied for 'sixteen 'hours.
Pat: 'How many 'hours?
Marty: Six'teen.
Pat: Are you kidding? 'Sixteen 'hours?

Because of the pervasiveness of the alternating rhythmic pattern, when English speakers encounter a new word, they tend to pronounce it according to this pattern. To see that this is true, pronounce the very long word at the end of the first teaching exercise for prosody (see pages 196–7) or the long nonsense word from the film *Mary Poppins*:

supercalifragilisticexpialidoscious

Note that (a) there is an alternation of strong and weak syllables on every other syllable and (b) there is one stressed syllable which is more prominent – i.e. longer, louder and higher in pitch – than all the others. As is typical in English, relatively long utterances will tend to have the most prominent syllable near the rightward utterance-boundary before the pause – here, it is on the syllable *do*.

Consider the phrases and sentences in Figure 4.2. Notice that in

one of a 'kind
in a 'minute
'three of them
where's his 'hat
why'd you 'go
'different from
the 'sofa
what's your 'name
was he 'angry
'cut them
five to 'two
are you 'coming
'tell him
dinner for 'four
ham and 'eggs
in a 'book
she can 'run
it has 'happened

FIGURE 4.2 Sentences and phrases with the final content word stressed

almost every case, the stress mark is in front of the last syllable of the
phrase or sentence, indicating that that syllable is stressed. The only
exceptions are (i) multisyllabic words, where the stress occurs on a particular syllable, which may or may not be final, and (ii) function words,
which ordinarily are monosyllabic and unstressed when they occur in
context.

When phrases are joined together into longer utterances, the last
stressed word will normally receive a comparatively higher degree of
stress than other stressed words. This is most easily illustrated by considering the stress pattern of individual words and phrases when they
occur alone and in context with each other, as in the following example:

the 'wizard   my 'favorite
of 'Oz   'movie
the `wizard of 'Oz                   my `favorite 'movie
                                     'is
                                     `is my 'favorite 'movie

The `wizard of ^Oz `is my 'favorite 'movie.

As this example illustrates, the so-called "Nuclear Stress Rule" of
English (Chomsky and Halle 1968) assigns the strongest beat, or **main**

stress, to the last content word – i.e. to the rightmost stressed element before pause.

Stress and information

It may be remembered from Chapter 3 that stress, i.e. prosodic high-lighting, is related in a very important way to **information**. The general rule in all languages is that the most important information in a phrase or longer utterance will be highlighted, that is, will receive prominence through some kind of accentuation of a particular word or group of words. This accentuation may involve a noticeable (a) change in pitch – usually, but not always, a pitch rise; (b) increase in duration, or length, of a syllable; (c) increase in loudness; or (d) combinations of (a)–(c). In a language such as English, often all three of the prosodic features (a)–(c) occur together to signal prominence. In other languages, accentuation may be accomplished by only one of these prosodic features.

In all languages, prosodic highlighting serves a very obvious **deictic** function, which is to signal important information for the audience. Under normal, or unmarked, conditions, it is the content words (nouns, verbs, adjectives, adverbs) that are accentuated by pitch, length, loud-ness or a combination of these prosodic features. Function words (prep-ositions, articles, pronouns) and affixes (prefixes and suffixes) of various kinds are de-emphasized or **backgrounded** informationally by destressing them. The rightward orientation of phrase stress in English is therefore a consequence of the fact that content words tend to come after function words in the word order, i.e. the syntax, of English. Note that this means that prosody is intimately tied to grammar.

This focusing through prosody on content words and word roots, and the de-emphasizing or backgrounding of function words and affixes, is probably a universal for all languages. Although the mechanisms for accentuating linguistic elements vary from language to language, there are rather predictable ways of drawing attention to spoken items – i.e. by making the voice louder, by changing pitch, or by lengthening a word or phrase. Thus, prosodic accentuation is very unlike other aspects of phonology in that it shows a rather direct relationship between sound and meaning, i.e. it is highly **iconic**.

FOREGROUNDING DEVICES	PROSODIC ELEMENT	BACKGROUNDING DEVICES
loud or varied	Tone of voice	soft or unvarying
high or varied	Pitch	low or unvarying
long or varied	Syllable length	short or unvarying
minimal	Coarticulation	maximal

Both word order and stress placement are used to indicate to a listener which parts of an utterance are to be considered shared, known (**given**) or backgrounded information and which parts are to be taken as new or focused information. In the unmarked or usual case in English, utterance-initial position is reserved for shared or known information, while new information is introduced in utterance-final position. As a consequence, the least marked stress pattern for an English utterance contains the main stress (or **tonic accent**) on the last content word.

However, sometimes speakers will accentuate a word in another part of the sentence, indicating that this word is to be taken as the new or focused information. For example, if someone asks a question such as *Who's Pat?*, one might answer as in (1a) below, to indicate that *Pat's* is the given information since it has been introduced already in the question. The new information is *the director*, which receives the main stress, giving added prominence to the lexically stressed second syllable of the content word, *director*. Other stressed syllables in the context of the main stress may remain the same or be downgraded to a lower degree of stress in order to further accentuate their contrast with the main stress, thus giving additional prominence to the information highlighted by the main stress.

On the other hand, if someone asks *Who's the director?*, one can answer as in (1b), indicating that the first part of the sentence is given (already introduced) information, while the second part is new. At the same time, one might opt to use the same word order for the answer as was used in the question, producing (1c) instead of (1b) as the answer, with *PAT* still highlighted (as shown by **capitalization**) and the rest of the sentence de-emphasized.

(1) (a) Pat's the diRECtor.   (main stress on last content word)
     (b) The director is PAT.   (main stress on last content word)
     (c) PAT's the director.   (main stress on first content word)

It is also possible to give the focal lexical item an extra degree of stress in each of these cases as shown by capitalization and italic, producing emphasis or contrast, as in:

(2) (a) Pat's the di*REC*tor.   (not the TEAcher)
     (b) The director is *PAT*.   (not MARty)
     (c) *PAT*'s the director.   (not MARty)

The fact that emphasis or contrast can be increased by placing increased stress on a particular portion of speech is another iconic aspect of prosodic highlighting, in that the listener is signaled to pay special attention to the emphatically or contrastively stressed item or items. In fact, even normally unstressed syllables of words or function words can receive an emphatic or contrastive stress, as the following examples illustrate:

I didn't say *PRO*duce, I said *RE*duce.
This guy says his name is Elvis, but of course, not *THE* Elvis.
You gave me *HIS* coat; *THAT's* mine.
You gave me the *COAT*; now could you give me the *HAT*?

Thus, the main stress rule may be violated to indicate emphasis or contrast. In addition, as Cruttenden (1990) has observed, the main stress rule has some exceptions, in that:

(1) Final sentence adverbials are not stressed.
  e.g. I don't know how to 'do it fortunately.
    He's going back to 'America wisely. (Cruttenden 1990: 13)
(2) In sentences beginning with a *wh*-word functioning as an adjective before a noun, that noun receives the main stress.
  e.g. What 'seeds did you use?
    Which 'course did you take? (Cruttenden 1990: 14)
(3) Some sentences describing events have the main stress on the subject rather than the verb, as in the second of each of the following utterance pairs:
  Watch 'out! That 'building's falling down.
  What was that 'noise? Oh, it was just a 'car backfiring. (Cruttenden 1990: 12)

Although these cases would appear to violate the main stress rule, each has a ready explanation in informational terms. In the first case, the sentence adverbials can be seen as parenthetical, or backgrounded, information relative to the foregrounding of the main sentence. In the second case, the subject of the sentence is the focus of questioning and therefore receives the main stress on its rightmost element. In the third case, the proper explanation is that the event is highlighted by placing the main stress at the beginning of the unit describing the event.

Pause groups

As pointed out in Chapter 1, a speaker plans an utterance in advance to some extent (though the plan may be changed after production of the utterance has begun) in terms of the amount of speech which will be spoken on one breath. An utterance of more than a few words may be spoken on one continuous breath or broken into two or more smaller **pause groups**, i.e. stretches of speech surrounded by pauses. These may or may not represent individual breath groups, as it is possible to reserve breath over an intervening pause. Short pause groups may indicate that a speaker is thinking while talking, putting together a message or matching a message to its desired linguistic expression bit by bit. Short pause groups can also be produced deliberately, as a way of simplifying a message or of emphasizing the information in an utterance, by slowing down its presentation and giving listeners more time to absorb and digest it. Longer pause groups, which are more challenging for the listener, tend to background a message as the presentation of information is speeded up, making it possible to focus only globally and so in some cases to catch only the gist or key points.

Thus, a speaker who breaks up the utterance below into several pause groups might give an impression of some difficulty remembering or communicating the information. Alternatively, when the message is spoken as four separate pause groups, it may suggest a "weighty" or especially important message, as compared to the more ordinary, less remarkable piece of information communicated when the same words are spoken as a prosodically unifed message between pauses. As a context for the short pause groups in this example, one might imagine a situation in which the speaker is trying to recall or to accurately report to the authorities the previous night's activities of a missing person.

/ He went jogging / and then / he came home / right afterwards. /

/ He went jogging and then he came home right afterwards./

Intonation contours can be described in relation to pause groups and breath groups. A **tone group** can be defined as that part of an intonation contour which extends between two pause points. An intonation contour is made up of one or more tone groups. Thus, an intonation contour, like a breath group, may be continuous across a pause, especially if it is a short (under 1 second) pause.

A speaker may opt to break an utterance into two or more prosodic units, i.e. pause groups or tone groups, either for ease of production (e.g. to avoid running out of breath or to allow time to search in memory for a certain word) or to create some special effect on the listener (generally, to emphasize or dramatize a point). Note that a major pause (1–2 second) right before a word serves to highlight that word, as shown by the placement of the colon in:

There's only one thing we want: peace.

There seems, then, to be a natural association between pause groups and several other aspects of utterance structure. A tone group is defined with reference to a pause group, and these two groupings are related to semantic or informational groupings of words. Words which group together semantically (**sense groups**) or in the train-of-thought process during speech (**thought groups**) tend to be organized in terms of pause groups and tone groups. *In sum, word groups which form idea units will also form prosodic units.*

A different length of pause indicates different amounts of **juncture**, i.e. different degrees of physical separation of the words and of functional separation of the messages they carry (Pennington 1989: 27–8), as can be seen in the following example, where a single slash mark represents a short pause (1 second or less) and a double slash mark indicates a longer pause (2 seconds or more):

['ɔː // "noːʊ]
O h . N o !   (2–3 second pause between words)

['oʊ / 'noːʊ]
O h , n o !   (0.3–0.5 second pause between words)

['ə'noːʊ]
O h n o ! (no pause between words)

A 2–3 second pause between the two words suggests a functional separation of the message conveyed by *Oh.* and that conveyed by *No!*. For instance, *Oh.* could be the close of an interaction with another person who is conversing with the speaker, while *No!* is an unrelated reaction to something happening in the context of speech – perhaps something just noticed such as a toddler about to grab a cigarette out of an ashtray. Where the two messages are so separated, they will be spoken on two different intonation contours, with the first falling in a definitive, "closed" meaning (see discussion below).

A short pause of 0.3–0.5 seconds, which is about the smallest readily detectable break in speech, indicates that the reaction signified by *no!* is related to the understanding signified by *Oh,*. In such a case, we can expect that *Oh,* will have a non-falling terminal contour, signaling the link with the coming word *no!*. Where there is no pause between the two words, understanding and reaction are merged into one complex response in a conventionalized two-word expression of surprise or distress, with reduced stress on the first component of the expression.

Several natural effects relate to the presence of a junctural point in speech and serve to emphasize the presence of an upcoming boundary. Such effects include (besides falling pitch) lengthening of a syllable, its vowel or its final segment(s) before pause – so-called **pre-pausal lengthening**. Glottal stopping, which sharpens the edges of words, is another effect of juncture. As Giegerich (1992: 280) observes, rather than eliding the words in the following utterance, they may be kept distinct by glottal stopping (. indicates juncture):

[ði:z.ʔɑ:.ʔoʊld.ʔɛgz]
These are old eggs.

As a junctural phenomenon, a glottal stop often co-occurs with the oral closure period of a final obstruent; however, it may also arise in post-vocalic position preceding a final stop, as discussed in Chapter 2. Another junctural effect also covered in Chapter 2 is loss of voice in utterance-final position – either over a whole segment or in the final phase of a segment. Such utterance-final devoicing, which is most common in final voiced obstruents, may be interpreted as early loss of vocal cord vibration in anticipation of an upcoming pause.

Contextual effects related to stress and prosodic grouping

The timing of syllables in English is determined by the placement of the stresses. Stressed syllables or words are forcefully articulated and spread out temporally as compared to unstressed syllables. In phrases, the unstressed syllables of function words are compressed and blended together in anticipation of the stressed content word, showing clearly that they form a unit consisting of one content word and its **pre-modifiers**. As a result of destressing and coarticulation, unstressed affixes and words tend to weaken in several ways. In casual speech, these effects are sometimes referred to as **leveling** of unstressed speech.

One type of leveling under reduced stress in informal speaking conditions is **neutralization** of vowels, in most cases resulting in schwa. As mentioned in Chapter 3, an unstressed syllable may contain a reduced vowel. The most weakly stressed syllables are the ones that tend to have the reduced vowels. The pronunciation of English vowels is also influenced by position in the word in relation to any unstressed syllables – for example, unstressed endings added to a content word. The pronunciation of a particular vowel within a word depends to some extent on the number and type of unstressed syllables, if any, following it. In this sense, reduced vowels are a coarticulatory effect related to stress.

Consonants may also weaken under conditions of weak stress, changing their articulation to a more open sound or assimilating to the place of articulation of a neighboring sound. Sometimes, the sound which results is a kind of **blend** of two phones which are kept distinct when a word or phrase is carefully pronounced, as in:

Got you! ['gɑ˘čə]   *That's you.* [˘ðə'žu:]

In some cases, a vowel or consonant drops out completely, as happens in contractions:

It's here, isn't it? [ˋɪts'hi:ər/'ɪz˘nɪʔtˈ]

In everyday English conversation, dropping of the initial consonants of destressed pronouns is common, as in:

his hat [˘ɪz'hætˈ] *in her bag* [ˋɪnər'bæ:g]

In unstressed positions, whole syllables or words can drop out in casual speech, as in:

suppose ['spouz], ['pouz]   *believe* ['bli:v]
probably ['prɑ˘bli:], ['prɑ˘li:]
What did you say? [ˋwʌʔ˘jə'se:ɪ]

Another stress-related effect is **elision** (linking) between words pronounced as one phrase. Common kinds of elision in English include the following:

(a) **Bridging** via an existing sound, which serves as a transition between two words:

  when I ['wɛñaɪ]   *is a* ['ɪžə]   *far away* ['fɑřə'we:ɪ]

(b) Emergence of a **transitional glide** between two words that would not occur in either word spoken in isolation:

  go away [ˋgow̌ə'we:]   *know it* ['no:w̌ɪʔtˈ]
  say it ['se:ǰɪtˈ]   *my eyes* [ˋmaɪǰa:ɪz]

Note that the bridging sound is the nearest glide to the articulatory position of the preceding vowel.

(c) **Consonant attraction**, in which the final consonant of a word is pronounced as though it began the next following word:

  bad apple [ˋbæ'dæpl̩]   *big eyes* [ˋbɪ'ga:ɪz]
  his arm [˘hɪ'za:rm]   *you're on* [˘jə'rɑ:n]

Note the placement of the stress mark to indicate the perceptual beginning of the second syllable in each of the phrases given as examples above. In the examples of (a) and (b), the second stress mark is placed over the bridging phone or transitional glide phone to indicate that the syllable boundary occurs during its production. In the examples of (c), the stress mark indicating the perceptual beginning of the second syllable is placed before the attracted consonant.

Another contextual effect is the coming together of two like consonants which occur in sequence across two words. In such cases, linking of the two like stops produces a long closure period, making a long consonant, as in the following examples:

Stop Pete! [ˈstɑpˈʰiːtˀ]
Get Tom! [ˈɡɛtˈʰɑːm]
Kick Ken! [ˈkʰɪkˈʰɛːn]

In such cases, it is accurate to put the stress mark over the long consonant, as it bridges between two syllables. Note that where a double consonant is indicated in the spelling of English, as in *stopper*, *getting*, *backing*, this is not normally pronounced as a long stop but rather as a single consonant sound which bridges between the two syllables or which undergoes consonant attraction to the next syllable:

stopper [ˈstɑp̆ʰər] or [ˈstɑ˘pʰər]
getting [ˈɡɛɾɪŋ] or [ˈɡɛ˘ʰɪŋ]
backing [ˈbækʰɪŋ] or [ˈbæ˘kʰɪŋ]

Regional and social variation in the form and effects of utterance-level stress and prosodic grouping

At the level of whole utterances, phrases and syllables, the New Englishes can be contrasted in several respects with the older varieties. At the utterance level, there seems to be a tendency in some of the New Englishes to overgeneralize the main stress rule so that it applies to a final content word even when the rule might be overridden because of considerations of information focus. For example, an Indian English speaker, as noted by Bansal (1990: 228), might counter the statement "You just weren't listening" with:

I was ˈlistening

with stress on the repeated item, *listening*, rather than a stress on *was* to emphasize or contrast what the previous speaker has just alleged. An Indian English speaker might also stress *so* in *I think so* (Bansal 1990: 228), though *think*, as the last content word, would be the stress carrier in this utterance according to the main stress rule. There may also be a tendency in phrase stress to regularize the placement of main stress in a position other than that dictated by the main stress rule. For example, some Indian English speakers place the main stress within a noun phrase on the first content word or on an adjective preceding a noun (Bansal 1990: 228).

Similar tendencies have been noted in some Asian varieties such as Hong Kong and Singapore-Malaysian English, where the main stress of phrases and sentences tends to be on the last word, whether or not it is a content word (Platt 1984: 395, 409). In addition, Hong Kong English speakers may neutralize the stress difference between given and new information and between content and function words (Bolton and Kwok 1990: 154).

For these varieties, the relationship between stress and information that is a feature of other varieties of English appears to be lost or altered. Speakers of some varieties may also be less prone to exploit stress for purposes of emphasis or contrast. For example, Trudgill and Hannah (1985: 103) state that "[c]ontrastive stress is rare" in West African English, where contrastive or emphatic meaning is commonly expressed through grammatical means by *it*-extraction, as in:

It's the hat I want, not the coat.

At the level of phrases and syllables, many of the New Englishes represent exceptions to the principle for English of stress-timing. These include Filipino English (Wells 1982: 647), Hawaiian English (Vanderslice and Pierson 1967), Hong Kong and Singapore-Malaysian English (Platt 1984: 395, 409), Indian English (Bansal 1990: 227; Kachru 1984: 359; Trudgill and Hannah 1985: 106), and Caribbean and African varieties of English (Lanham 1990: 250; Lawton 1984: 258; Trudgill and Hannah 1984: 99; Wells 1982: 642). All of these varieties tend towards **syllable-timing**, meaning that each syllable tends to be stressed and so to be of approximately equal duration.

In addition, contextual effects related to stress do not occur in all varieties of English, possibly because the difference between strong and weak stress is not great. In particular, vowel neutralization does not occur in unstressed syllables in all varieties. A somewhat stereotyped middle class Scottish English accent referred to as "Kelvinside" in Glasgow and "Morningside" in Edinburgh tends to maintain unreduced pronunciations in function words and uniform stress and non-coarticulation in all syllables of multisyllabic words (Macafee 1983: 32). A less pervasive tendency away from reduced vowels can be seen in Welsh, where a full vowel rather than schwa has been observed for orthographic *o*, as in *condemn*, and for the final vowel of *sofa*, pronounced at a more open position as [a] (Trudgill and Hannah 1985: 29). Similarly, Trudgill and Hannah (1985: 18) report that "broad" Australian speakers have a fully open vowel in the second syllable of *ever*, i.e. [eva].

In Hong Kong English, strong vowels are maintained in many of the syllables where schwa occurs in other varieties – e.g. in the first syllable of the words *society*, *familiar* and *conclusion* – and a similar tendency is found as well in Singaporean English (Wells 1982: 646), Indian English (Kachru 1984: 359; Trudgill and Hannah 1984: 106), some African varieties (Wells 1982: 642) and Jamaican English (Trudgill and Hannah 1985: 98). The vowel in a weak syllable with /l/ or /n/, which in British and American varieties of English is lost, resulting in syllabic consonants in words such as *button* /bʌtn̩/ and *apple* /æpl̩/, is retained as a full vowel in West African English, viz. /bɔtin/, /apul/ (Trudgill and Hannah 1985: 103).

In Indian English: "Suffixes tend to be stressed, and function words which are weak in other varieties of English (*of* /əv/, *to* /tə/, etc.) tend not to be reduced" (Trudgill and Hannah 1985: 106). In such cases, the stress in these syllables may in fact not be greatly reduced. In Filipino English, the relationship of vowel neutralization, stress and informal speech style has been further disrupted. In this variety, schwa vowels occur in formal style in words such as *alcohol* ['alkəhəl] and *nation* ['nejšən], whereas full vowels are preferred in the non-initial syllables of such words in conversational style – ['nejšon], ['alkohol] (Wells 1982: 648). This pattern of vowel variation perhaps indicates the influence of local languages on the informal style and the stronger influence of English on the formal style.

Two essentially opposite effects can be noted in relation to phonological leveling in the New Englishes. One is a blocking of phonological leveling and loss of syllables in the varieties of English such as those which occur in Singapore, Hong Kong, and in many parts of Africa where syllable-timing keeps syllables relatively strong and distinct, thus preventing strong coarticulation and assimilation of unstressed to stressed syllables. The other, essentially opposite, effect found in the New Englishes is that of extreme destressing or "overleveling." These are cases in which very reduced syllables tend to drop out, as in the following examples from Indian English:

/'əstənt/ *assistant*
/'ınstju:t/ *institute*   (Bansal 1990: 226)

Reduction or loss of initial unstressed syllables is common in informal English speech in many varieties. It occurs in a large group of words beginning with unstressed vowels, when these occur in a larger utterance context, including *about, around, arithmetic, America, electric, eleventh, equipment, especially, excuse, expect, imagine, occasionally, unless, until*. Reduction or loss of the initial syllable of *because, between, refrigerator* and *remember* is also common.

These sorts of effects are usual in informal American English, and are the norm in both stressed and unstressed contexts in rural varieties such as Appalachian speech. For the latter variety, Wolfram and Christian (1976) show the following reduced forms:

Loss of initial phoneme in personal pronouns, definite article, and demonstratives
. . . if I get back wif [*with*] 'er [*her*]. (p. 49)
You could pick 'em [*them*] while 'ey [*they*] was hot. (p. 54)
An' [*and*] 'e [*the*] one I was gonna shoot disappeared. (p. 55)
'at [*that*] old man jumped 'at [*that*] big buck. (p. 55)
You wanna use 'is [*this*] or you wanna use 'at [*that*]. (p. 54)

Syllable loss in negatives
didn't [dɪn], *couldn't* [kʊn], *wouldn't* [wʊn]
wasn't [wən], *isn't* [ɪn] (p. 60)

Initial syllable loss in nouns and verbs
He's a 'lectrician [*electrician*].
I don't 'member [*remember*]. (p. 50)

Elision is a common coarticulatory effect in Scottish and American varieties of English. A special case of bridging is the "intrusive r" which occurs in some non-rhotic English accents such as Boston, New York City, RP, Australian English and New Zealand English – but not South African English (Trudgill and Hannah 1985; 26). For example:

idea of [˘aɪˈdɪə̆rəv]   *Cuba and China* [ˈkjuː˘bər̩ n̩ˈčaɪ˘nə]

In contrast, in many of the New Englishes, elision is not a common feature, and in some (e.g. Hong Kong English), syllables can be kept distinct by means of glottal stopping and doubling or lengthening of medial consonants, as in:

backing [ˈbæʔk̚.ˈkʰɨŋ]   *stopping* [ˈstɑʔp̚.ˈpʰɨŋ]

Variation is also apparent across varieties of English in pausing behavior and its effect on the grouping of speech into units. Currie (1979) maintains that junctural pauses tend to be shorter in Glasgow speech than in Edinburgh speech, and Welkowitz, Bond and Feldstein (1984) suggest that pause length may vary across different varieties such as Canadian English and Hawaiian English. There may also be differences in frequency of pauses for different groups of speakers, as some speaker groups – e.g. South African Black speakers (Lanham 1990: 250) – divide speech into shorter breath groups, while others – perhaps Puerto Rican English speakers – divide speech into longer breath groups.

Intonation

Pitch and intonation

In English, as in many other languages, pitch is an important component of accentuation, or prominence, both at the level of individual words and at the level of longer utterances. In general, we distinguish between pitches which are relatively **steady-state**, i.e. which do not change level perceptibly, and those which change by **stepping** or **sliding** up or down to another pitch level, as illustrated in the figure below. English intonation characteristically slides or transitions gradually from one pitch level to the next rather than stepping up or down abruptly from one pitch level to the next. Thus, English intonation is best represented by "humps" and "waves" rather than by "angles" and "steps".

Sliding contour   *Stepping contour*

The pitch of the voice is determined by the frequency with which the vocal cords vibrate. The frequency of vibration of the vocal cords is in turn determined by their thickness, their length and their tension. The **modal pitch** of the voice, i.e. one's natural average pitch level, depends on the size of the vocal cords. In general, men have thicker and longer vocal cords than women and children do. As a result, the modal pitch of a man's voice is generally lower than that of a woman or a child.

In addition to its modal pitch, every individual voice has a **pitch range** which can be achieved by adjustments of the vocal cords. By tightening the vocal cords, a person can raise the pitch of the voice (**vocal pitch**); by loosening them, one can lower vocal pitch. These adjustments allow speakers to use pitch changes to achieve certain meaningful effects in speech.

There is also a natural variation in pitch associated with the amount of air that is expended during speech. When the airflow through the glottis is great, it causes the vocal cords to vibrate quickly. As airflow is reduced, the effect on the vocal cords is diminished, and the frequency of vibration decreases. Although it is possible to override these natural effects – e.g. by changing the tension of the vocal folds – in the unmarked case, the pitch of the voice will descend naturally over an utterance as the speaker's breath is used up. This effect is called **downdrift**.

As a result of downdrift, there is a natural iconic association of falling pitch with finality and related meanings such as assurance or definitiveness. Conversely, there is a natural association of non-falling (steady-state or rising) pitch with non-finality and related meanings such as lack of assurance or non-definitiveness. The difference between falling and non-falling or rising intonation is represented by Cruttenden (1981) as that between "closed" (assertive) and "open" (non-assertive) meaning.

The pitch of the voice falls when the speaker has finished giving all of the intended information – when an utterance is finished – and wants to signal the end of a turn at speaking. As long as the pitch has not fallen, it is an indication of unfinished information or an unfinished interaction. Typically, then, pitch falls at the end of a statement and stays level or rises slightly at the end of a phrase where more information is coming, as illustrated in the following example:

George bought a dozen eggs, a carton of milk and a bag of sugar.

The more uncertainty or incompletion is indicated, the more vocal pitch tends to rise. Whereas in the example above there was a low rise in pitch on each item in the list, for the following utterance, there will be a final high rise in pitch to indicate a high degree of uncertainty or incompletion in the meaning:

George bought only one bag of sugar?

A yes/no question can be seen as half of an interaction. Since it indicates uncertainty (lack of information) and incompletion, it generally ends in a high rise, as in:

Did George buy any fruit? - Yes.

In the above example, the answer of "yes" completes the interaction with falling pitch.

Rather than a high rise, so-called *wh*-questions (question beginning with *who, where, when, why, which* and *how*), though they ask for information that is unknown to complete an interacion, typically end in high but falling pitch, as in:

Who's that? Why did he do it? How can I get there? Where's Ann?

It seems likely that non-native speakers might tend to produce *wh*-questions with a rising intonation, on the pattern of *yes/no* questions.

So-called **tag questions** may have rising or non-rising pitch, depending on whether they are really meant to ask questions or not:

George is really smart, isn't he? vs. *George isn't back yet, is he?*

In a similar case, English speakers may use the expression *you know* to ask a question or not, as shown by the pitch:

It's the store on M Street, you know? vs. *I like her, you know.*

Even an utterance in the grammatical form of a yes/no question can become a non-question, i.e. a statement, if the pitch falls:

Isn't she lovely! Doesn't my baby speak well.

In these last two examples, the speaker does not ask a question but states a belief, expecting the hearer to have the same opinion.

Generally, the term **intonation** is reserved for talking about the pitch patterns of sentences or longer discourses, rather than individual words or phrases. However, individual words or phrases may in some cases constitute an entire utterance in natural speech, as can be seen in the different intonation contours for *okay* in Figure 4.3.

As these examples illustrate, intonation, like other aspects of accent, is highly iconic, i.e. it means just what it seems to mean. Thus, a pitch **fall**, or **proclaiming** contour (Brazil, Coulthard and Johns 1980), marks what the speaker believes or proclaims. In this contour, initial high pitch draws attention to an item, and a fall to low pitch signifies completion of a thought or a statement – i.e. the end of an utterance. A **high rise** is against the neutral interpretation, marking something the speaker questions or does not believe. A heightened pitch signals heightened emotion or awareness such as surprise, irritation or drama, and the rising contour indicates "open" meaning. The non-falling or **low rise** pitch pattern indicates incompletion of a thought or a statement, a non-committed response, or openness to other participants to the interaction.

Contour	Meaning	Example	

		o
		  k
		    a	

FALL	neutral/factual	y.	(I accept this.)
		y ? ? a k o	
HIGH RISE	contradictory/ unbelieving		(I don't accept this.)
LOW RISE	non-committal/ unfinished	k a y . . . o	(I'm listening.)
FALL–RISE	with reservation/ uncertain	o y, k a	(but I'm doubtful.)
RISE–FALL	with commitment/ definite/emphatic	k a o y!	(Definitely.)

Source Adapted from Brazil, Coulthard and Johns 1980: 110; Ladefoged 1982: 103

FIGURE 4.3 The iconicity of intonation: intonation means just what it seems to mean

The two compound patterns combine the meanings of falling and rising intonation in interesting iconic meanings. The **fall–rise** pattern, which is a combination of the fall and low rise patterns, has the meaning of both, i.e. both closed and open meaning. This signifies both definiteness and indefiniteness simultaneously, in the sense that a referent is instantiated but the utterance is not yet completed or in the sense that the speaker feels some hesitancy, reservation, doubt or uncertainty. The **rise–fall** pattern incorporates the fall of completion or assurance of the first pattern with the emotional overtone of a high pitch in the middle of the utterance. This is a so-called **swell tone** used for emphatic meaning: as the tone swells, the meaning or emphasis increases and, along with it, the sense of the definiteness of the speaker or the definitiveness of the information conveyed.

Brazil, Coulthard and Johns (1980) point out the importance of **key**, or relative pitch level, in a discourse context, e.g. for indicating affect or emotion and certain kinds of sociocultural meanings. Most importantly, the key of an utterance shows the speaker's attitude toward the information that s/he is conveying. The neutral, unmarked, **mid** key – which is the speaker's modal pitch – is used to make a statement in a neutral manner. In contrast, **high** key indicates an informational contrast, as shown in example (a). Because high key implies a contrast even when one is not explicitly present in the discourse, it can be used to single out individual words for special attention, as in example (b).

```
                        Y                      HIGH
            H                 a                 MID
         ar                 l
(a) I'm going to    vard, not    e !
```

```
        n                              HIGH
     e                                 MID
    v       t   t.
(b) I'd    er  do  h a
```

Low key is used when the speaker wants to assert that two items in successive tone units are in some sense equivalent, as in (c):

```
    t                                  HIGH
     o                                 MID
      l
(c) I    d you already, du
                      mmy.             LOW
```

Here the low key on *dummy* signals that it is to be interpreted as conferential to *you*.

In general, a topic which is continued throughout a discourse will be indicated as sustained by use of low key and non-falling pitch – a **referring** contour (Brazil, Coulthard and Johns 1980) – after its first mention, which occurs on a higher key with falling pitch. For example, the following values for fundamental frequency, in cycles per second (from Brown, Currie and Kenworthy 1980: 76) are typical for second and third mentions of nouns.

	First mention	*Second mention*	*Third mention*
gardens	130–110	110	
houses	120–90	100	*housing* 90

New topics or continued instantiations of topics are signaled by high key, usually accompanied by pitch fall. Thus, a speaker who wishes to emphasize a certain topic may repeatedly reintroduce it as "new" information. The repeated instantiations by high key give such a topic the added informational force of the accumulated prosodic force. A speaker may also signal a desire to keep the conversational floor, i.e. not to relinquish the conversational turn, by using high key at the end of an utterance, i.e. a pitch rise, to draw attention to a continuing topic (Brown, Currie and Kenworthy 1980: 135).

Regional and social variation in intonation

Some varieties of English may constitute partial exceptions to the generalization about English as having the type of intonation which glides smoothly up and down rather than skipping abruptly from one pitch level to the next. For instance, Russ (1984) describes "intermediate tones [which] skip suddenly from one pitch level to another" (p. 46) in Liverpool English. African-based varieties of English also constitute an exception, as they may show the influence of the stepping tones of many African languages (Wells 1982: 643). Such varieties are not restricted to the African continent, as Berry (1976) observes in his description of intonation in Guyanese English as "reminiscent of the terrace-tone languages of West Africa in which the pitch changes by discrete steps from syllable to syllable in an overall pattern of downdrift" (p. 270). Berry (1976) gives the following example:

'Give the old-'man a 'packet.

I have noted similar pitch patterns in Hong Kong English, such as the following from a 20-year-old male polytechnic student when asked "Do you find it difficult to get the information you need?"

I find it uh quite difficult to uh to to find out the information.

In some varieties of English, e.g. those spoken in Ireland, Liverpool and Hawaii, the terminal high rise in yes/no questions is replaced by an earlier rise, with high pitch maintained until the tonic word or phrase, followed by a fall (possibly itself followed by a steady pitch or a slight rise), as in:

Ireland: *Would you like some tea?*
(Wells 1982: 436)

Liverpool: *Did you go to the new supermarket?*
(Cruttenden 1986: 141)

Hawaii: *You need a general catalog?*   *You get one book?*
(Vanderslice and Pierson 1967: 446)   (Carr 1972: 53)

In Hawaiian English, question tags comprising *yea* with high rising pitch are frequent. In Welsh English, question tags are emphasized by a "swell-tone" (rise–fall pattern) on the tag, which makes it more definite or emphatic.

In the conversational English of many varieties, the speaker may try to involve the hearer by having the pitch rise rather than fall at the end of a clause or utterance. In the following example, the high rising pitch on *black* and *past*, in leaving the message open by use of non-falling pitch and in drawing attention to the end of a clause by the use of high pitch, simultaneously signals the non-definitiveness of the utterance and the attentiveness of the speaker to the audience:

It was black and a fish swam past. (Britain 1992: 103)

The tendency to have high rising pitch in statements is common in the conversational English speech of the residents of northern urban areas in Britain – including Liverpool, Birmingham, Manchester, Tyneside, Glasgow and Belfast (but not Edinburgh) – and in Wales (Cruttenden 1981: 83; 1986: 139; Macafee 1983: 36–7), Australia (Guy, Horvath, Vonwiller, Daisley and Rogers 1986; Horvath 1985), New Zealand (Britain 1992; Britain and Newman 1992), Canada (James, Mahut and Latkiewicz 1989), and the United States (Ching 1982). It has been reported for Indian English as well (Bansal 1969: 144).

Horvath (1985: 123) shows that in Australia the use of high rising intonation in statements is an innovation in that three-quarters of the recorded instances are from teenagers and only one-quarter from adults. The pattern for males and females is as shown in Figure 4.4 (with the vertical axis representing the probability of use of the high rising contour in a statement).

This pattern of usage illustrates a phonological change led by women "from below" (Kroch 1978), i.e. from the lower working class. In New Zealand, the use of high rising intonation in statements appears as an innovation led by Maoris and women of European descent. As in

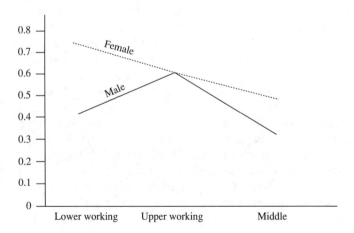

Source Horvath 1985: 126

FIGURE 4.4 Probability of use of hgh rise contour: gender × socioeconomic class

Australia, for New Zealanders these contours "are positive politeness markers used to emphasize speaker–hearer solidarity and to assist in the cooperative management of talk" (Britain 1992: 98).

The rising pitch on statements seems to have a function similar to utterance-final particles such as *ne* in Japanese or *a/ha* in Cantonese and Singaporean Mandarin. Its function can also be compared to the English discourse marker *you know*, which solicits listener participation (Schiffrin 1987). In the view of Horvath (1985), rising pitch on statements, like rising tone in general, *"requests the heightened participation of the listener"* [italics in original] (p. 132). Like rising tone, it also suggests a question, such as might be asked with *you know?* or *see?* at the end of a phrase to solicit the listener's attention or feedback. Thus, it can be suggested that the high rising tone at the end of a statement is an implied question of this sort.

Voice quality

The nature and communicational functions of voice quality

The final topic within the general subject of prosody is **voice quality**, defined as the long-term and stable characteristics of a given voice which span stretches of speech. **Voice quality** is the term used to describe the auditory impression made by a certain mechanical setting of the speech organs over stretches of speech. The term **voice setting** is sometimes used in the same way as voice quality but can also mean the physical postures of the articulators which produce a particular voice quality. (Other terms are **articulatory setting**, **vocal setting** and **voice set**.) Different individuals and groups of speakers have different ways of setting their tongue, jaw opening, lip shape and vocal cords to achieve a characteristic voice quality.

Voice quality can be thought of as the most global and longest-term aspect of prosody, i.e. that aspect which spans the longest stretches of speech and underlies all other aspects. In this way of thinking, intonation and stress, as well as the articulation of vowels and consonants, are produced within the limits of the voice quality set by the articulators and the breath stream coming up from the lungs. For example, if the setting of the vocal cords is very tense, it is not possible to produce as full a range of pitch as when they are set at a more moderate level of tension. As a second example, if the voice is set at low volume – i.e. soft voice – the possibilities for producing stress contrasts are thereby reduced. As another example, if the jaw is set at a relatively close position – i.e. with only a moderate vertical mouth opening – this limits the possibilities for production of the low vowels. As a final example, if the tongue is set with a forward thrust, all phonemes will tend to be produced as raised and fronted variants.

The voice setting, which is manifested in the nature and volume of the breath stream passing through the glottis and in the posture of the articulators, can be thought of as the prosodic foundation on which intonation is produced. The general intonation pattern then sets the bounds for the rhythmic pattern of an utterance. Within this rhythmic pattern, individual stressed syllables occur and these, in turn, set the context for the production of the individual segments of speech. As illustrated in Figure 4.5, which is an elaboration of Figure 1.1, the vowels, since they are the main segments to be prolonged, and so to spread across stretches of speech, can be seen as existing at a lower level in the hierarchy of phonological production than consonants, which define the boundaries – the closures or edges – of articulation.

In the words of Esling (1987):

> Voice setting is a part of accent. It is generally what we have identified when we say that we recognize an individual by his/her 'voice'.

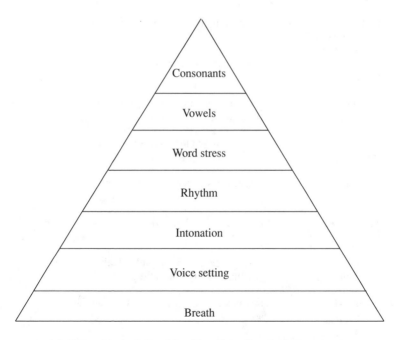

FIGURE 4.5 Hierarchical relationship of breath to phonological parameters

In this sense, accent refers to all of the speech-sound information that an individual produces, within which voice setting acts as the background or field, stress and intonation are overlaid as prosodic waves on that field, and phonemic segments appear as particles in rapidly changing succession, bearing a relationship to both the medium-term (prosodic) and long-term background (setting) elements. (p. 45)

Some examples of voice quality are given in Figure 4.6.

Different voice qualities are associated with the speech of different languages, geographical dialects, and socially defined varieties – e.g. those varieties spoken by groups of speakers defined by ethnicity, socio-economic background or gender. Voice quality can also help identify peoples' momentary attitudes and moods, as well as their more permanent emotional and psychological state, i.e. their personality (Esling

Tense voice: (nervousness, anxiety)	tight vocal cords, tending to raise pitch
Harsh/hoarse voice: (anxiety)	very tight vocal cords, giving voice a raspy quality
Creaky voice: (superiority, fatigue)	vocal cords are tight but with low pitch
Slack voice: (relaxation)	loose vocal cords, tending to lower pitch
Nasal voice: (whining, nastiness)	velic opening throughout speech allows air to exit continually through the nose
Palatal voice: (mocking)	tongue is raised to palate for all articulations; all consonants have [j]-glide, all vowels are high
Retroflex voice: (rural)	tongue tip is curled upwards and backwards
Back voice: (masculine)	tongue is pulled back somewhat for articulation of all sounds
Front voice: (feminine)	tongue is far forward for all articulation; many articulations made with the tongue tip
Labialized voice: (baby talk)	lip rounding or spreading accompanies all articulations

FIGURE 4.6 Examples of voice quality and associated settings and connotations

1987: 451; Laver and Trudgill 1979: 14–17; Scherer 1979: 159). In sum, voice quality is an important aspect of the geographical, the social and the personal identity of speakers.

Situational and psychological correlates of voice quality

Because of its associated physiological correlates, voice quality is a sign of the speaker's overall physical and mental condition. Speakers who are elderly, tired or in very poor health often have a creaky voice quality, as a result of a tense posture of the vocal cords and their slow and somewhat irregular vibration. One manifestation of psychological tension is a tense setting of the vocal cords, which shows in the voice as a harsh or strained quality that is generally accompanied by heightened pitch. Conversely, a generally relaxed state of mind and body results in a relaxed vocal posture as well, producing a lax or slack setting of the vocal cords that lowers pitch and may produce breathy voice as well. As a consequence, slack voice gives an impression of relaxation or laziness, while tense voice gives an impression of tension or irritation.

A loud voice, which would be appropriate in situations where it is necessary to get someone's attention, might also indicate a state of high emotion, such as anger, surprise or excitement. If part of a speaker's normal voice set, a loud voice might be interpreted as a sign of the speaker's confidence, or, less positively, of an aggressive or dogmatic personality. A soft voice, which would be usual in trying to calm someone down or in an intimate conversation or one in which secret, private or very serious matters are discussed, can also be indicative of shock or terror, or of a sad or depressed state. As a normal vocal feature, a soft voice might be interpreted as an indication that the speaker is a gentle, shy or timid person.

A high-pitched voice – including **falsetto** or **false voice** – expresses surprise and is also used for joking and discussion of non-serious matters. As an indicator of the speaker's emotional state, a high voice suggests joyfulness or pleasurable feelings. As a stable trait, high pitch is associated with a non-threatening, pleasant or playful personality, and with femininity. Less positively, it might be viewed as an indicator of someone who is childish or who cannot be taken seriously. A low-pitched voice, which might be used in talking about serious matters or expressing authority – e.g. in giving orders or telling someone off – might also be a sign of controlled anger or stifled rage. It can therefore be taken as a threatening voice quality symbolizing a threatening state of mind or personality or, more positively, as indicative of seriousness and confidence.

Variety in pitch, which would be usual in animated conversation or in telling a story, signals interest or excitement in the topic of conversation or the person(s) being spoken to. As a permanent style of speaking, highly variable pitch suggests an excitable or attention-seeking individual, or a dramatic personality. A voice with little variation in pitch would be normal in reading academic material aloud or in attempting to sound objective and not to express one's attitude or emotions – e.g. in reading a resolution aloud on which people must vote. Outside of such contexts, monotonous pitch gives an impression of boredom, inattentiveness or resignation. If it is a person's normal voice, then that person might be seen as unexcitable, boring, shallow or lacking in personality.

A monotonous rhythm is used appropriately in calling out or in giving emphatic commands. It is also the kind of rhythm used to imitate a machine (e.g. a robot or a computer) talking. A person who speaks with little variety in rhythm is assumed to be controlling his/her speech and to be intentionally or unintentionally distant or uninvolved. People who are, or who are perceived to be, highly controlled or uncommunicative might show little variety in their speech rhythm. These people might be viewed in a negative light as over-careful, or, in the worst case, as inhuman.

A speaker might employ very precise articulation of individual phonemes and words when teaching low proficiency students or when giving information to non-native speakers. Speakers also sometimes articulate carefully when they are thinking a lot about what they are saying, selecting their words with care, and weighing their impact both before and after they are spoken. Such a speaking style can therefore give an impression of heightened attention or anxiety, as attending to the audience, or as trying to be precise. As an indicator of personality or character traits, this sort of voice suggests a meticulous, non-spontaneous, artificial or pedantic person.

Because different voices have different natural and symbolic associations, they are often exploited in acting, pretending or playing various roles. In English and some other languages, labialized articulation can signify baby talk – i.e. talking to a baby or to another person in a babyish style. A combination of retroflex and labialized articulation made the American actor, Jimmy Stewart, seem ingenuous – a combination of childlike and rural. A palatalized articulatory setting, sometimes with nasalization, is used in English for baby talk as well as for mocking. The combination of nasal voice and a spread lip setting in the speech of the American actor, Jack Nicholson, gives a sinister impression – a man who mocks and smiles at the same time.

By raising the larynx – e.g. by raising the chin and leaning the head backwards – an adult voice can be made to sound more like that of a child, as this stretches the vocal cords and raises the pitch as a consequence. This is a setting that might be used for the voice of a cartoon character (e.g. Mickey Mouse), a doll or an adult playing a child (e.g. PeeWee Herman). In contrast, producing a voice with a lowered larynx creates a deeper, more adult voice and so might be the voice adopted by a child attempting to imitate an adult, especially a male adult. An army drill sergeant might "bark out" orders in a harsh shout while also placing his chin on his chest, thereby lowering the larynx and making the voice lower and more "commanding". In films, a harsh or breathy voice is often used to disguise the voice over the telephone, as the harshness or breathiness covers up, and to some extent substitutes for, the normal identifying resonances of the voice.

Regional and social variation in voice quality

Different voice qualities or settings have been recognized for different varieties of English. A pervasive nasal quality is often said to characterize "broad" American and Australian speech (Wells 1982: 604), though this characterization seems to be a stereotype of Australian English (Horvath 1985: 21ff). The pitch range of American Black English speakers, West Indian English speakers and women in general (Brend 1975; Smith 1985) is said to be wide as contrasted to the narrow pitch range of rural Southern (White) speakers, the "Texan drawl" (Wells 1982: 92) and men in general. Texans and Canadians are reported to have relatively deep voices or "lowered larynx voice" (Wells 1982: 93), which also seems to be generally characteristic of North American males. In contrast to the louder speech and "raspy" or "tense breathy" voice quality of some male English speakers, females tend to have a softer voice and a laxer type of "breathy" speech (Smith 1985: 73). Collins and Mees (1992: 78–9) describe the American English voice setting as combining apico-alveolar articulation with uvularization, nasalization and lax voice.

In Vancouver, Canada, Esling (1991: 127) reports laryngo-pharyngealized voice for "middle working class" speakers, velarized voice for "upper working class" speakers, palatalized voice for "lower middle class" speakers and nasal voice for "middle middle class" speakers. My own data on the speech of Americans in the rural Southeast suggests a social distribution of voice qualities similar to that found by Esling in Western Canada. In the non-coastal interior region of North Georgia, Tennessee and Virginia, a palatalized voice setting has the attributes of "urban", "female" and "careful" speech as compared to a backed (i.e. velarized, larynx-lowered, retroflexed) voice setting having the attributes of "rural", "male" and "casual" speech (Pennington 1982: 286–7).

A creaky voice quality is reportedly common in British RP speech (Wells 1982: 92) and in the speech of working class (but not middle class) speakers in Norwich (Trudgill 1974: 186), while the voice quality of Cockney speakers is described as "harsh" (Wells 1982: 331). Working class speech in Liverpool is velarized as a result of a high back tongue position (Knowles 1978; Russ 1984: 46) – a setting also noted for RP (Collins and Mees 1992: 79). In North Wales, an even backer voice setting is common, involving a constriction in the pharynx (Wells 1982: 93). Speakers in the Scottish lowlands are reported to have tense voice (Wells 1982: 93) – i.e. with a tense setting of the vocal cords – and in Edinburgh and Glasgow, a typical articulatory setting is said to be one in which the jaw protrudes out beyond the top lip (Esling 1994b; Macafee 1983), producing a distinctive lip shape and secondary modification of segmental phonemes. Tense voice is also a characteristic of Hong Kong English, while lax voice, a narrow jaw opening and a retroflex tongue position characterizes Indian English.

As noted by Esling (1994a), different voice qualities may receive a positive or negative evaluation from listeners through their association with different social groups:

> *Nasal voice*, for instance, carries high social prestige when associated with certain accents (viz. RP, Standard Edinburgh English), but stands out as an undesirable feature to many listeners when associated with other accents. Evaluations of this sort are quite subjective. (p. 49–51)

Voice quality is thus a means by which listeners make general assessments of speakers' social traits through their identification with certain groups and with the characteristics of those groups, according to community norms as well as listeners' personal viewpoints.

A prosodic continuum

Some linguists refer to voice quality as not belonging strictly to the domain of linguistics but rather to the larger domain of communication – including gestures and other forms of non-verbal communication – termed the "paralinguistic" domain. There is, however, a problem with removing voice quality from the domain of language per se. This is because, as recognized by Bolinger (1986), the domains of the "strictly linguistic" form of prosody (i.e. intonation), which is intimately bound up with grammatical meaning, and of voice quality, which is intimately bound up with affective meaning, are not clearly distinguishable. As Bolinger (1986) observes:

> [S]ometimes pitch goes more or less out of control; the sweep of the melody as a whole and the size of the jumps that mark the accents exceed what one expects in ordinary discourse. This is the effect of EMOTION. With excitement there are greater extremes of pitch; with depression the range is narrowed. Of course one can always pretend, and then the uncontrolled becomes controlled. Anger faked uses the same wide range as anger genuine. One can simulate great surprise by asking a question with an extremely high pitch at the end: the pattern remains the same, but it is stretched. Since no human utterance can be totally without emotion, one can never be certain where the 'grammar' of an utterance ends and its 'emotion' begins. Intonation lies on the last frontier between primitive and civilized communication. (p. 13)

Moreover, since certain intonational patterns are regularly associated with certain grammatical constructions – types of phrases and sentences – and certain voice qualities are regularly associated with certain emotions and social roles, these patterns become emblematic of those constructions, emotions and social roles, and maintain those meanings even when divorced from their characteristic grammatical and lexical moorings.

It is then a short step to phonological markers and stereotypes which indicate meaning that can override and contradict the lexical meaning of the words and can therefore be used to intentionally deceive or confuse. Thus, when a person's voice says one thing and his/her words say another, we tend to believe the voice, not the words. In addition, when certain voice qualities are regularly associated with certain social roles or socially defined groups, they are easily recognized by people for what they symbolize and so can be used to parody or to ridicule.

From the foregoing discussion, it can be concluded that prosody – taken as a complex of voice quality, intonation, rhythm, stress and phonological fluency – fulfils a wide range of communicative functions. In English, prosody functions as:

(1) a direct, iconic indicator of the significance of information (e.g. as of greater or lesser importance);
(2) an emblematic indicator of a grammatical pattern (e.g. statement vs. question);

(3) a symptom of an emotional state or attitude (e.g. uncertainty vs. certainty);

(4) a signal of a certain stance or role taken by the speaker (e.g. condescension or authority);

(5) a marker of a socially or geographically defined group (e.g. speakers from a certain region or ethnic group);

(6) a symbol of a particular social role (e.g. femininity vs. masculinity);

(7) a defining characteristic of a particular type of interaction (e.g. "adult talk" vs. "baby talk");

(8) a representation, whether genuine or not, of a speaker characteristic, condition or role;

(9) an index of a speaker's individual identity.

In sum, the dividing lines between prosody in its function as marking out information units and as communicating various types of expressive and social meanings are by no means clearcut. The range of meanings of prosody, as summarized in Figure 4.7, can be described as a continuum from **presentational**, in which the relationship between sound and meaning is simple and direct, to **representational**, in which the relationship between sound and meaning is more complex and indirect (cf. Bolinger 1985: 98). The most presentational type of meaning is the deictic, or signaling, function of accent to indicate new or important information. This aspect of prosody is the most tied to the immediate context, the most situationally variable and changing, and the least symbolic socially and culturally. It is therefore the most universal aspect of prosody.

Somewhat less simple and direct is the relationship between sound and meaning shown in the attitude expressed by intonation / voice quality. This type of meaning, rather than being a direct indicator, is a somewhat less direct symptom of the speaker's emotional state. At a more abstract level, prosody is a representation of a speaker's longer-term psychological, social and cultural makeup. At this more abstract representational level, prosody relates to the larger communicational context

PRESENTATIONAL	REPRESENTATIONAL
Iconic	Symbolic
Immediate context	Larger context
Situational	Characteristic
Temporary	Long-term
Least socially loaded	Most socially loaded
Most universal	Most culture-bound

FIGURE 4.7 Two poles of a prosodic continuum

and to characteristic, long-term qualities of the speaker. Because of its connection to characteristics of people, it is the most socially "loaded" and culture-bound form of prosody.

Considering the physiological interrelations and the fuzzy functional boundaries between voice quality and other aspects of prosody, it seems counterproductive to separate out this aspect of language from the general discussion of prosody, especially when the underlying purpose is to help language learners achieve full communicative competence in a second language. It can be concluded that in terms of both physiology and function, voice quality is beneficially added to the curriculum in phonology and oral language skills.

If the voice setting and other aspects of prosody are as basic as I am claiming them to be, then clearly pronunciation should be taught not only or not primarily in terms of the articulation of individual sounds, but in terms of the general characteristics of speech that span more than one segment, i.e. speech prosody. This is what is meant by a **top-down** focus for the pronunciation curriculum, as described in Pennington (1989), where a number of specific teaching suggestions are provided. In Chapter 6 of the present text, a protocol for "top-down" analysis and diagnosis of student pronunciation is offered.

Prosody activities

1. Transcription practice

Transcribe the phrases of Figure 4.2 as they might be pronounced in rapid speech, including phones, diacritic markings and stress marks.

2. Matching intonation contours to context

Match each sentence plus intonation contour with an appropriate context from the pairs of questions/statements above them.

(a.) Where's my lunch?
    What's in the bag?

Your lunch is in the bag.

(b) What is your son doing?
    I can't believe my eyes!

My son / is practicing / the piano.

(c) Who's making the coffee?
What are you making?

I'm making the coffee.

(d) What happened to Pat last night?
Why didn't you come to the party last night?

Pat cut her finger / and I had to take her to the hospital.

(e) When are you going to eat tonight?
What will you be doing around 9:00 pm tonight?

I'm planning to eat around nine.

(f) Do you do your laundry on Saturday?
Do you want to go for a drive in the country on Sunday?

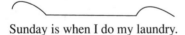

Sunday is when I do my laundry.

3. Imitation practice

Practice imitating a particular person's voice or a dialectal or non-native accent of English that you are familiar with and teach this to other class members. Try to give them clear instructions about how to set their vocal organs so that they can achieve a good imitation.

4. Creating prosody exercises

Try to create exercises to deal with the following pronunciation problems of non-native speakers:

* the tendency to make all final syllables of words CV by adding an epenthetic vowel (*schwa paragoge*) to the end of each word (e.g. Brazilian Portuguese speakers);
* syllable-timed rhythm (e.g. Cantonese speakers);
* non-elision or glottal stopping between syllables or words (e.g. German speakers);

- pervasive nasality (e.g. Spanish speakers);
- non-apical (blade) articulation (e.g. Japanese speakers);
- palatalization (tongue raising), especially of stops (e.g. Russian speakers).

5. Adapting material for prosodic practice

Prepare the riddles below as material for students to practice English prosody by dividing each riddle into breath groups as you see fit and marking possible intonation contours. You may try to mark the entire contour, as shown in the first two items, or you may mark only the direction of the terminal contour at the end of each breath group.

Note that in telling a story, a joke or a riddle, the speaker often pauses slightly after key words or phrases, to ensure that the hearer will catch them and to build suspense or interest. Otherwise, the point of the story, joke or riddle might not be understood or might not be as effective. As a consequence, these types of discourse are often broken up into more breath groups than might occur in other types of speech. Thus, the second riddle might have a break after the key phrase "Frankenstein's monster", even though (unlike the first riddle) there is no grammatical break between clauses at that point.

Also note that the terminal contour of any breath group before the final one will be non-falling, i.e. low rising or relatively steady-state, since it does not signal the end of a thought group; whereas the terminal contour of the final breath group will always fall, since each of the riddles is a *wh*-question.

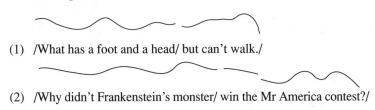

(1) /What has a foot and a head/ but can't walk./

(2) /Why didn't Frankenstein's monster/ win the Mr America contest?/

(3) What did one magnet say to the other?

(4) Why is a cup of coffee like an elevator?

(5) What gets answers but never asks questions?

(6) What is the noisiest part of a tree?

(7) Why did the man stand behind the mule?

(8) What's the difference between a hill and a pill?

(9) What will be dirtier after taking a bath than before taking one?

(10) What's the difference between sunrise and sunset?

(11) What has a heart in its head?

(12) What bus crossed the ocean?

(13) What word begins with "e" and ends with "e" and has only

one letter in it?

(14) How do you communicate with a fish?

(15) What has four wheels and flies?

(16) What gets wetter the more it dries?

(17) What did the cannibal say when he had a stomachache?

(18) What man never does a day's work in a lifetime?

(19) What has a mouth and doesn't talk, and a bed that it doesn't

sleep in?

(20) What ten-letter word starts with gas?
(Answers are provided at end of the Activities section.)

6. Designing an activity to practice prosody

Design an activity to practice one of the three aspects of prosody in A,
B or C below.

A. *A limited response activity for practicing juncture*

Design a limited response activity or sequence of activities to practice
hearing and producing junctural distinctions, using all or some of the
material below.

Why choose	Why cheat	Why chop	Why chip
White shoes	White sheet	White shop	White ship
Why tie	My tie		
White tie	Might tie	Right tie	Light tie
White eye	Might I	Right eye	Light eye

For example, students might be required to listen to short texts such as
the following for the first pair of expressions (*Why choose* / *White
shoes*) and to supply the correct expression or to decide whether the
expression as supplied by the teacher or another student is the semantically appropriate one for the context.

When the young thief, wielding a knife, said to his would-be victim,
"Your money or your life!" the man pulled out a 44 Magnum revol-
ver and calmly replied: "_____?"

When Marty went to visit Pat, who was taking a rest in the Shady
Arms Retreat, they met in a common room full of people. "A lot of
the people here are trying to find themselves; they are not sure who
they are, or they think they are someone else. For example, that guy
over there thinks he is a great concert pianist, and the woman next to
him thinks she is a European princess.

"And the man in the white coat and _____, I guess he thinks he's a doctor?" "No," Marty replied. "The guy thinks he's God. He just happens to *be* a doctor."

B. *A dialogue to practice stress*

Construct a dialogue involving questions and responses between a customer and a sales clerk at a bakery counter that will practice the following contrasting stress patterns:

'beside the rolls	'one of each	'six of them	'two of those
beside the 'rolls	one of 'each	six of 'them	two of 'those
'several more	a 'dozen of these	it's 'too much	not 'too many
several 'more	a dozen of 'these	it's too 'much	not too 'many

C. *A pair activity to practice intonation*

Use some or all of the material below as a jumping-off point to develop a pair activity involving objects or pictures in which students practice discriminating the functions of asserting and questioning where the only clue is falling vs. rising intonation.

Her hair is long.	His eyes are brown.
Her hair is long?	His eyes are brown?
He's the tallest one.	That's the biggest one.
He's the tallest one?	That's the biggest one?
There are three yellow ones.	That's the only blue one.
There are only three yellow ones?	That's the only blue one?
There are none left.	That's the last one.
There are none left?	That's the last one?

7. Critique of syllabus for English stress

Critique the following syllabus for developing basic competence in English stress in two one-hour lessons per week, as part of a six-week beginner ESL course (adapted from Clennell 1986: 96–7).

Objectives
By the end of the course, learners will be able to:

• recognize basic stress patterns for words and sentences;
• produce a clear distinction between stressed and unstressed syllables;
• distinguish words on the basis of stress;
• differentiate between basic sentence rhythms.

Weekly schedule.

WEEK 1. Word stress recognition focusing on months in the context *When did you arrive here?*, using the calendar, pictures representing months or seasons and cuisenaire rods of different sizes to show stress patterns. For example: JANuary, APril, deCEMber.

WEEK 2. Stress patterns associated with words for food items, reinforced by pictures or actual food items. For example ONion, poTAto.

WEEK 3. Stress patterns associated with countries and nationalities, using maps and pictures from around the world. Simple sentence patterns can be practiced in an identification game and reinforced by use of cuisenaire rods. For example: picture of man beside Eiffel Tower – he's a FRENCHman; picture of a woman next to the Great Wall – she's chiNESE.

WEEK 4. Recognition and production of weak forms in exercises to identify objects in pictures and their location, reinforced by use of rods. For example: in FRONT of the DOOR; on TOP of the TAble.

WEEK 5. Authentic listening material with gap filling for weakly stressed words; practice in asking and giving information at the market. For example: I'd like a KIlo of ORanges; do you have any toMAtoes?

WEEK 6. Recording and playing back roleplays or interviews of students at the market; aural discrimination test.

8. Sociolinguistic mini-research: stress in multisyllabic words

Develop a research project in which you and/or your students will test members of your community, other teachers or students to determine the stress patterns in the following two sets of words:

SET A	SET B
voluntary	communal
momentary	integral
military	applicable
sedentary	abdomen
secretary	controversy
commentary	torment (verb)
inventory	finance (verb)
trajectory	unique
auditory	address
lavatory	chauffeur

The words of Set A vary in the level of stress on the third syllable. The options are:

(1) tertiary stress;
(2) weak stress;
(3) ultra-weak stress;
(4) loss of the vowel of the third syllable and possible trilling or devoicing of /r/ in combination with the preceding voiceless aspirated stop /t/.

The words of Set B vary in the placement of the strong stress on either the first or the second syllable.

Since the placement of stress may vary depending on the context of the word, it might be a good idea to have subjects say each word in isolation as well as in a phrase or sentence context which you supply or ask the subject to invent.

As in the mini-research projects in other chapters, it will probably be interesting to categorize your subjects into groups by their similar characteristics and then to compare and contrast the responses of those with similar characteristics to those who are classified in different categories – e.g. graduate vs. non-graduate, male vs. female, older vs. younger people. It might also be useful to compare the responses of different groups in the various contexts by computing their index scores as before.

9. Action research: stress patterns of individual words

Conduct an action research project with your students to find out what problems they have with the stress of individual words in English and how you might go about remediating their problems.

Analyze both production and perception of stress in words of two or more syllables and consider whether to focus on perception and/or production based on the problems you uncover. Regularly monitor your progress and adjust your teaching plan and activities as needed throughout the action research.

10. Action research: teaching ideas for prosody

Try out one of the teaching ideas below and then assess the results, following the procedures outlined for action research in Exercise 10 of earlier chapters. As outlined in Chapter 3, in designing your project, you will need to decide whether to carry out the research:

- in one or two classes;
- with or without a research partner;
- in your own class(es) and/or in someone else's;
- by trying out lessons simultaneously or sequentially.

Once you have designed your project, you will need to attend to its ongoing implementation and evaluation by:

- monitoring the effectiveness of instruction;
- making any necessary changes in curriculum or teaching approach;
- retrospectively assessing the teaching process and effects of instruction.

Answers to riddles in activity 5

(1) a bed
(2) He had too many imported parts.
(3) "I'm attracted to you."
(4) They both give you a lift.
(5) a doorbell
(6) the bark
(7) He thought he'd get a kick out of it.
(8) One gives you a hard time going up; the other gives you a hard time going down.
(9) a bathtub
(10) a day
(11) lettuce
(12) Columbus
(13) envelope
(14) drop him a line
(15) a garbage truck
(16) a towel
(17) "It must have been someone I ate."
(18) a night watchman
(19) a river
(20) automobile

Teaching ideas for prosody

1. Syllable awareness

A. *Pronouncing different types of syllables*

Each individual vowel or combination of consonant(s) and vowel below is a possible **syllable** in English. Practice the syllable units below as a way to get accustomed to pronouncing each type as a unified group of sounds planned and spoken together on one breath.

o	**e**	Vowel
po	**le**	Consonant + Vowel
pro	**ple**	Consonant + Consonant + Vowel
spro	**sple**	Consonant + Consonant + Consonant + Vowel
u		Vowel
up		Vowel + Consonant
ups		Vowel + Consonant + Consonant
cups		Consonant + Vowel + Consonant + Consonant
crups		Consonant + Consonant + Vowel + Consonant + Consonant
scrups		Cons. + Cons. + Cons. + Vowel + Consonant + Consonant
scrulps		Cons. + Cons. + Cons. + Vowel + Cons. + Cons. + Cons.

(For many learners, it will be useful to practice the pronunciation of English nonsense syllables or one-syllable words spoken in isolation. In this way, the learner can become accustomed to the units and timing of English words.)

B. *Grouping of words by number of syllables*

Work with a partner to group the words below into columns according to the number of syllables.

NUMBER OF SYLLABLES

1	2	3	4	5

WORDS TO GROUP INTO COLUMNS

military	poll	coming	machinist	politician
politics	millet	mechanical	miller	militaristic
problematic	communal	pro	mechanistic	mechanize
machine	probing	police	communist	probe
come	problem	mill	militia	commune

Follow-up questions
Does *military* consist of three or four syllables? How many syllables are there in *militaristic*?

Does *militia* consist of three or four syllables?
Why is *politician* not a five-syllable word?
Why do the words *machine, police* and *commune* not have three syllables, and why do *come* and *probe* have only one syllable?

C. *Noticing stress patterns in words of more than one syllable*

Look at the words that you have just grouped into columns and listen to your teacher pronounce each of them. You will notice that for words of more than one syllable, one of the syllables is stronger than the others. This stronger syllable is usually **louder, longer** and **higher in pitch** than the syllables around it. Listen again as your teacher pronounces the words in each column and underline the part of the word that is the strongest. This part of the word is called the *stressed* syllable.

NOTE: For the one-syllable words, you can underline the whole word.

Look at the two-syllable words that you have just marked. You will notice that some of them have the stressed syllable first, while others have the stressed syllable second. Write a "1" next to those which have the stressed syllable first and a "2" next to those that have the stressed syllable second. The unstressed syllables in these words are sometimes referred to as *weak* syllables.

Now look at the three-syllable words that you marked. Some of these have the stressed syllable first, while others have the stressed syllable second. Again, mark the place of the stressed syllable by writing a "1" or a "2" next to the word. For those words with the stressed syllable in the middle (that is, second), the two syllables on either side are weak. Have your teacher pronounce these words to hear how much stronger the middle syllable is as compared to the first and third syllables. For those words with the stressed syllable first, however, the third syllable is somewhat stronger than the syllable in the middle, that is, stronger than the syllable that occurs right next to the stressed syllable. Yet, the third syllable is not as strong as the first syllable of the word. In such a case, we can say that the first syllable receives a *strong* stress and the last syllable a *medium* stress.

This last type of word illustrates an important principle of English rhythm, that of *alternating stress*. This principle means that non-weak stresses tend to recur at regular intervals with one (or sometimes two) weak syllables in between. In the three-syllable words in your list that have the strongly stressed syllable first, one weakly stressed syllable follows, and this is in turn followed by a syllable with a medium level of stress, that is, with a level of stress which is stronger than the second syllable but not as strong as the first syllable.

The four-syllable words in the list illustrate three different positions of the strongest stress: initial syllable, second syllable and third syllable. Mark the one four-syllable word that has the strongest stress on the first syllable with a "1". Note the medium stress on the third syllable. In the converse situation, when the strongest stress is on the third syllable, the first syllable of the word had a medium stress. Find the three four-syllable words which show this stress pattern and mark them with a "3". Note that the second and the fourth syllables in all these words receive a weaker stress than the syllable to their left. Now locate the one four-syllable word that contains the strongest stress on the second syllable. What are the stresses of the other syllables?

There is one five-syllable word in the list. In this word, the strongest stress is on the fourth syllable. Which syllables receive medium and weak stresses?

D. *Pronouncing a very long word*

The following word is the longest word in the English language which you can find in an all-purpose dictionary:

pneumonoultramicroscopicsilicovolcanoconiosis

Look up this word in a dictionary. What does it mean? We can break this word down into its parts to practice their pronunciation and to see what each part means.

pneu	'breath, of the lungs'
mono	'one, single'
ultra	'extremely'
micro	'small'
scopic	'visible'
silico	'of silicon, a common non-metallic element of the earth's crust
volcano	'of volcanic origin'
coni	'cone-like or cone-shaped'
osis	'abnormal or diseased condition'

The word describes a disease of the lungs which is commonly referred to as "Black Lung Disease". This disease occurs among coalminers. It involves breathing in coal dust, which forms cone-shaped deposits in the lungs.

Work with the same partner or a different one to pronounce this word according to the directions that follow for Partner A and Partner B.

Partner A

Pronounce the syllables of this long word. Every time your partner taps, pronounce a strong syllable in the word. Pronounce the weak syllables in between taps. The strong syllables are written in big letters below to remind you to make them long and loud. They are written higher than the weak syllables to remind you to pronounce them with higher pitch than the weak syllables.

Partner B

Tap a regular rhythm with approximately one-second intervals using your pencil or pen. Tap only for the syllables written in large letters. This will help your partner keep a regular rhythm in pronouncing this long word. Tap extra-strong for the syllable that is underlined, the last strong syllable, to remind your partner that this syllable receives the strongest stress. It is a general fact of English that the last strong syllable in a word, phrase or sentence usually receives the strongest stress.

MO	UL	MI	SCO	SI		CO	CA	CO	<u>O</u>
pneu	no	tra	cro	pic	li	vol	no	ni	sis

2. Phrase stress

Working with a partner, practice giving emphases to different words in the contexts below, by substituting each option in the blank spaces, as shown in the example for number 1.

Partner A: It wasn't _____, was it?
Partner B: No, it was _____.

Example for number 1:
Partner A: It wasn't *on the TABLE*, was it?
Partner B: No, it was *on the DESK*.
Partner A: It wasn't *IN the desk*, was it?
Partner B: No, it was *ON the desk*.

Note that for the first two lines of the dialogue, the noun in the prepositional phrase receives the strong stress, whereas in the second two lines, it is the preposition that receives the stress. Without this stress pattern, the four-line mini-dialogues do not make sense in terms of which information is known or assumed and which information is not known or assumed.

Practice the dialogue several times until you are able to place the stresses correctly, according to the meaning. As you perform the dialogue, try to produce phrases on one breath, with linking, contractions and schwa vowels where these would occur in normal casual speech.

PARTNER A: It wasn't	PARTNER B: It was
(1) on the table in the desk	(1) on the desk
(2) a black van a green car	(2) a black car
(3) a bottle of wine a glass of beer	(3) a bottle of beer
(4) one of us two of them	(4) one of them
(5) a little boy a big girl	(5) a little girl
(6) a three-bedroom house a two-bedroom apartment	(6) a three-bedroom apartment
(7) the apple cider the cherry pie	(7) the apple pie
(8) a blue jacket a purple overcoat	(8) a blue overcoat
(9) an old woman a young man	(9) an old man
(10) six o'clock in the morning seven o'clock in the evening	(10) six o'clock in the evening

3. Stress and intonation in context

A. *Contrastive stress contexts*

Work in a pair to build short dialogues around one of the sentences in each set below. Then perform your dialogues for the other student pairs and have them guess which of the sentences you selected.

(1) (a) WE did not go to that restaurant last Saturday night.
    (b) We did NOT go to that restaurant last Saturday night.
    (c) We did not go to THAT restaurant last Saturday night.
    (d) We did not go to that restaurant LAST Saturday night.
    (e) We did not go to that restaurant last SATURDAY night.
    (f) We did not go to that restaurant last Saturday NIGHT.

(2) (a) MARTY is hardly ever on time for dinner at my house.
    (b) Marty is HARDLY ever on time for dinner at my house.
    (c) Marty is HARDLY EVER on time for dinner at my house.
    (d) Marty is hardly ever ON TIME for dinner at my house.
    (e) Marty is hardly ever on time for DINNER at my house.
    (f) Marty is hardly ever on time for dinner at MY house.

(3) (a) MERCURY isn't running in the final race at Pimlico today.
    (b) Mercury ISN'T running in the final race at Pimlico today.
    (c) Mercury isn't RUNNING in the final race at Pimlico today.
    (d) Mercury isn't running in the FINAL race at Pimlico today.
    (e) Mercury isn't running in the final race at PIMLICO today.
    (f) Mercury isn't running in the final race at Pimlico TODAY.

(4) (a) PAT used to eat only strict vegetarian food.
    (b) Pat USED TO eat only strict vegetarian food.
    (c) Pat used to eat ONLY strict vegetarian food.
    (d) Pat used to eat only STRICT vegetarian food.
    (e) Pat used to eat only strict VEGETARIAN food.
    (f) Pat used to eat only strict vegetarian FOOD.

(5) (a) I don't THINK you could stand that for long.
    (b) I don't think YOU could stand that for long.
    (c) I don't think you COULD stand that for long.
    (d) I don't think you could STAND that for long.
    (e) I don't think you could stand THAT for long.
    (f) I don't think you could stand that FOR LONG.

B. Getting to know each other questions and answers

Working with a partner, ask and answer a series of questions such as the following, which are appropriate for a first-time meeting between two people. If you and your partner already know each other, then you can each make up questions to ask for information you do not already have about each other.

> What's your name?
> Where are you from?
> How long have you been here?
> How long have you been studying English?
> Where do you work?
> Where do you live?

After asking the series of questions, each partner then reviews the information by putting the answers together in a series of clauses joined by *and*. The speaker should make an effort to pronounce each clause as a unit on one breath, with linking and other types of coarticulatory effects, foregrounding the key information units in each clause (i.e. the answers to the questions) and backgrounding the rest of the information in each clause (i.e. the presupposed question). The speaker should also make use of lengthening and low rising intonation on the last syllable of each clause before *and* to indicate that more information is coming until the last syllable of the last clause, which should have falling pitch.

> "So your name is RICARDO, and you're from BOLIVIA, and you have been here for only TWO WEEKS, and you have been studying English for TWO YEARS, and your major is ENGINEERING, and you do NOT HAVE A JOB yet, and so you do NOT WORK anywhere, and you live on RODNEY ROAD."

4. Voice quality

A. *Expressing emotion by voice quality*

Tone or quality of voice expresses one's meaning in a rather direct and transparent way. Thus, heightened emotions such as happiness, excitement, surprise or fear are expressed in heightened or exaggerated voice qualities such as high or varied pitch and stress. Conversely, depressed emotions such as sadness, hopelessness or boredom show in lowered or depressed voice qualities such as low or monotonous pitch or stress.

Working with a partner, try showing different meanings by pronouncing the following syllables with different voice quality. Your partner should guess which emotion you are expressing.

[mmm]   [aaa]   [ooo]

B. Expressing routine, predictable information by voice

Working with a partner, speak each of the sentences below, trying to show one or the other of two possible meanings by using voice quality, stress and intonation. In one possible meaning of each sentence, the speaker expresses that the event is unexpected, unusual or out of the ordinary. In the other possible meaning, the speaker expresses that the event is expected, usual or routine. Your partner should guess which meaning you intended, based on how you use your voice to say the sentence.

(1) Your mother's here.   POSSIBLE MEANINGS
                                   She is not expected.
                                   It is a routine visit.

(2) The phone's ringing.   POSSIBLE MEANINGS
                                   I am surprised by this.
                                   We both expected it to ring,
                                   and you are to answer it.

(3) I'm still waiting.

POSSIBLE MEANINGS
I want you to know that I am willing to continue waiting.
I've been waiting for a while and you already know this.

(4) Your lunch is ready.

POSSIBLE MEANINGS
I don't expect you to know this.
It's ready as usual.

(5) The water's boiling.

POSSIBLE MEANINGS
I just noticed this and am surprised.
I know it's been boiling for two or three minutes already.

(6) The dinner's burning.

POSSIBLE MEANINGS
I just noticed this and am alarmed.
I expected this to happen as you are not paying attention to your cooking.

(7) You left the lights on.

POSSIBLE MEANINGS
This has never happened before.
You usually forget to turn them off.

C. *Your voice shows your true feelings*

If a person's words say one thing, and that person's voice says something different, which one do you believe? Generally, we believe the voice more than the words because tone of voice is directly tied in with a person's physical and emotional state. Also tone of voice is what we notice most.

Tone of voice or voice quality carries more communicative weight in speaking than do the words themselves. In fact, a certain tone or quality of voice can turn the message of an utterance completely around, to the opposite meaning. For example, the following utterance can be turned from a statement to a question, from excitement or joy to irritation or anger, from shock or disbelief to routine acceptance, just by changing the tone or quality of the voice:

The plane's leaving now.

For effective communication, it is important to pay attention to voice quality and tone in others and to use voice to get your own message across as intended. This is especially true in speaking a second language, where your words may not always express exactly what you intend.

To practice producing and interpreting different qualities and tones of voice, make a tape recording in which you try to give several different interpretations to each of the sentences (1)–(5) below, according to the interpretations (a)–(g). Then exchange tapes with a classmate, and each of you will try to match the utterances with the interpretation that was intended. Where your interpretation disagrees with that of your classmate, let others listen to your tape and help decide what message is conveyed by voice quality in the unclear cases.

1. The plane's leaving now.
2. This thing cost $5,000.
3. Your mother arrived last night.
4. It's thundering and lightening.
5. The film is about to begin.

Interpretations for different voice qualities

(a) The speaker is making a statement of fact.
(b) The speaker is questioning whether the statement is true.
(c) The speaker is questioning a statement that s/he can hardly believe.
(d) The speaker is excited or joyful about the fact or event.
(e) The speaker is irritated or angry in relation to the fact or event.
(f) The speaker is shocked by the fact or event.
(g) The speaker is bored by this expected information or routine occurrence.

5 Phonology and orthography

Connecting written and spoken language in language teaching

The relationship of the written and spoken versions of a language is exploited in many and varied ways in language teaching. In the area of vocabulary, new words are commonly introduced by pronouncing written words aloud. When new vocabulary items are encountered in a conversation class, the teacher will often write these on the board so that students can make cognitive connections between the spoken and written versions of lexical items. In the teaching of grammar, sentence patterns are generally introduced first in the written form and then practiced in the spoken form. In reading classes, students might be encouraged to read what is written aloud, while in pronunciation classes, students might be expected to repeat words and sentences written in their books or on the board.

The interconnections between speaking and writing provide a rich source of information about a language. Literate speakers of a language are accustomed to making these connections and to learning the spoken form of a new language, at least in part, in relation to its written form. For non-literate or semi-literate adult language learners, proficiency in speaking and writing are often equally important goals, so that for this population, too, the connections between speaking and writing are a common focus of instruction. In many typical language learning contexts, then, it is probably unrealistic to expect adult language learners not to make connections between the spoken and written forms of the language, and not to use information gleaned from written forms as a source of information about spoken forms.

As language teachers, we must, however, recognize some of the potential problems of emphasizing the written language in a spoken language context. For adult learners, an emphasis on the written language or the reinforcement of the spoken language by the written language can cause the learner to develop associations of spoken and written forms that are highly misleading. A main problem is the lack of reliability of the written form of a word as a guide to its pronunciation. In

English, there are many words or parts of words that are spelled exactly the same way but which are pronounced entirely differently. For example, compare the pronunciation of *ough* in *tough*, *though* and *thought*, or of *ea* in *break* and *breakfast*.

Of particular importance for English in this connection is the large number of reduced vowels which are not pronounced as they are spelled but rather as schwa. Consider, for instance, the *a* in the second syllable of *breakfast* vs. the *a* in *fast*, or of *man* vs. *workman*. In a large number of cases, the vowels in the stem of a word in different grammatical forms may be either full or reduced. For example, in *democracy*, the noun, the vowels in the first and third syllables are reduced, while that in the second syllable is not. In contrast, in the adjectival form of the word, *democratic*, the second syllable contains a reduced vowel while the first and third syllables contain full vowels. In such cases, the placement of stress, which is not at all indicated by spelling (though it to a large extent follows a predictable pattern depending on the particular suffix attached to the stem), is a critical determinant of the correct pronunciation.

To summarize, English spelling (and the same can be said of many languages) is not a reliable indicator of pronunciation in a great majority of cases because of idiosyncratic factors having to do with (a) the history of individual words and (b) the placement of stress. Notice, for example, that the first vowel of *demon* is a fully stressed /i:/, while the second is reduced to schwa under the influence of reduced stress; in *demonic* the first vowel varies from speaker to speaker between a /ə/ vowel that carries reduced stress and the vowel /i:/ with medium stress, while the second vowel is a fully stressed /ɑ/; in *demonstrate* and *democratic* the first vowel, which carries primary or medium stress, is /ɛ/, while the second is schwa; in *demonstrative* and *democracy*, the first vowel is the reduced schwa and the second vowel is full (/ɑ/). Clearly, a language learner who bases pronunciation on spelling alone will not have adequate information for a large part of the English lexicon. Equally clearly, however, there are some regular patterns and clues to pronunciation that can be found in sets of words.

Perhaps of even greater importance for English is the fact that the written language does not portray any of the extensive coarticulatory effects that occur in everyday conversational pronunciation. As a result, a student who relies on the written form as a guide for the spoken language will not only fail to pronounce individual words correctly, but will also pronounce the language with what is from the point of view of natural English pronunciation a highly artificial separation of the stream of speech into individual words.

Besides the difficulties inherent in the writing system of English in relation to pronunciation – difficulties which cause problems for children when they are first learning to read and write – the second language learner may experience some difficulties with English pronunciation that are related to the spelling system of the native language. We can imagine that a learner whose native language has quite regular correspondences between sound and spelling, or whose native language has different values for the alphabetic symbols that are used to spell English words, will experience some difficulty in trying to learn the system of English spelling and its relationships to pronunciation.

By the time a learner has become an accomplished reader in the native language – which for most people would occur by the time they reach a lower secondary level in their education – the spelling patterns of the mother tongue will have become internalized and so will influence the perception of sound–spelling correspondences in learning a new language. In addition, since many English words have been borrowed into other languages, the system for representing the sounds of these borrowed words in the native language may also be known to the language learner and may be a source of additional interference (Pennington 1994). For example, a speaker of Japanese who has seen a certain brand of *kohi*, *biru* or *miruku* advertised in Japan may have a harder time learning to pronounce the English words *coffee*, *beer* and *milk* than if s/he were not familiar with the renderings of these words in their borrowed Japanese forms.

A language teacher who is aware of the potential influence of spelling patterns in both the target and the native language on the learner's pronunciation in the second language will want to be well informed about the spelling system of English and its many and varied relationships to pronunciation. In this way, the language teacher will be in a better position to reinforce productive and regular spelling patterns for students, while weaning them away from a reliance on unreliable correspondences between (a) the written and spoken forms of English and (b) the spelling patterns of the native language and the spoken forms of the target language, English.

Historical and present-day patterns in English orthography

Sources of variability in English phonology and orthography

Writing systems are – at least in the present age – quite conservative in comparison to phonological systems. While some variability in spelling, or orthography, is tolerated in speech communities, a uniform writing system is essential to maintain written communication with speakers outside the local speech community. In contrast, variability in phonology within and between speech communities which share the same written conventions is expected and normal.

The fact that written documents have a much longer survival period than individual humans means that the conventions of the written language of one generation can easily be preserved into the next generation, whereas those of the spoken language are more difficult to maintain from one generation to the next. Even given the possibility of preserving voice on audiotape, speech, which is inherently much more variable than writing, cannot be maintained in a uniform state. Thus, while some varieties of English differ dramatically in their spoken form and are barely – if at all – mutually intelligible, "conventional English orthography is a reasonably adequate system of representation for both British and American English, and the vast range of English dialects that exist within each country and around the world" (C. Chomsky 1970: 295).

Our strange language

When the Englishe tongue we speak
Why is "break" not rhymed with "freak"?
Will you tell me why it's true
We say "sew" but likewise "few";
And the maker of a verse
Cannot cap his "horse" with "worse";
"Beard" sounds not the same as "heard";
"Cord" is different from "word".
Cow is "cow" but low is "low".
"Shoe" is never rhymed with "foe";
Think of "hose" and "dose" and "lose";
And think of "goose" and not of "choose";
Think of "comb" and "tomb" and "bomb";
"Doll" and "roll," "home" and "some";
And since "pay" is rhymed with "say",
Why not "paid" with "said", I pray?
We have "blood" and "food" and "good";
"Mould" is not pronounced like "could";
Wherefore "done" but "gone" and "lone"?
Is there any reason known?
And in short it seems to me
Sounds and letters disagree.

Author unknown

FIGURE 5.1 Poem illustrating difficulties of English spelling

Although there exists a reasonably adequate and consistent system of orthography for the representation of English in all of its spoken varieties around the world, the relationship of sound to spelling and the phonological value of individual alphabetic letters and combinations of these in English is a highly complex one. Part of this complexity is a consequence of the economy of the English orthographic system, which makes do with twenty-six letters to represent all of the possible meaningful combinations of sound in the language. Part of its complexity is the result of historical changes in the spoken form of the language, including its phonology and lexicon, as well as of historical changes in orthography, which, though far less frequent than changes in phonology, do occur from time to time.

There are several sources of change and variability in languages that affect their phonological systems and their spelling conventions, or **orthographic systems**. Two main sources are historical **sound change** and the mass importation of **loan words** via **lexical borrowing** from another language. These two principles affect writing in two ways. The first effect is that they create changes in the values of individual symbols, destroying the optimal principle for orthography of one-to-one correspondence – i.e. "one sound, one symbol" or "same sound, same symbol". As a result, **graphemes** – individual letters or orthographic symbols – that formerly had distinct values may overlap partially or completely in their new values, as when *f* and *ph*, *j* and *dg* coalesce in phonemic value, both in each case representing the same sound. At the same time, as a result of such historical effects, one graphemic symbol or combination of symbols may not always have the same value, as when *oo* indicates /ʌ/ in *blood*, /u:/ in *boot* and /ʊ/ in *book*.

The second type of effect on orthography occurs later, when sound change and lexical borrowing eventually initiate change in the orthographic system to reflect the pronunciation of the phonologically changing or lexically importing language. Thus, in present-day English, many common words which have historically ended in *ight* are beginning to appear spelled instead as *ite* in advertisements and signs. Sooner or later, we might expect even the relatively infrequent words spelled with the initial Greek consonant combinations that violate the usual spelling patterns of English – e.g. *psychology*, *ptomaine* and *pneumonia* – to simplify graphemically to represent their simplified pronunciation.

Both of these types of change, viz. sound change and lexical borrowing, generally occur gradually and item by item, according to natural phonological processes and lexical diffusion, or **analogy** (the term used in historical linguistics). Consequently, for a period of time their effects leave the language quite inconsistent in its spelling. These two types of change in languages can also lead to the coexistence of two different spellings for a single lexical item. In addition, the spelling conventions of one language, when applied to another language, may introduce irregularities into its spelling system. There are also many idiosyncratic factors which affect spelling patterns in languages, such as changes in fashion, the influence of spelling patterns of individual phonemes or words, and the effects of print media.

Multiple acceptable spellings occur in English words such as *adviser/advisor* and *cigaret/cigarette*. Where two different spellings exist for the same word, dictionaries will usually list one as "preferred", though not uncommonly different dictionaries will show different preferred spellings for the same word. Often, the less preferred spelling in American English is the preferred one in British English orthography, which differs from American English in regular ways in a few sets of words. For example, in British English, *re* rather than *er* is preferred in words such as *theatre/theater*, *centre/center*; *s* rather than *z* in *civilisation/civilization*, *naturalisation/naturalization*; *our* rather than *or* in words such as *honour/honor*, *neighbour/neighbor*, *colour/color*; *mme* rather than *m* in *programme/program*.

In Canadian and Australian English, the two orthographic systems, British and American, coexist; e.g. *centre* (British) and *program* (American) are both preferred spellings. A similar mixture of patterns can be found throughout most of the English speaking world, in addition to adjustments of English spelling patterns in some words to better reflect local pronunciation and sound–spelling correspondences. Thus, Macafee (1983) reports spellings in Glasgow, Scotland, of *buld* for *build* and *wull* for *will* as reflecting a "lowered, retracted realisation of /ɪ/" (p. 39). Her book also contains (ch. 5) many sample twentieth century literary texts in which the influence of the native variety is apparent in the style of English orthography adopted by Scottish writers.

As the sound systems of languages change and as they import words from other languages, the orthographic system becomes less and less consistent, and the correspondences between graphemes and phonemes move towards a many-to-many relationship. While such diversity of patterns makes the orthographic system less efficient, at the same time it opens up possibilities for special effects using unusual spellings. Thus, people in advertising realize that the spelling of *light* as *lite* in beer and cigarette (or cigaret!) advertisements connotes a free-spirited ("lite"), modern lifestyle, while people in the travel and leisure industries are aware that the British spellings of *theatre* and *centre* connote high quality and prestige.

When more than one subsystem for spelling exists, writers wishing to achieve a special effect may take advantage of this fact. For example, the **canonical**, or dictionary, spelling of a word may not be employed when the writer wishes to achieve a certain effect of dialect pronunciation or conversational style. In seeking to record casual speech or dialect in English, a writer might employ any of the following **pronunciation–spellings**:

> *roit* (right)
> *dat* (that), *dis* (this), *de* (the), *den* (then)
> *cuz/coz* (because, cousin)
> *doin'/doin* (doing), *runnin'/runnin* (running)
> *nuthin* (nothing), *sumpin* (something)
> *bidnis* (business), *wadn't* (wasn't)
> *durty* (dirty), *wull* (will)
> *winder* (window), *widder* (widdow)
> *gonna, gunna* (going to), *wanna* (want to) *oughta, orta* (ought to),
>   *useta* (used to), *hafta* (have to) *sorta* (sort of), *kinda* (kind of)
> *woulda* (would've), *coulda* (could've), *shoulda* (should've), *musta*
>   (must've), *hadda* (had to, had've)
> *gotcha* (got you), *watcha* (what you)
> *didja* (did you), *couldja* (could you), *wouldja* (would you)

Innovative spellings such as these can initiate permanent changes in the orthography of a language.

Historical influences on English spelling

Before the Battle of Hastings, a West Saxon scribal tradition had developed in England that evolved a relatively uniform script (Scragg 1974: 11). After the Norman Conquest in 1066, when English was replaced by French as the official language of the Britons, the pronunciation and the orthography of English went through a period of great diversification and change. English spelling did not regularize until the modern period, in the seventeenth century, after printing started to become well-established, and dictionaries started to prescribe the "correct" forms of English words.

Spellings in the Middle English (ME) period, beginning around AD 1100 and continuing up to about AD 1600, were extremely irregular, varying from region to region and from person to person. For example, the following is a sample of spellings cited in the *Oxford English*

Dictionary (OED) for the word *disease* from the fourteenth to the seventeenth century:

> *disease* **14th-15th** dissease; **14th-16th** disese; **15th** disees, disesse, dysese, dysesse, dessayse, deshaese, **Scottish** discese; **15th-16th** dysease, desease; **16th** desesse; **17th** discease

The existence of this variety of spellings is actually a boon for linguists, as it provides them with records of possible dialectal variation in pronunciation as well as potential differences in pronunciation which occurred at different socioeconomic levels during the Middle English period.

One source of English spellings in the fifteenth century was Caxton, who introduced the printing process to England. As has already been noted, the spelling conventions of English at that time were not yet well-established. Moreover, Caxton, though a native of England, had lived most of his life in Holland, and many of those he employed in printing English documents were non-native speakers of English. It can be surmised that this group of people, who were not fully conversant with the English spelling patterns of the time, were nevertheless influential in the development of spelling conventions in the late ME period.

For example, Caxton and his printers are thought to be responsible for introducing an initial *gh* into many English words which had previously been spelled *g* (Stubbs 1980: 49). Examples are *ghost* and *ghastly*, where these spellings survive, as well as *gherle* (*girl*) and *ghoos* (*goose*), where they do not. These spellings, which represent a possible confusion of English and Dutch orthographic patterns, illustrate how idiosyncratic factors – including the influence of one individual – may profoundly influence a language.

The style of handwriting at the time also contributed some idiosyncratic spellings to the English language. When a writer used a feather quill or similar writing implement, certain letters in the Middle English period were written simply as one or more vertical strokes. Thus, *i* was written as one vertical stroke (*ı*), *u* and *n* as two vertical strokes (*ıı*), and *m* and *w* as three vertical strokes (*ııı*). As a consequence, any word that contained a sequence of these letters became illegible (Stubbs 1980: 52). The solution in some cases was to change the spelling of the words.

For example, the *o* in *monk* and *wonder* – both of which had previously contained a *u* vowel between a three-stroke and a two-stroke grapheme, resulting in an identical series of seven vertical strokes – were the result of a conscious attempt to improve legibility and avoid graphemic confusion. The *o* in *women* – which had previously contained an *i* vowel between two three-stroke graphemes, also resulting in seven vertical strokes in a row – was introduced in a similar attempt to compensate for a weakness in the mode of handwriting that stemmed from the nature of existing writing implements and the conventions for using these.

The representation of the first vowel of the word *women* by an *o*, though intended to remedy a serious problem in the written form of the language, in fact resulted in an inconsistent and opaque orthography which has for centuries puzzled literate English speakers, natives and non-natives alike. In recent times, attempts to modernize this orthographic anachronism by innovative spellings such as *wimin* and *wymyn* (e.g. in some feminist and literary publications) have reintroduced a more consistent correspondence between sound and spelling.

During the course of its historical development, many words from other languages have been imported into the English language, and these imports have greatly affected the orthographic conventions of the language. Many lexical importations into English during the Old English (OE) period (8th to 12th centuries), were Scandinavian. A large number of words in English beginning with *sk*, *sc* and *sh* can be traced back to the period of Scandinavian influence on OE.

In the late OE and early ME period, French culture and language were tremendously influential in England. Over 25% of the core, non-specialized lexicon of English is French in origin – some (e.g. Scragg 1974: 40) place the proportion of French items in English as high as 40% – and the spelling patterns of French were imitated in many English words which were not originally French. Thus, for example, the French spelling of *qu* was adopted in the ME period for English words formerly spelled *cw* such as *queen* and *quick*, and non-original *s* was added to the English word *island* in the ME period by analogy to the French word *isle*.

Some scholars have argued that the French influence in the medieval period went far beyond lexical borrowings, affecting the grammatical and phonological systems of English in profound ways. A few have even suggested that the language which was continued as "English" in the seventeenth century was actually a new linguistic variety, i.e. a creolized mixture of French and English (Bailey and Maroldt 1977). The French–English creole theory has been offered as an explanation for the massive phonological and grammatical changes which occurred during the ME period.

There were many changes in this period which affected the phonological system and hence the orthographic system of English. One of the most massive changes, termed the **Great Vowel Shift** (GVS), affected the whole vowel system in a kind of chain reaction. This shift

/f/

f	*fat, after, if*
ff	*stuff, official*
gh	*enough, roughneck, tougher*
ph	*physics, apostrophe, graph*
pph	*sapphire*

/k/

k	*keep, cookie, took*
ck	*package, crackling, sack*
c	*cool, cane, laconic, picnic, ironic*
cc	*accolade, accordion*
cu	*biscuit, circuit*
ch	*chemistry, school, lachrymose, tech*
cch	*saccharin*
que	*conquer, plaque*
cque	*lacquer, racquet*

/s/

s	*sip, eraser, ask, bus*
ss	*massage, passtime, dress*
sc	*scene, scissors, reminiscent, coalesce*
c	*city, racing, space*

/z/

z	*zip, lazy, hazy, topaz*
zz	*buzzer, fuzz*
s	*easy, cousin, is, does*
ss	*scissors, dissolve, dessert*
x	*xenophobic, xylophone*

/š/

sh	*shy, ashen, fishnet, hush*
ch	*chef, moustache*
si	*tension, emulsion*
ssi	*profession, mission*
shi	*cushion, fashion*
ti	*station, option*
ci	*precious, ancient*
sci	*conscience, conscious*
ce	*ocean, gaseous*
su	*censure, cocksure*
ssu	*fissure, tissue, assure*

/ž/

g	*regime, rouge*
ti	*equation*
si	*division, fusion*
su	*closure, pleasure*
zu	*azure*

(Continued)

FIGURE 5.2 Different spellings for one consonant phoneme

/č/

c	*concerto, cello*
ch	*chip, teacher, rancher, reach*
tch	*butcher, watch*
ti	*question, mention*
tu	*nature, century*
ce	*cello*

/ǰ/

j	*jury, ajar, injure*
g	*giant, agent, pungent, sponge*
dg	*ledger, lodge*
di	*soldier*
du	*educate*

FIGURE 5.2 (*Continued*) Different spellings for one consonant phoneme

is therefore often described as a type of **chain shift**, in which the movement of one vowel to a new position within the system caused the other vowels within the system also to move to new positions. The movements of the ME vowels in the GVS can be represented as shown in Figure 5.3.

This diagram is meant to represent a series of changes in the pronunciation of English vowels which are thought to have begun with the shifting of the low vowels to a higher position. It is not known why this shift began, though there are many theories seeking to explain these changes in the values of the English vowel phonemes. What is fairly widely accepted is that the movement of one vowel in the system precipated a shift in the position of the vowels throughout the system, via the "domino effect" that is a chain shift.

The chain shift known as the Great Vowel Shift is most commonly thought (cf. Russ 1984: 21ff for an alternative account) to have begun when words containing long /a:/ shifted to the position of /ɔ/, and words

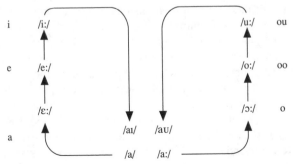

FIGURE 5.3 The English Great Vowel Shift

containing short /a/ (as in *mate*, *name* and *grave*, which were then two syllables, as the final *e* was still pronounced) lengthened the vowel. This long vowel, spelled with the letter *a*, was raised to a mid front position, /eː/. (The loss of the sound of final *e* in this set of words may well have had something to do with the change.) Now these *a* words (formerly /a/ → /ɛː/) had taken over the position previously occupied by the /eː/ words (such as *meat*, *heed* and *beet*). As a result, the phoneme in this set of words shifted up to a new, higher position, eventually becoming /iː/. By a similar process, the vowel in the set of long /iː/ words (e.g. *mine*, *bite* and *ride*) shifted to a new position, falling back down to the original *a* position, but with diphthongization, to /aɪ/.

With the lowering of the high front vowel to a non-back position close to that of the original /a/ which started the shift, the chain reaction of the non-back vowels comes almost full circle. The /a/ vowel, whose original articulatory position was apparently low and **non-peripheral** – i.e. neither front nor back – shifts its position to a fronter and higher place of articulation; this shift precipitates raising and then lowering of vowels in a **push-chain** that kicks /iː/ (which can raise no further without becoming a consonant, /j/) back to a low and non-front position, as diphthongal /aɪ/.

The same logic is generally employed to describe the shifting of the back vowels in English, beginning with raising of the /aː/ words to the position of /ɔː/ (as in *grown*, *bone*), moving those with ME /oː/ (e.g. *boot*) to the position of /uː/, and ending with a lowering of the words spelled *ou* (as in *house*, originally /huːs/) to the position of the diphthong /aʊ/. Again, the first step of the shift involves a movement to a more peripheral (i.e. more front or more back) position, the intermediate steps involve raising, and the last step involves lowering and tensing/diphthongization.

It can be observed that the GVS radically altered not only the position of individual vowels in English, thereby causing major changes in the phonetic values of the graphemes, but also the nature of the vowel system as a whole. In the terms introduced in Chapter 3, it seems that the pre-GVS vowel system of English was essentially a sonority-based, Type 2 system, which seems to have survived in Scotland – or else to have been reintroduced there, perhaps as a simplification of the more complex color-based, Type 1 system of the South. In contrast, the post-GVS system of English vowels, which is the system that has survived into the present day in the Old Englishes – i.e. the RP and RP-influenced varieties such as the standard varieties in South Africa, Australia and New Zealand, as well as North America – is a Type 1, color-based system. Interestingly, many of the New Englishes appear to be adopting a vowel system which is more like that of the English spoken before the Great Vowel Shift.

The overall logic and the details of the change in vowel qualities which are termed the Great Vowel Shift, although of great interest to linguists, are of minor importance for the language teacher. What a language teacher might find worth knowing is that at some time in the distant past, before the Great Vowel Shift, the values of English vowel symbols matched more closely to those of other IndoEuropean languages such as Spanish and German, and so more closely to the values for those symbols in phonetic transcription.

The sound–spelling correspondences for English vowels have changed radically since Old English, partly as a result of sound change, partly as a result of the adoption of French (and Latin – see below) spelling patterns, and partly as a result of many other idiosyncratic historical events. Nevertheless, many regular orthographic patterns can still be discerned in the English lexicon, as can be seen in Figure 5.4.

A major change in the history of the language was the loss of many

I. Vowel phonemes with little variation in spelling

A. /æ/ is always spelled *a*: *apple, happy, hat.*

B. /ɛ/ is usually spelled *e*: *end, pep, men.*
In a few words, /ɛ/ is spelled *ea*: *head, read* (past), *breakfast.*
In one word, /ɛ/ is spelled *ai*: *said.*

C. /ɪ/ is usually spelled *i*: *it, him, pig.*
In words beginning with *cy*, except *cycle*, /ɪ/ is spelled *y*: *bicycle, cyclic, cylinder, cylindrical.*
In one word, this sound is spelled *o*: *women.*

D. /ɑ/ is spelled *a* before *r*: *car, bar, starry.*
/ɑ/ is spelled *o* before *t*: *hot, lot, got.*

E. /ɔ/ is spelled *o* before *r*: *port, glory, bore.*
/ɔ/ is spelled *a* before *ll* or *w*: *all, call, saw, law.*
/ɔ/ is spelled *ou* or *au* before *ght*: *ought, bought; caught, taught.*

F   /ʊ/ is spelled *u* before *ll* and *sh*: *pull, full; push, bush.*
/ʊ/ is spelled *ou* in modal verbs: *would, could, should.*
/ʊ/ is spelled *oo* before *k*: *book, took, look.*
/ʊ/ is spelled *oo* before *t* and *d*: *foot, soot; good, stood.*
Notice, however, that /u:/ is also represented by the spelling *oo*: *food, boot, boom, zoo.*

G. /ʌ/ is spelled *u*, or it is spelled *o* when a vowel follows the next consonant: *up, cut, fuss, come, mother, coming, wonder.*

H. /ə/ may be spelled by any single vowel in an unstressed syllable: *sofă, capăble; bullĕt, compĕtition; competĭtive, flexĭble; cŏnnect, Washingtŏn; circŭs, circŭmstance.*

(*Continued*)

FIGURE 5.4 Common spelling patterns of English vowels

II. Long and short vowels

A. The (a) (monophthongal) sounds below are termed **short** vowels, and the (b) (diphthongal) sounds are termed **long** vowels.

(a) Short vowels			(b) Long vowels		
a	/æ/	*rat, ran*	/e:/	*rate, rain*
e	/ɛ/	*bed, her*	/i:/	*bead, here*
i	/ɪ/	*lid, grim*	/aɪ/	*lied, grime*
o	/ɑ/	*rod, hop*	/o:/	*road, rode, hope*
u	/ʌ/	*run, luck*	/u:/	*rune, ruin, Luke*

Note that silent final *e* makes a preceding vowel long (tense).

B. In most cases, the phonemes /e:/, /i:/, /aɪ/, /o:/ and /u:/ are spelled with two vowels. Generally, the first vowel is the letter of the alphabet which represents the phoneme, i.e. the name of the letter of the alphabet: /e:/ *a*; /i:/ *e*; /aɪ/ *i*; /o:/ *o*; /u:/ *u*. The second vowel may be right after the first vowel, or it may be after the following consonant.

/e:/	*a*	*paid, day*; *date, naming*
/i:/	*e*	*seem, mean, receive, people*; *scene, here, Pete*
/aɪ/	*i*	*tie, lie*; *time, fine, lining*
/o:/	*o*	*coat, hoe, going*; *home, spoke, smoking*
/u:/	*u*	*true, fruit*; *flute, tune* [u:] or [ju], *pruning*

C. A double consonant between two syllables keeps a vowel short. A single consonant between two syllables indicates a long vowel.

(a) Short vowels		(b) Long vowels	
a	*tap, tapping*	*tape, taping*
	happen, latter	*hate, hating, later*
e	*bet, betting*	*beat, beating*
	better	*beater*
i	*dinner*	*dine, dining*
	written	*write, writing*
o	*hop, hopping*	*hope, hoping*
	totter	*toe, toting*
u	*rudder*	*rude, ruder*
	tunnel	*tune, tuner, tuning*

FIGURE 5.4 (*Continued*) Common spelling patterns of English vowels

final inflections, resulting in various types of simplifications of endings and in the pervasive "silent e" of English. In addition, certain sounds which had once been pronounced, such as *gh* following a vowel (as in *ought, taught*), *k* and *g* before *n* (as in *knew* and *gnu*), or *c* following *s* (as in *science* and *sceptor*), lost their consonantal articulation (see Figure 5.5).

During the late ME period and into the early Modern English (ModE)

A. Beginning of a word

w	before r	*write, wrong, wrestle*
g	before n	*gnat, gnaw, gnu*
k	before *n*	*knee, know, knight*
p	before *n*	*pneumonia, pneumatic, pneumonic*
p	before *s*	*psoriasis, psychology, pseudonym*
p	before *t*	*ptomaine, pterodactyl, ptosis*
h	before vowel	*hour, honest, heir*

B. After initial consonant

u	after *g*	*guarantee, guard, guess*
h	after *g*	*ghost, ghastly, ghetto*
h	after *r*	*rheumatic, rhythm, rhapsody*
h	after *w*	*white, why, where*
c	after *s*	*science, scenic, scent*

C. Middle or end of a word

g	before *n* or *m*	*reign, feign, diaphragm*
b	after *m*	*dumb, thumb, plumber*
b	before *t*	*debt, doubt*
t	before *en*	*soften, listen, fasten*
s	before *l*	*island, aisle*
l	after *a* and before *f*	*half, calf*
l	after *ou* and before *d*	*could, would, should*
gh	after *ou* or *au*	*through, dough*
gh	after *ou* or *au* and before *t*	*ought, thought, taught, caught*
gh	after *i*	*high, thigh*
gh	after *i* and before *t*	*night, right, height*

D. Silent final *e* to make a preceding vowel long (tense)

i	*time, like, mine*
e	*scene, here, Pete*
a	*hate, sane, fame*
u	*flute, tune, tube*
o	*bone, home, tote*

FIGURE 5.5 Silent letters

period, beginning around AD 1600, Latin – which had also been influential in the OE period – became a major influence on the English lexicon and thus, indirectly, on its morphological, orthographic and phonological systems. Greek also exerted some influence, sometimes as the source of the Latin words. An example is the word *paradigm*, borrowed as the Latin *paradigma*, from the Greek *para + deiknynai*, meaning "to show side by side". During this period, borrowings and newly coined words were imported into English from Latin, which was revered as an ancient and learned language that was especially appropriate for writing. The newly coined words were often spelled **etymologically**, i.e. spelled in such a way as to show their historical derivation, or supposed derivation. Late examples are *submarine* and *submerge*, from the Latin prefix *sub-* "under"+ Latin *mare* "sea" or *mergere* "to plunge".

At that time, it was also common to change the form of English words to conform to Latin morphology and orthography. For example, the French word *anormal* "not normal" (originally from Latin *a-* "not" + *normalis* "normal") was given a new spelling and derivation in English with the more obviously Latin prefix *ab* "from", yielding ModE *abnormal*. Another interesting example of this latinizing tendency in the English language is the derivation of *Columbus* (*-us* is the Latin masculine singular nominative ending) as the English name of the Italian sailor, *Colombo*, who is credited with the discovery of the New World of the Americas.

The tendency to invent Latin words and to latinize existing words continued through the nineteenth century, when many of the words which appear to be Latin in origin were coined. Even today specialized scientific terminology may be built on Latin (or Greek) roots, affixes and morphological rules – as when a new plant species is named by coining a word or descriptive phrase in Latin (or Greek), or by adding a Latin (or Greek) ending to the name of the person or place associated with its discovery.

A conservative estimate of words of Latin origin in the present-day English core lexicon must put the number – as for words of French origin – at somewhat over 25%. However, when specialized terminology is included, the percentage rises considerably, possibly to as high as 30% of this expanded English lexicon. Like French borrowings, these Latin borrowings and coinages exerted an influence on the underlying orthographic system of English and on its pronunciation as well. Also like French, the conventions of Latin orthography exerted an independent influence, as noted by Scragg (1974).

Although many unusual spellings can be traced to borrowings and invented words, in general, spelling irregularities simply indicate the irregular history of individual words in English, as can be seen in Figure 5.6.

By the end of the eighteenth century, orthographical correctness had begun to be an important indicator of status, as it represented the possession by the privileged classes of literacy and education. By the nineteenth century, spelling contests, called **spelling bees** in the United States, started to be common practice in grammar schools and secondary schools. ("Bee" in this original meaning, which was current in the eighteenth and nineteenth centuries, meant "a gathering of people".) The attention to spelling in the present day includes not only classroom

/iː/	encyclopaedia	amoeba	people	fjord	picayune	chamois
	Caesar					
	aegis					
	archaeology					
/ɪ/	been	sieve	busy	parliament	mysterious	mischief	counterfeit
	breeches			marriage	hysterical	kerchief	forfeit
							foreign
/eː/	matinee	crepe	lingerie	Mae	gauge
	negligee	suede			
	melee				
/ɛ/	aesthete	said	says	friend	Oedipus	jeopardy	their
	aerial	again					heifer
		against					heir
/æ/	aunt	(or /ɑ/)	plaid	meringue
	laugh	(or /ɑ/)		
/uː/	shoe	lieutenant	Sioux	canoe	lieu
/juː/	vacuum	beauty	(lieu, lieutenant)
/ʊ/	bosom	woman	wolf	could
				should
				would
/oː/	beau	chauffeur	sew	yeoman	brooch
	plateau				
/ʌ/	blood				
	flood				
/aɪ/	aye	eye	height	geyser	coyote	maestro	diamond
			stein				
			seismograph				

FIGURE 5.6 Some unusual spelling patterns for English vowels

and school spelling bees, but also state and national spelling contests. As in most highly literate cultures, the use of correct orthography is considered a mark of education and, to some extent, social status, in the English speech community worldwide.

The legacy of historical changes in English orthography

In English, idiosyncratic factors, historical sound changes, lexical borrowings and borrowed spelling conventions such as those described above, impacted orthography, "and our spelling is thus the result of overlaying, for nearly a thousand years, of one tradition upon another" (Scragg 1974: 14). The historical changes to the language and the

Hints on pronunciation for foreigners

I take it you already **know**
Of **tough** and **bough** and **cough** and **dough**?
Others may stumble, but not you
On **hiccough, thorough, slough** and **through**?
Well done! And now you wish, perhaps,
To learn of these familiar traps?
Beware of **heard**, a dreadful word,
That looks like **beard** and sounds like **bird**,
And **dead**: it's said like **bed**, not **bead** –
For goodness sake, don't call it **deed**!
Watch out for **meat** and **great** and **threat**.
(They rhyme with **suite** and **straight** and **debt**.)
A **moth** is not a **moth** in **mother**,
Nor **both** in **bother**, **broth** in **brother**.
And **here** is not a match for **there**,
And **dear** and **fear** for **bear** and **pear**,
And then there's **dose** and **rose** and **lose** –
Just look them up – and **goose** and **choose**,
And **cork** and **work** and **card** and **ward**,
And **font** and **front** and **word** and **sword**.
And **do** and **go**, and **thwart** and **cart** –
Come, come, I've hardly made a start!
A dreadful language? Why, man alive!
I'd learned to talk it when I was five,
And yet to write it, the more I tried,
I hadn't learned it at fifty-five.

Source Adapted from a letter published in the London *Sunday Times*
          (January 3, 1965), from J. Bland

FIGURE 5.7 Poem illustrating difficulties of English spelling

multiple orthographic traditions that have informed English spelling
have created the following present-day classes of lexical items (note
that these are not mutually exclusive categories):

- those containing **Latin and Greek spellings**
  from Latin, *datum* (sg.)/ *data* (pl.), *quantum* (sg.)/ *quanta* (pl.),
      alumnus (sg.)/ *alumni* (pl.)
  from Greek, *criterion* (sg.)/ *criteria* (pl.), *phenomenon* (sg.)/
      phenomena (pl.), *schema* (sg.)/ *schemata* (pl.)
- those containing **archaic spellings**
  programme, shoppe, racquet, briquet/briquette
- those containing **silent letters**
  the *gh* in *night, light, right*

the *g* in *gnarl, gnaw, gnat,*
the *p* in *ptomaine, psychology, pneumonia*
the *c* in *scene, science, ascetic*
the *b* in *dumb, doubt, plumber*
the *e* in *mate, mite, mute*

- **homographs** (words with the same pronunciation and spelling, but different meanings)

  see ('view with the eyes')/*see* ('a bishop's territory')

  neat ('tidy')/ *neat* ('domestic bovine')

  bat ('to wink')/ *bat* ('a nocturnal flying mammal)/ *bat* ('a wooden implement used for hitting a ball in various games')

  bow ('the forward part of a ship')/ *bow* ('incline the head and/or the upper part of the body')

  set ('put down')/ *set* ('a group of matching items')

- **homophones**, or **homonyms** (words with the same pronunciation, but different spellings and different meanings)

  write, right, wright, rite

  wear, where, ware, where're, weir

  there, their, they're

  too, to, two

  hair, hare

  beat, beet

  know, no

- **heterographs** (words with the same pronunciation and meaning, but different spellings)

  adviser/advisor, theater/theatre

  traveling/travelling, fulfil/fulfill, jewelry/jewellery

  cigaret/cigarette, pipet/pipette

  dialog/dialogue, catalog/catalogue

  judgment/judgement, acknowledgment/acknowledgement

  civilization/civilisation, realization/realisation

  reflection/reflexion, connection/connexion

  license/licence, practise/practice (verb)

  honor/honour, neighbor/neighbour, mustache/moustache

  plow/plough, donut/doughnut

  draft/draught, sluff/slough

  cooperate/co-operate, coeducational/co-educational

  tire/tyre, pajamas/pyjamas

- **heteronyms** (words with the same spelling, but different pronunciations and meanings)

  desert ('abandon')/ *desert* ('expanse of arid land')

  supply ('provide')/ *supply* ('limberly')

wind ('natural movement of air')/ *wind* ('twist')

sewer ('person who sews')/ *sewer* ('subterranean conduit to carry effluent')

refuse ('garbage or trash')/ *refuse* ('deny')

bow ('a tied ribbon')/ *bow* ('the forward part of a ship') or
　bow ('incline the head and/ or the upper part of the body')

lead ('direct')/ *lead* ('a heavy soft gray metal')

recreation ('something created anew')/ *recreation* ('leisure time activities')

Archaic spellings sometimes have an impact on pronunciation, as speakers initiate **spelling-pronunciations**, i.e. pronunciations of the lexical items that are based on the archaic spellings, seeking to give each grapheme a particular phonetic value. For example, the rhythm and humor of the following poem depends on its being read aloud with the initial *k*s and *g*s being pronounced, including the last one (which is added to the normal spelling of the colloquial word *nosh* 'to eat with relish'):

A gnat gnawed a gnarring gnu
Watched by a knight on his knees in a canoe –
"What a view of you have I," he said,
"And gosh, what a gnosh!"

M. C. Pennington

The large number of silent letters, homophones, homographs and heteronyms in English forms a rich basis for many different types of word play, poetry and other kinds of creative uses of language, as the poems in this chapter illustrate. At the same time, the existence of all this variety in English spelling gives an impression of English orthography as extremely complicated and inconsistent, as these illustrative poems suggest.

It is common in the history of languages for people to decry any irregularities that exist in the correspondences of sound and meaning and for would-be reformers to seek to make changes in the orthographic system of a language to make the correspondence between sound and orthography more consistent. In the United States, for instance, Benjamin Franklin proposed to reform English spelling by eliminating the letters *c*, *q*, *w*, *x*, *y* and *i*. At the same time as he wished to eliminate these "unnecessary" letters completely, Franklin thought it would simplify English spelling to replace the digraphic symbols *th*, *sh* and *ng* – since they each represent a single phoneme – by new, single graphemes, and to add new vowel symbols to ease the burden of the vowel symbols *a*, *o* and *u*, which represented many different sounds.

In the present day, the SR1 (Spelling Reform One) movement in

Australia initiated by Lindgren (1969) has had some success in regularizing the spelling of /ɛ/ as *e* – e.g. substituting *gess* for *guess*, *frend* for *friend*, and *hed* for *head* (Sampson 1985: 197). The popular success of this spelling reform in Australia stands as a rather unusual case, since deliberate attempts at spelling reform, no matter how sensible, rarely result in major changes to orthography. In fact, any spelling changes which do occur in a language, either through deliberate intervention or through unconscious simplifications or regularizations of patterns, tend to be limited in their effects – e.g. to a certain set of words or contexts for those words (such as advertising), or to a certain group or locale (as in the Australian case just mentioned). Because of the limited nature of such reforms, they have the effect, as often as not, of increasing the variety and hence the irregularity of sound–spelling correspondences.

At the same time, in recent years, deliberate attempts to address the problems in English orthography faced by beginning readers have achieved some limited success. In Britain, a simplified Initial Teaching Alphabet (Downing 1965) was widely used as a bridge to English orthography in the 1970s, though its popularity has waned in the last decade. In the United States, speakers of non-standard varieties, especially Black English Vernacular, have been encouraged to learn to write first in a form of dialectal orthography and then are taught to replace the non-standard orthographic forms gradually by standard orthography. Some educators have suggested that young students should learn to write "naturalistically", allowing orthographic patterns to develop based on gradually increasing experiences with print (Edelsky 1982). In such an approach, childrens' misspellings, simplifications and overregularizations of English orthography are accepted as a stage on the way to learning the correct patterns. Each of these approaches represents a realistic attempt to deal with the difficulty of mastering standard English orthography for reading and writing, though none is widespread in education today.

The nature of the present-day English orthographic system

"No English word is ever spelled in such a way that it gives no information about pronunciation" (Stubbs 1980: 54). At the same time as there are predictable relations in English between the orthographic and the phonological systems, relationships between phonemes and graphemes vary, and not all of the regularities of English spelling are tied to phonology. For example, the English grapheme *c* is pronounced /s/ or /k/ depending on context, and *e* corresponds to /iː/ in a group of open-syllable words (e.g. *me*, *she*, *he*) but to /ɛ/ in a group of closed-syllable words (e.g. *men*, *shell*, *hen*). Moreover, the pronunciation of words changes when certain affixes are added, even when the orthography remains constant, as in *nation* /neːšən/, *national* /næšənəl/. English spelling can perhaps best be described as not one uniform system of rules but rather a great complex of context-dependent rules – some of which are strictly phonological and others of which involve morphology – accounting for relatively small subsets of lexical items.

It is in fact very common in English for meaning relations and grammatical relations to be preserved in spelling, even when pronunciation varies, as in the following sets of related items: *nation/national/nationalize* (or *nationalise*), *resign/resignation*, *grade/gradual*, *critic*, *critical*, *criticize* (or *criticise*). Thus, English orthography is to a large extent based on morphological relations among words, that is, English orthography transparently connects words related in form and meaning. In fact, English spelling can be said to combine aspects of morphology and phonology in a system sometimes termed **morphophonemic**.

If we look at relatively small subsets of the English lexicon, we can find many phonological regularities which are not indicated orthographically but which are nevertheless predictable for that set of words. For example, a regular pattern of alternation of long or tense and short or lax vowels is seen when endings are added to stems, as in the following sets of pairs (each of which could be expanded to a longer list):

a	/eː/	*nation*	/æ/	*national*
		ration		*rational*
	/eː/	*sage*	/ə/	*sagacious*
		able		*ability*
i	/aɪ/	*hide*	/ɪ/	*hidden*
		ride		*ridden*
		bite		*bitten*
		wide		*width*
o	/oː/	*phone*	/ɑ/	*phonic*
		cone		*conic*
		melody		*melodic*
		photo		*photography*

As in the examples for vowels given above, it can be said that "the conventional spelling of words corresponds more closely to an underlying abstract level of representation within the sound system of the language, [sic] than it does to the surface phonetic form that the words assume in the spoken language" (C. Chomsky 1970: 288). The orthographic patterns of English in such items may make reading more efficient since the reader is led to ignore phonetic detail in favor of semantic relationships among words (C. Chomsky 1970: 293). According to N. Chomsky and Halle (1968), "conventional orthography is [thus] a near optimal system for the lexical representation of English words" (p. 49).

In all of these cases, "the principle adhered to is that phonetic variation is not indicated in the lexical spelling when it is predictable by general rule" (C. Chomsky 1970: 291). Such regular alternations are felt by adult native speakers of English to be automatic. As noted by N. Chomsky and Halle (1968):

> Orthography is a system designed for readers who know the language, who understand sentences and therefore know the surface structure of sentences. Such readers can produce the correct phonetic forms, given the orthographic representation and the surface structure, by means of the rules that they employ in producing and interpreting speech. It would be quite pointless for the orthography to indicate these predictable variants. (p. 49)

Yet children and non-native speaking adults have to learn the underlying phonological system in order for these alternations to become automatic, and this process certainly must take a period of years. In the meantime, it may be valuable for these connections to be the explicit focus of instruction in a language course designed for literate adults.

Spelling rules in English

A few regularities of English spelling have been codified in rules that native speakers often learn as children in school. None of these English spelling rules applies 100% of the time, though there are some regularities that apply consistently in subsets of words. For example, the "*i* before *e*" rule applies in a large number of cases, though it has many types of exceptions. This rule, learned in school by many English speaking children, is an attempt to describe which words are spelled *ie* and which *ei* in English. It goes like this: "*i* before *e* except after *c* or when sounded like /e:/, as in *neighbor* and *weigh*". Thus, *believe* and *relieve* are spelled *ie*, but *perceive*, *conceive* and *receive* are spelled *ei*.

In English, a final silent *e* is said to make a vowel "long" (diphthongal or "tense") whereas absence of this silent *e* makes the vowel of the word "short" (monophthongal or lax). Long and short vowels according to this form of description are provided in Figure 5.4. The "double the consonant" rule says that a final consonant in an accented syllable (i.e. a monosyllabic word or a polysyllabic word with the accent on the last syllable) must be doubled to maintain the "short" pronunciation of the vowel when followed by a syllable beginning with a vowel. Otherwise, it is pronounced as a "long" vowel. Examples are:

supper	/ʌ/	vs.	*super*	/u:/
hopping	/ɑ/	vs.	*hoping*	/o:/
latter	/æ/	vs.	*later*	/e:/
dinner	/ɪ/	vs.	*diner*	/aɪ/
herring	/ɛ/	vs.	*here*	/i:/

(See also Figure 5.4.)

The double consonant thus provides a sort of "barrier" to the tensing effect of the "silent *e*" or other following vowel.

The "keep the *e*" rule states that the final *e* is retained – unless *i* follows – to maintain a "soft" sound (i.e. a fricative or affricate instead of a stop) in words ending in *ce* and *ge*. Hence *peace + able → peaceable* and *manage + able → manageable*, but *rate + able → ratable* and *ice + ing → icing*. The "*y* to *i*" rule states that a final *y* becomes *i* before a suffix not beginning with *i*, as in *hurry + es → hurries, friendly + ness → friendliness*. The main exception to this rule is words in which *e* precedes *y*, as in *honey + ed → honeyed*.

While it is clear that these rules might be of some assistance in learning the spelling patterns of small sets of words, they are also clearly limited in their utility, both by their specificity and by the number of exceptions to each of them. Still, it would seem valuable to instruct students who have trouble with English spelling in their writing or with the correspondence of spelling and pronunciation about whatever regularities do exist in the system.

Relating orthography to pronunciation in the language lesson

In a language lesson, the spelling patterns of lexical items cannot easily be avoided, even when the focus of instruction is on spoken rather than on written language. Moreover, making explicit connections in instruction between phonology and orthography may be of benefit to students who are highly motivated to learn both the written and spoken forms of the language. For those students who are predisposed to focus on the written language, perhaps as a result of prior instruction, and to use it as a basis for intuiting patterns in the spoken language, work on sound–spelling correspondences will expose them to the wide variety of patterns that exist in the English lexicon and so perhaps improve their ability to pronounce individual lexical items. Browne and Huckin (1987), for example, offer work on English sound–spelling correspondences as a major part of their pronunciation tutorial program for foreign technical professionals.

As a concomitant to work on vocabulary in any language skill area, activities can be devised to work on differences in spelling patterns of tense/lax or long/short vowel pairs. In work on vocabulary, grammar, listening or speaking, a unit might be organized around morphologically related word sets and the changes in pronunciation associated with the addition of different suffixes and the shifting location of stress.

As a way to help wean students from a strict reliance on the spelling of individual lexical items as the basis for conversational pronunciation, students can be instructed in the effects of reduced stress and coarticulation. Work on how sounds change in context might contrast the careful, hyperarticulate pronunciation of words in isolation with normal conversational pronunciation of those words when they occur in the stream of speech. Alterations of pronunciation in context that occur as a result of coarticulation might be instructed in part through introduction of pronunciation-spellings.

By drawing the language learner's attention to (a) the internal patterns of the English spelling system and (b) the ways in which the orthographic system relates to the phonological system of the language, the language teacher provides a detailed source of information about segmental and prosodic aspects of English. Furthermore, in drawing the learner's attention to the ways in which orthography and phonology diverge, and to the patterns of conversational English pronunciation which supersede orthography, the language teacher offers valuable contrastive information on the English language as a written and a spoken medium. In both of these approaches – that which reinforces regularities within the orthographic system and its relationship to phonology and that which emphasizes differences and irregularities – explicit instruction can help the learner to internalize the rich and complex system that is English phonology.

Orthography activities

1. Analysis of the *i* befor *e* rule

Find exceptions to the "i before e" rule and put these into sets such that all of the words with the same pronunciation of the *ie* or *ei* combinations are grouped together. You should find at least six sets of exceptions besides the set *neighbor, weigh, neigh* that is accounted for in the exception statement of the rule.

Now, consider the following restatement of the "*i* before *e*" rule:

i before *e* for the sound [i:] except after *c*; otherwise, *e* before *i*.

How does this rule compare to the original formulation in terms of how many of the different sets of *ie* and *ei* words are covered by its formulation?

2. Comparison of alphabetic systems

Compare and contrast the spelling system of English to that of another language written using the Roman alphabet. Do all of the letters have the same phonological values as they do in English? What are the main points of divergence? Which system seems the most consistent?

3. Comparison of English orthography to a non-alphabetic system

Compare and contrast the English orthographic system with that of another language written with symbols other than the Roman alphabet. What are the points of similarity and difference, and the strengths and shortcomings of each system?

4. The teaching of English spelling in an academic English course

If you are teaching pronunciation in an academic English course where students will need to read and write well in English, what do you think is the best way to handle spelling?

5. Teaching orthography as a complement to listening

How might instruction in the spelling patterns of English be used to reinforce or complement work in listening comprehension?

6. Two approaches to the teaching of English spelling

Two widely used approaches to teaching word recognition and spelling for beginning readers are the **phonics** and the **whole-word** approaches. These two approaches are based on quite different principles. Phonics is an approach that teaches sound–spelling correspondences and involves much letter-by-letter reading aloud. A whole-word approach teaches students to recognize individual words by the whole shape of the word without breaking lexical items into individual graphemes. Phonics is based primarily on establishment of sound associations for graphemes, while whole-word reading is based primarily on meaning associations for words or morphemes. Therefore, phonics reading lessons will associate words which have sounds in common, while whole-word reading lessons will associate words which have morphemes in common. Why do you think some educators have advocated moving away from phonics and towards whole-word approaches to word recognition in basic reading? What do you think might have caused some of these educators to now be returning to phonics or to a mixed whole-word and phonics approach?

7. A novel approach to teaching sound–spelling correspondence

In New Zealand, an approach to teaching phonics has been highly successful with children who lag behind their peers in learning to sound out words as a basis for reading. In this approach, the child comes to associate individual sounds with phonemic units by learning from teacher modeling how to sound out written words phoneme by phoneme while pushing small round game pieces (such as the pieces used to play Tiddly Winks, Bingo or Go) slowly one by one into squares representing the individual sounds of the word.

For example, the sound–spelling correspondence for the word *meet* would be taught with reference to three contiguous squares (e.g. drawn by the teacher on a piece of paper), each with an associated game piece placed initially under its square. By watching the teacher perform the actions first, the child learns how to sound the word out slowly and continuously by pushing the first counter into the first square while saying /m/, the second counter into the second square while saying /iː/, and the third counter into the third square while saying /t/. Eventually, the child will learn to associate sounds and letters and so be able to sound out new words using this same procedure, as a basis for reading.

Consider the nature of this approach and why it has been so successful in helping children to develop a basic knowledge of sound–spelling correspondences.

8. Sociolinguistic mini-research: spelling change

Carry out an investigation on your own or with your students to review brand names of consumer goods (e.g. grocery store products), or advertising or informational copy in popular magazines, national or local newspapers to find cases of spelling simplifications which bring orthography more into line with phonology in English (e.g. *I'll* for *I will*, *brite* for *bright*, *n* for *and*, *nuff* for *enough*, *cuz* for *because*, *fax* for *facsimile*). Classify the cases as to the type of simplification which they represent:

- loss of graphemes representing phonemes no longer pronounced (contractions, "silent letters" such as *gh*)
- loss of graphemes representing phonemes often deleted in colloquial or informal pronunciation (e.g. final *d* after *n*, initial weak syllables, loss of all but initial syllable in shortened forms of words);
- generalization of a common sound–spelling correspondence (e.g. addition of "silent e" to make a word "long", use of *u* to represent [ʌ] or schwa, *z* instead of *s* for [z], *x* for [ks]).

Also review your sources to see if there are cases of the opposite tendency, viz. spelling complexifications which increase the distance between orthography and phonology in English or which make use of rare, archaic or foreign orthographic patterns (e.g. *Exxon, Crispettes, Parisienne*). Consider the sources and the motivation for the complex orthography in each case.

Consider the frequency of each of these categories of orthographic simplification and complexification in the sources that have been consulted and draw some conclusions about where and under what circumstances these simple and complex orthographic variants occur. On the basis of your analysis, make generalizations about present-day English orthography and predictions about the future of English spelling.

9. Action research: spelling problems related to pronunciation

Design and carry out an action research project to find out:

(1) what problems your students have in pronunciation that might be related to spelling and/or in spelling that might be related to pronunciation; and
(2) how you might go about remediating these problems.

For students whose focus in learning English has been on the written language, it is common for pronunciation to be based to a small or large extent on the way words are spelled. For example, such students tend to pronounce all vowels in a word as full and to have difficulty pronouncing common words correctly if they have unusual spellings (e.g. *women, breakfast*). This is a type of error which native speakers sometimes make in reading aloud but generally not otherwise.

For students whose focus in learning English has been on the spoken language, pronunciation-based spelling errors are often present in their written work, particularly such unedited work as classroom notes, first drafts of compositions and essay examination questions. Some of the pronunciation-spelling errors made by non-native speakers are the same as those made by novice writers who are native speakers of English, suggesting that these errors are based on overgeneralization of the existing sound–spelling correspondences of English. Other errors may be related to the pronunciation or the sound–spelling correspondences of non-native speakers' first language.

In coding pronunciation-spelling errors, it is therefore of value to try to determine the source of the error as:

- native language;
- spoken English;
- indeterminate (i.e. not sure or could be both).

By having an idea of the possible source of the error, the teacher is in a better position to tackle the problem at its source and to provide appropriate remediation.

In developing a profile of your learners' errors in these two areas, you may wish to look at how the type or frequency of errors varies depending on task – e.g. in spontaneous/informal vs. preplanned/formal speech or writing. In so doing, you may wish to test one or both of the following hypotheses:

(1) Spelling-pronunciation errors occur with greater frequency in preplanned and formal tasks than in spontaneous and informal ones.
(2) Pronunciation-spelling errors occur with greater frequency in spontaneous and informal tasks than in preplanned and formal ones.

10. Action research: teaching ideas for orthography

Try out one of the teaching ideas below and then assess the results, following the procedures outlined for action research in previous chapters. As before, in designing your project, decide whether to carry out the research in one or in two classes, with or without a research partner, in your own class(es) and/or in someone else's, and by trying out lessons simultaneously or sequentially. Attend to the ongoing implementation and evaluation of your action research project monitoring the effectiveness of instruction, making any necessary changes in curriculum or teaching approach, and retrospectively assessing the teaching process and effects of instruction.

Teaching ideas for orthography

1. *Activities for intermediate/advanced learners*

A. Exercises on morphologically unrelated words

(1) *Find the rhymes*

Have students work in pairs to pronounce the poem "Our strange language" and to fill in the blanks according to the directions below:

Directions
Work with a partner to say the following poem aloud and to find the missing words. Each missing word:

(1) is spelled the same – except for the first letter – as the other word in quotation marks on the same line; and
(2) rhymes with the last word of the preceding line.

> *Our strange language*
> When the Englishe tongue we speak
> Why is "break" not rhymed with "freak?"
> Will you tell me why it's true
> We say "sew" but likewise "_____";
> And the maker of a verse
> Cannot cap his "horse" with "_____";
> "Beard" sounds not the same as "heard";
> "Cord" is different from "_____".
> Cow is "cow" but low is "low".
> "Shoe" is never rhymed with "_____";
> Think of "hose" and "dose" and "lose";
> And think of "goose" and not of "_____";
> Think of "comb" and "tomb" and "bomb";
> "Doll" and "roll," "home" and "some";
> And since "pay" is rhymed with "say",
> Why not "paid" with "said", I pray?
> We have "blood" and "food" and "good";
> "Mould" is not pronounced like "_____";
> Wherefore "done" but "gone" and "lone"?
> Is there any reason _____?
> And in short it seems to me
> Sounds and letters disagree.

                                             Author unknown

(Answers are provided in Figure 5.1.)

(2) *Team activity for homographs and heteronyms*

The teacher prepares 2 sets of 12 cards, on each of which is written one of the following words:

set	bow
see	sewer
neat	desert
bat	supply
recreation	wind
refuse	lead

Before beginning the game, the teacher gives the definition of *homograph* with the example *butt* ('to ram', 'the end of a cigaret') and *heteronym* with the example *tower* ('one who tows', 'a tall, thin building or structure'). Students are divided into two teams, and each team lines up on one side of the room. The teacher shuffles the two sets of cards, mixing them randomly together, then places the cards on a table or other surface in the front of the room. The teacher flips a coin to decide which team is to take the first turn. That team is labeled Team A; the other, Team B. Teams alternate turns, and within teams, students take turns according to their order in line.

The game begins when the first player on Team A turns over a card, holding it up for all to see, then pronounces the word on the card and gives a definition or description of the meaning of the word pronounced. If the pronunciation and meaning given are correct, Team A receives 1 point, the card stays turned over, and the first player is allowed to turn over another card. If, however, the pronunciation and/or the meaning given are incorrect, the card is turned back over face down, Team A receives no points, and play moves to Team B. The play also goes to Team B if the second card turned over does not match the first card turned over. In both of these cases, the play goes to Team B without Team A scoring another point, and both cards are turned back over face down.

If the second card turned over matches the card already turned over (i.e. if it is spelled the same), the player pronounces that word and then gives a second definition or description of its meaning. The new meaning given must be different from the one already given. The pronunciation may or may not be the same, depending on whether the words are homographs or heteronyms. If the pronunciation and meaning are judged by the teacher to be correct, Team A receives another point, and the cards stay turned over. If the player errs in pronunciation or meaning, no point is given and the cards are then returned to their original face-down position. In both of these cases, the next play goes to Team B, whose first player follows an identical procedure. When that student has finished, the next play goes to the second player on Team A, then the second player on Team B, etc.

Every time a match is made, the cards remain turned over. The game ends when all cards have been turned over. The team with the highest score wins.

B. Exercises on morphologically related words

(1) *Vowel alternations*

(a) *Whole-class activity*
For the sets of related words below, students fill in the blanks with the correct vowel letters as the teacher pronounces each of them. Some sets of words will all have the same vowel or vowels. In other sets, the vowel may not be the same in each word.

n___tion	n___tional	n___tionality	n___tionalism
mechan___ze	mechan___zation	mechan___c	mechan___cal
sch___l	sch___lar	sch___larly	sch___larship
phot___	phot___graph	phot___graphy	phot__graphic
pr___duct	pr___duce	pr___duction	pr___ductivity
expl___n	expl___natory	expl___nation	
___pply	___pplicable	___pplication	
red___m	red___mable	red___mption	
___ble	___ble-bodied	___bility	
s___th	s___thern	s___therly	
blasph___me	blasph___mous	blasph___mer	
hist___ry	hist___rical	hist___rian	
ab___nd	ab___ndant	ab___ndantly	
pron___nce	pron___nciation		

(b) *Small group activity*
Students play a "Concentration"-type game in groups of 3–4. The game is based on the word families introduced in exercise (a) above. Each group receives a set of cards that contains each of the words from exercise (a) spelled out in full on an individual card. (Each group can make its own "deck" of cards before play begins, or the teacher can make them in advance.) The cards are shuffled and then arranged face down in 6 parallel rows of 7 or 8 cards each. The object of the game is to match related cards by turning them over.

In each group, 1 student serves as "Expert", and 2–3 as "Players".

The game begins when a Player turns over a card and pronounces the word on the card. If it is pronounced correctly according to the Expert, the Player receives one point and is allowed to turn over another card. If that card matches the card already turned over (i.e. if it is a related word), the Player pronounces that word. If it is judged to be correctly pronounced, the Player scores another point and is allowed to turn over two more cards, continuing in the same way until no match is made. Then the turn passes to the next Player.

Every time a match is made, the cards remain turned over. In this way, a later Player can continue to match cards previously turned over. The game ends when all cards have been turned over, and the Player with the highest score wins. It is suggested that the game be played enough times for every Player to have a turn as Expert.

(2) *Silent letters*

Students work alone or in pairs to find a word related to each of the words below but for which the silent letter of the word shown is spoken.

bom*b*	_____	sign	_____
de*b*t	_____	desi*g*n	_____
		resi*g*n	_____
solem*n*	_____	mali*g*n	_____
hym*n*	_____		
condem*n*	_____	(adapted from C. Chomsky 1970)	

2. Activities for low-level learners

A. Long/short vowel pairs

Small group or pair activity for low-level learners

Students work in pairs or groups of 3 to list the words that can be made by adding a "silent e" to the words listed, all of which contain "short" vowels. Students can be encouraged to use a dictionary to see if the words with the "long" sounds exist. To finish the activity, students must make a sentence for each short and long vowel word and then recite these to the class.

at	____	led	____	hid	____	tot	____	cut	____
mad	____	let	____	pin	____	ton	____	fun	____
rag	____	pep	____	bit	____	hop	____	pun	____
gap	____	net	____	lip	____	rod	____	pup	____

B. Spelling of different vowel sounds

Small group activity for low-level learners

This exercise, based on the Chilton technique, requires groups of 3–5 to list under time pressure as many words as they know in two columns, based on a key word for each column. The key words selected should be two whose pronunciation is not clearly differentiated by the learners (e.g. contrasting words with /iː/ and /ɪ/, /æ/ and /ɑ/, /uː/ and /ʊ/, /oː/ and /ɔ/).

Each group chooses a "Scribe" to do the writing. The others will brainstorm for words as the Scribe writes them down. The teacher or another student times the groups for 2–3 minutes. Then the teacher checks the lists to see if the words are correctly grouped into the two columns, having students repeat the words in chorus. The teacher may also take the opportunity to point out different spelling patterns in the two columns of words. The group with the most correct words in the two columns wins. This activity can be repeated in one class period for different word pairs 2–3 times without loss of interest.

Example	KEY WORD 1:	*owed*	KEY WORD 2:	*odd*
Student lists		load		rod
		go		law
		rowed		taught
		snow		caught
		know		thought
		toe		ought
		etc.		etc.

C. Homonyms matching exercises

(1) *Exercise on /eː/ vowel*

Students work with a partner to pronounce the words and then to draw a line connecting each pair of homonyms.

Example
great – – – – – – grate

break

weigh   brake

reign   ate

eight   wait

weight   rain

way

(2) *Mixed vowel exercise (focus on /e:/)*

Students work with a partner to circle the pairs of homonyms on each numbered line.

(1) sleigh   sly   slay
(2) sail   sale   sell
(3) pale   pail   pal
(4) mall   male   mail
(5) die   day   dye

6 Pronunciation in the language curriculum

A place for phonology in the language classroom

Questions of curriculum in second language phonology

Your ideas about the teaching of pronunciation have probably been shaped by your own individual experiences as a language learner and, for those readers who already have teaching experience, as a teacher. They may also have been shaped by whatever you have read about the teaching of pronunciation. Whether you believe pronunciation should be taught explicitly or allowed to develop without explicit instruction, as an autonomous course or as a skill integrated into other language skill areas, for every language teacher, the question of the place of pronunciation in the language curriculum needs to receive an answer of some kind.

The most important perspective for deciding what to teach is to look at your students, their problems with English and their future needs in the way of English language skills. Whether or not the learners are adults does not in itself determine the advisability of instruction in pronunciation. One could argue that older learners, unlike children, will not improve in phonology without explicit attention to this aspect of language. If so, then instruction may be able to help them focus their attention more than they might otherwise on the phonological aspects of a language. The desires of the learners must also be considered, and many adult learners desire explicit attention to pronunciation. In some cases, such a desire can be satisfied through optional language laboratory work, though in other cases, students will expect classroom lessons to incorporate some explicit attention to phonology. In virtually every case of learning a second language, students expect feedback on their pronunciation, though the form of the feedback must always be tailored to the audience.

Listening activities are an important part of the pronunciation lesson. However, they cannot be the whole lesson. It is doubtful that work on listening comprehension, or even listen-and-repeat lessons performed in a language laboratory, can alone be expected to improve pronunciation.

Like other forms of active, productive behavior, pronunciation can be expected to improve through practice, in particular, through the kinds of pair and group activities that are at the heart of modern, communicative and learner-centered methodology for language teaching.

The learner's attention and motivation are key to activating change, facilitating the change process and maintaining progress in phonological acquisition. In the definition of Crookes and Schmidt (1991), motivation is closely linked to attention (p. 484) and incorporates elements of "choice, engagement, and persistence, as determined by interest, relevance, expectancy, and outcomes" (p. 502). Thus, instructional approaches for second language phonology should seek to motivate and engage learners to make a greater self-investment in their own phonological development by considerations of such factors as learners' interests and goals, interactional dynamics and classroom climate, and appropriate feedback and reward systems.

Motivation can be generated in the pronunciation class by presenting interesting and relevant lessons that offer positive reinforcement and feedback on performance and that help students progress towards their own personal learning goals. As Firth (1992a) reminds us:

> Both the teacher and the student must remember that pronunciation change is gradual in nature. Pronunciation inaccuracies do not miraculously disappear; instead, production becomes more accurate by stages. A realistic set of expectations and positive, constructive feedback from peers and the instructor will help keep motivation among students high. (p. 181)

The curricular goals of engagement and self-investment as well as the students' own learning goals are also achieved by (1) encouraging learners to monitor and self-correct their own pronunciation and (2) helping them to develop the insight and skills needed to do so. In this way, language learners increase their level of interest, involvement and responsibility in pronunciation learning, while the teacher functions as a motivator, facilitator and "expert" consultant who helps them fulfil their individual goals. In this type of instructional program, learners improve their pronunciation through an active, focused and cooperative effort with the teacher to train attention on pronunciation and to work to change it.

The teacher's role in this sort of partnership with learners is similar to that of a coach, as noted by Morley (1991), who describes the pronunciation or speech "teacher-as-coach" in the following terms:

> The work of a pronunciation/speech coach can be viewed as similar to that done by a debate coach, a drama coach, a voice coach, a music

coach, or even a sports coach. A coach characteristically supplies information, gives models from time to time, offers cues, suggestions and constructive feedback about performance, sets high standards, provides a wide variety of practice opportunities, and overall [sic] supports and encourages the learner. (p. 507)

In classes that combine structured pronunciation lessons and pronunciation/speech "coaching", students have opportunties to learn the phonology of a second language as a focused area of instruction and managed self-development, and not only as a by-product of work on other language skills.

Goals for pronunciation in a second language

Even if you decide that there is no place for explicit instruction in pronunciation, the question of the **implicit** instruction in pronunciation which students receive daily in any class that involves speaking or listening activities still needs an answer. In addition, the question of **feedback** must be resolved: What kind and what amount of feedback on pronunciation is desirable?

The logical starting point for decisions about what to teach in the area of phonology is to consider appropriate goals. Probably the most obvious, justifiable and pressing goal in the area of phonology is **intelligibility**. For beginning students, this is the most immediate need, as no communication can take place without a certain level of mutual intelligibility among speakers. Thus, a strong focus on pronunciation is justified at a beginning level of instruction.

At intermediate and advanced levels, student needs in the area of phonology will be more variable than at the beginning level. Some students will have achieved basic intelligibility in phonology by the time they reach an intermediate level of proficiency in other language skills, whereas for others, problems in phonology may obscure intelligibility even after the student has achieved a relatively high score on a standardized test of English proficiency.

Beyond the goal of basic intelligibility, there are several possible goals in this area of language. In the majority of cases, native pronunciation seems to be an unrealistic goal. **Fluency** is one goal that is important for many students who will leave their home country and use the second language in the host country, as over-hesitant speakers are likely to have difficulty communicating with native listeners for any length of time. **Accuracy** in terms of audience-determined norms is also an important goal, especially for those who must convey information to other native speakers, such as teaching assistants in undergraduate courses, supervisors in businesses or people who must speak to clients over the telephone in the target language.

On the other hand, neither of these goals may be especially important for those using the second language for limited communication, or for those who communicate in the second language primarily with others who speak the same first language. In such limited circumstances, the goal of intelligibility is probably adequate for the purposes of many.

For many speakers, however, even all of these goals taken together – intelligibility, fluency and accuracy – are too modest. Those who wish to function well in the target culture will need to aim to master those aspects of pronunciation that define a person's attitude, mood, orientation to the audience and to the topic, and other basic characteristics of the speaker's personal, social and cultural orientation. For speakers who wish to communicate on an equal footing with native speakers, goals focusing on casual and expressive ability in phonology are important. For a non-native speaker who uses a formal or non-expressive style of pronunciation (e.g. with aspirated stops in final position, with monotonic rhythm or with full vowels in unaccented syllables) may be unconsciously evaluated by many native speakers as "stand-offish", formal, or even unfriendly.

According to Morley (1991), a variety of types of learners can benefit by attention to phonology in "a broadly-constructed communicative approach" (p. 490):

In ESL settings

1. Adult and teenage refugees in vocational and language training programs.
2. Immigrant residents who have been in an English-speaking country for 5 to 15 years.
3. A growing population of nonnative speakers of English in technology, business, industry, and the professions in English-speaking countries.
4. College and university faculty members and research scholars in virtually every field of higher education.
5. Graduate and undergraduate students in higher education in English-speaking countries.

In EFL settings

1. International business personnel, scientists, technologists, and other professionals whose careers demand the use of both effective written and spoken English as a lingua franca.

2. College and university professors and academic research scholars in many disciplines in higher education.
3. Students who ultimately wish to enter English-speaking colleges and universities to pursue undergraduate and/or graduate degrees. (Morley 1991: 490–2)

As in all other aspects of curriculum decision-making, the nature of students, their level and the goals of the language program will all determine what other goals (if any) are appropriate. Whether the learners are to remain in the country of origin or are intending to study or work in a country where English is spoken, whether they will maintain the first language as primary or not, what their specific needs for use of the second language are – these and other concerns are paramount in determining a curriculum for pronunciation that will be appropriate and useful for a specific group of learners.

Phonological objectives beyond the basic goal of intelligibility have to do with what is feasible under the constraints of the course (e.g. in terms of time available) and in the context of other decisions about what to teach and on what schedule. For example, the instructor must decide whether to focus on those individual sounds or areas of prosody which most students have trouble with, or on basic distinctions between prosodic patterns (e.g. related to communicative function) or between categories of sounds (e.g. based on manner of articulation).

Benefits of attention to phonology for other curricular goals

Work on pronunciation, whether in the form of feedback or in the form of explicit lessons, can help to further other instructional goals in the language curriculum. In listening comprehension, work on individual sounds can help the learner to pick out individual words in the stream of speech. Work on the more global prosodic properties of speech such as rhythm can aid the learner in comprehending stretches of speech and in determining which words and phrases are the focus of information. In conversation or other speaking activities, work on the pronunciation of individual sounds can increase intelligibility of individual words, while work on prosody can increase fluency.

Recognition of words in reading may also be aided by work on the pronunciation of those words. Moreover, since all aspects of language proficiency are related, as spoken fluency increases, so does fluency, or automaticity, in reading and writing. Thus, work on spoken fluency may aid the development of a kind of fluency in listening, reading and writing.

Many aspects of grammar involve systematic phonological processes and may thus be reinforced by work on the relevant aspects of phonology. For example, the derivation of one part of speech from another by means of a grammatical ending often involves a change in pronunciation which is systematic across a whole set of words, as illustrated in Figures 3.5 and 3.7. As another example, the inflection of verbs in the past tense is based on phonological principles, viz. that of assimilation of voicing in context, in combination with the principle of separation of like sounds through addition of an epenthetic vowel. The *-(e)s* ending of the third person singular present tense of verbs, the plural of nouns and the possessive of nouns is attached according to the same basic principles. In addition, the alternations of different forms of a verb in different tenses (e.g. *bite, bit, bitten*) sometimes take place according to a regular phonological principle such as an alternation of tense and lax vowels in the verb root.

At the level of phrases, prepositional phrases (e.g. *in a minute, at 5:00, on time*) and noun phrases not modififed by an adjective (e.g. *a pencil, the book, his car*) generally contain one stressed word in final position and one or more unstressed words preceding the stressed word. The structure (and the comprehension) of these units may be reinforced by some attention to their phonology. Complex verb phrases that contain one or more auxiliaries (e.g. *will not have been talking, must have been seen, is going to be leaving*) will generally be at least partially unstressed and weakened, and in some cases, contracted. Here again, work on the pronunciation of these units will aid production and recognition in context.

Targetting areas for instruction, remediation or feedback

As in all things in life, it is not possible to do everything that we would wish to do. There is never enough time. Furthermore, students will get bored or overwhelmed if the teacher tries to cover too many areas in too much detail. Hence, as in all teaching, a choice must be made as to which pronunciation areas to teach and which errors or problems to focus on in instruction, remediation and feedback on performance.

First, the teacher will need to do an analysis or diagnosis of students' pronunciation to find out what kinds of problems the learners are experiencing with the second language. The most basic type of analysis might work from transsegmental to segmental aspects of phonology. Appendix A, Hierarchical Analysis of Student Pronunciation, provides a guide for on-the-spot analysis of and feedback on student pronunciation. The guide divides pronunciation aspects into Level 1 concerns, the most serious and major areas needing attention – including ultra-low or ultra-high values for prosody throughout speech and pervasive segmental problems – and Level 2 concerns, those of lesser importance – including segmental and transsegmental problems involving individual lexical items or expressions. It also offers teachers a four-step process, with examples, in Part III for giving students feedback on their pronunciation according to the Level 1 and Level 2 concerns.

For a more extensive analysis, Appendix B, Pedagogical Classification of Pronunciation Errors and Problems, provides a guide for classifying learners' pronunciation difficulties preparatory to lesson design or as a basis for feedback to the whole class or individual students. As detailed and illustrated in Appendix B, the choice of what to teach or remediate in the area of phonology can be made by balancing four factors: (1) the most important errors or problem areas, (2) errors or problems that will benefit most from remediation, (3) errors or problems identified by the learners themselves as needing attention and (4) errors or problems in areas of language related to the learner's particular needs.

Errors or problems which can be classified in two or more areas of Appendix B are probably the ones that should be given the highest priority in instruction or remediation. It can be useful to focus specific attention on the pronunciation errors or problems in need of work, by telling students individually or the class as a whole which errors or problems you have identified and which ones you feel they should work on and why. In working with adolescents or adults, it is also a good idea to discuss the possible reasons that they are making these errors and the types of problems they can cause or are causing in their communication. Such information will make the learners more aware of their pronunciation errors or problems and the need to pay attention to them, while also motivating them to want to improve and so to be open to remediation and instruction in this area of language.

Lesson design for phonology

From mechanical to real pronunciation practice

Many people's objections to the teaching of phonology in language classes center on the non-communicative, mechanical nature of the activities. In reaction to these types of criticisms, authors such as Celce-Murcia (1983, 1987), Gilbert (1984), Kenworthy (1987), Naiman (1992), Pica (1984) and Wong (1987b) have attempted to develop communicative pronunciation activities. However, the term "communicative" is not always used in a consistent way and can mean many different things. As a consequence, many levels of language practice which are not strictly communicative have nevertheless been described using this popular term. Figure 6.1 illustrates several levels of language practice, from what might be termed **mechanical** to what might be termed **real**. Except for the first term, **mechanical**, all of the other categories on this scale have been referred to as "communicative" language practice.

In order to lay a foundation for examining and for developing lesson material for the teaching of pronunciation, it is useful to take a closer look at the different levels of a language lesson and to clarify the use of such terms as "communicative", "meaningful", "realistic" and "real" in relation to language teaching. To this end, Figure 6.2 provides an analysis of a language lesson that moves from basic to less basic levels toward a final goal of communication. Read from top to bottom, the figure represents a **standard progression** of a unit or lesson, which may or may not be reflected in detail in any particular lesson. The figure can thus be seen as providing a logical series of steps for a lesson or unit which may be varied for certain purposes or in certain approaches.

The unit structure, shown in the first column in the figure, has just two levels, beginning with presentation and moving to practice. This unit structure is reflected in the activity types of the next column, which fall into the two categories of presentation and practice. Under presentation, a focus activity focuses the learner's attention on the point to be mastered in the lesson. This focus activity is followed in the standard

Mechanical
(e.g. repetition of minimal pairs)

Contextualized
(e.g. repetition of key words in a listening passage)

Meaningful
(e.g. choice of correct word in a sentence or reading passage)

Realistic
(e.g. a roleplay of a situation similar to one faced in real life)

Real
(e.g. discussion of the students' real-life situation or concerns)

FIGURE 6.1 Levels of language practice

Unit structure	Activity type	Practice level	Cognitive load	Modality	Participation	Information
Presentation	Focus	Mechanical	Low inference	– Production	– Interaction	– Communicative
	Contextualization	Contextualized				
Practice	Controlled	Meaningful				
	Structured	Realistic				
	Free	Real	High inference	+ Production	+ Interaction	+ Communicative

FIGURE 6.2 Standard progression of a communicative language lesson or unit

progression by contextualization of the point that was taken out of context to provide a focus for the lesson. For example, a contrast of two sounds pronounced in isolation can then be used in words, phrases and sentences. These two activity types, focus and contextualization, reflect the presentation component of the unit structure.

In the category of practice, there are three activity types: controlled, structured and free activities. A controlled activity is one which offers little freedom or possibility of creativity on the part of the students but which involves some limited level of language use. Examples might be student pairs for dialogue practice or practice of the differences in pronunciation of minimal pair words in context. Activities which are somewhat structured but which allow for student creativity and freedom of choice in deciding how to complete the activity fall into the category termed "structured" activities. If all structure is relaxed, as when students are simply given a topic to discuss, with no direction or goal provided, this type of activity is termed "free".

As illustrated in Figure 6.2, a separate scale applies to practice level. Although this scale, like that for activity type, has five levels and although its categories relate to some extent to those of activity type, it is intended to be independent from that scale. Thus, the categories on these two scales may or may not correspond in a given case (e.g. practice classified as real might be the focus component of a lesson). The practice level scale begins with mechanical language practice such as repetition of minimal pairs. Contextualized practice in pronunciation might be the repetition of minimal pairs in sentence contexts.

Meaningful practice signifies language activities which require knowing the meaning of the items in order to complete the activity. "Meaningful" in this sense does not necessarily imply either "realistic" or "communicative". For example, a meaningful pronunciation activity might require a student to decide whether one out of a minimal pair of words has been used correctly in a sentence. While practice of this sort involves meaning, and is in that respect an advance on repetitive mechanical practice, it does not represent communication in any true sense of the word.

Practice is not realistic until it is similar to use of language in real life. Examples of realistic practice include simulations and roleplays of situations like those faced by students outside of class. Real practice goes one step further, in allowing students to bring real-life concerns and functions into the educational curriculum. Such practice might involve discussion or problem-solving related to the students' activities outside of the language class.

The scheme of Figure 6.2 includes four categories which have only two values. In general, lessons or units will begin at the low or minus level in each of these categories and move to a high or plus level in later stages. The category of cognitive load is meant to reflect the amount of information processing which the student must handle in order to perform the activities of the lesson. It is common for a lesson to begin with a light cognitive load and progress to a heavier cognitive load. Those aspects of a lesson which are not very cognitively demanding can be referred to as **low inference**, meaning that they require very little thinking or extrapolation from the immediate context of the input given to the student. **High inference** activities, on the other hand, involve considerable mental effort on the part of the learner, requiring extrapolation from the immediate context through inferencing and associations with other knowledge and experience. High inference activities are thus more challenging and creative than low inference activities.

In the category of modality, the standard progression of a unit or lesson is from non-productive to productive language use, e.g. from listening to speaking activities. In the category of participation, activities move from non-interactive to interactive. The category of the last column in Figure 6.2 is that of truly communicative language lessons. This is the category of information. Typically, a lesson begins with some kind of activity which does not require real communication because (a) the students are not required to manipulate any information but rather merely to *perform*, e.g. through repetition, and/or (b) the students all have the same information, so that no transfer of information can take place. Only when there is an actual transfer of information can we say that a communication has taken place. Hence, information-gap activities in which one person has information that the other must obtain are a type of communicative activity. Notice that this type of activity may or may not be realistic or real in the sense of these terms used here, though, in general, it is desirable for communicative activities to be realistic or real rather than artificial.

Designing the autonomous pronunciation lesson or unit

After analyzing students' pronunciation problems, the teacher may wish to design a pronunciation lesson or unit to work on a particular problem or group of problems which many or all of the learners have in common. An autonomous pronunciation lesson or unit will comprise a series of activities for teaching students how to discriminate, to pronounce and to contextualize a problematic segmental or prosodic aspect or contrast. In designing the lesson or unit, consideration should be given to the student population that the lesson is intended for and to the characteristics and constraints of the teaching situation. The teacher must also carefully plan how much time is to be spent on pronunciation and how phonology is to be integrated with other teaching goals and activities. A sample unit plan for working on the /r/–/l/ contrast in a language class is shown in Appendix C.

In the initial stages of the autonomous pronunciation lesson, the teacher isolates the prosodic point or the individual sounds that are to be the focus of the lesson and then draws attention to the pronunciation features or contrasts of the lesson focus through modeling, demonstration, explanation or some other type of awareness-building activity. As in other types of instruction, the pronunciation lesson might begin with a preview activity to attract the students' attention to the pronunciation point addressed, using something amusing, an interesting visual aid or model, or a tape recording of a native speaker to model the pronunciation point or of a student to illustrate a certain pronunciation problem. Examples of such activities can be found in exercises 1A, 3A and 4A in the Teaching Ideas for Consonants (end of Chapter 2). After addressing the production of the phonemic or prosodic aspect or contrast and giving the students some controlled practice on the teaching point(s), the teacher can then move to a practice activity that allows students to work in pairs or small groups.

Activity types for pronunciation may be borrowed and adapted from other types of lessons or content areas. Mechanical practice exercises may be of the traditional dictation or listen-and-repeat variety. Mechanical activities can be performed in student pairs or groups to make them more participatory. Any activity that can be performed with teacher control can become student directed by having one student in a group or pair perform the "teacher" role. We will now look at some types of mechanical activities and how these can be used for pair or small group work.

An AB comparison is any type of activity that compares two (or more) items in contrast (e.g. two commonly confused sounds). Such a task might, for example, ask students to decide whether a stimulus word is the same as or different from another word on the chalk board or on an exercise sheet. This type of activity can form the basis for a communicative exercise which asks the student to perform some activity X (e.g. stand up) if s/he hears word A and perform a different activity Y (e.g. sit down) if s/he hears word B.

A variation on the AB format asks students to pick the odd item in a series of items, e.g. the word which has a different vowel sound from all the others. This type of format is used for the pair matching exercise of 4E in the Teaching Ideas section of Chapter 2. Another variation is the

ABC multiple choice format in which the learner must choose the correct response from among a set of choices, only one of which corresponds to the target sound. As a pair or small group activity, students can be asked to circle the letter of the item that corresponds to a stimulus spoken by another student. Fill-in-the-blanks can be used as a format for pair or small group dictation in which students fill in missing words or sentences based on dictation by other students.

An important part of any student-managed exercise is checking afterwards, which is best done by the students themselves (at least as a first step befor more systematic checking by the teacher). As the students check their answers, they will be gaining additional practice in pronunciation and adjusting their pronunciation targets cooperatively. Given their natural orientation to their peers, cooperative checking is the most realistic – and for the students, the most meaningful – way to get students to monitor and refine their articulation.

The steps described below can be followed in developing a sequence of activities starting with mechanical practice and moving to meaningful practice and then to realistic or real activity. Activities in the "realistic" or "real" category – e.g. involving a simulation, roleplay or discussion – can be developed based on the material used for the mechanical and meaningful activities, if the items chosen are carefully selected with the ultimate goal of using them in a realistic or real activity.

I. *Background to lesson preparation*

A. *Consideration of student population*
Consider the student population that the lesson is intended for in terms of nationality, country (ESL/EFL status), age, educational level, proficiency level, reason for studying English, and any other distinguishing characteristics of the student population. Consider how these learner characteristics should affect your lesson design.

B. *Consideration of teaching situation*
Consider the possibilities and the constraints of the teaching situation in relation to such factors as curricular goals, class size, time and resources available. Be realistic about what is and is not possible, given the teaching context.

C. *Determination of teaching point*
Based on the consideration of I A–B, decide on the pronunciation point you will focus on, generally a phonological feature or contrast as it

applies in a specific grammatical structure, function, utterance context or set of lexical items, e.g.:

- tense/lax pairs with /i:/ vs. /ɪ/
- voiced/voiceless stops in final position
- the pronunciation of past tense endings
- rising vs. falling intonation in tag questions
- "teens" and "tens"

You should have a rationale for focusing on a particular teaching point at a given point in time.

II. *Lesson components*

A. *Presentation of pronunciation point*

Formulate a series of steps to present the basic teaching point or contrast using visual modeling, demonstration and simple instructions about how to produce the pronunciation point. If possible, use visual material, props, taped speech or other interesting material to raise awareness and reinforce the presentation. The presentation should concentrate on the mechanics of the pronunciation point and should move from an activity to focus the students' attention on the problem and on the key aspects of the pronunciation point to one which places it in a typical context or range of contexts. The presentation normally begins with the students listening but may progress to some limited and controlled production on the part of the students. A series of presentation activities is offered below for teaching the stress patterns and pronunciation of the "teens" numbers (i.e. those ending in *-teen*) and the "tens" numbers (i.e. those ending in *-ty*).

Example: Presentation on "teens" and "tens"

The teacher begins by playing a teacher-prepared tape of a native speaker counting to thirty, followed by pairs of native speaker voices, in which one speaker asks the other a question for which the answer involves a number between 13 and 99, sometimes spoken with and sometimes without context. Some of the conversations can be continued to indicate misunderstandings related to stress and the clarification of these. For example:

Speaker 1: How much did those shoes cost you?
Speaker 2: They cost me 49 dollars.
Speaker 1: I think you got a good deal.

Speaker 1: How many ties do you have in your closet?
Speaker 2: 17. I have 17 ties in my closet.
Speaker 1: I'd say that's about average for most guys.

Speaker 1: How many times have you seen *Gone with the Wind*?
Speaker 2: 14.
Speaker 1: Did you say you've seen that movie 40 times??
Speaker 1: No, 14.
Speaker 2: Well, that's bad enough!

The teacher then draws the students' attention to the following information on the chalk board. Different color chalks can be used to highlight the different patterns for tens and teens.

TEENS	TENS	
+10	NUMBER	10 ×
plus TEN		TEN times
weak STRONG	STRESS PATTERN	STRONG weak
or STRONG weak		
(counting, before a noun)		
[tʰiːn]	PRONUNCIATION	[tʰiː] or [ɾiː]
		[i] (only for *twenty*
		and *ninety*]

The teacher gives examples of the different stress patterns for the "teens" by:

(1) counting from 10 to 20;
(2) asking and answering "how many" questions for which the answer is a number between 13 and 19 (e.g. "How many days are there in a fortnight?", "What is the most unlucky number?");
(3) showing the contrast of stress where a noun follows or not as in contexts such as "Here are ____ pencils", "the number of pencils is ____".

The teacher then gives examples of the different pronunciations for the "tens" by:

(1) counting by tens from 10 to 100;
(2) asking and answering "how many" questions for which the answer is a number between 20 and 99 and modeling the different possible pronunciations. (e.g. "How old is this building?" "How many candies are in this packet?").

B. *Basic practice*

Develop a basic exercise (or exercises) for working on the pronunciation point introduced in II A. The exercise should focus on sound rather than meaning, though there may be some attention to the meaning of the individual words, grammatical structure or language function to build interest and avoid questions or confusion later on. The exercise may be in a whole-class, pair or small group format. It may include some listening practice but should also include some pronunciation practice. Try to make the exercise interesting while not at the same time moving too far from the basic teaching point or contrasts. It is all right to start out with hearing or pronouncing minimal pairs, but there should be some practice beyond this very mechanical type of exercise, e.g. a type of Bingo game such as that illustrated in the Teaching Ideas for Vowels (end of Chapter 3) or the types of pair exercises illustrated in the Teaching Ideas for Consonants (end of Chapter 2), or some variation on these.

Example: Basic practice on "teens" and "tens"

The teacher – and afterwards students working in pairs – can perform a dictation of items containing "teens" and "tens", and the students might be asked to circle the word they hear from two possibilities (e.g. *13* vs. *30*) on an answer sheet. For example:

"George is (13/30) years old."
"Carmen has (14/40) cousins."

Students might be given the dictation material or else allowed to make up their own items.

The exercise can be strictly mechanical and context-free or may be contextualized in various ways. Contextualization, which makes the activity less artificial and at the same time more challenging, can be accomplished in a number of ways, such as by setting the dictated items within larger numbers – possibly with additional answer choices (e.g. *1913* vs. *1930* vs. *9013* vs. *9030*), phrases (*13/30 sandwiches*), or whole sentence contexts (*George ate 13/30 sandwiches at the picnic*).

Notice that this basic activity, even when whole-sentence contexts are involved, requires only recognition of the correct item in context and not understanding of meaning.

C. *Meaningful practice*

Develop an exercise which follows up on II A and II B by contextualizing the contrast in a meaningful way. In other words, develop an exercise in which students must respond according to the meaning of items, and not only according to their sound.

Example: Meaningful practice on "teens" and "tens"

For the "teens" and "tens" material so far presented, a basic practice whole-sentence dictation might be followed up by comprehension questions. Or a highly controlled, teacher-presented dictation for basic practice may be followed up by students presenting their own meaningful dictations, with comprehension questions, in pairs.

Supplementary or alternative types of meaningful practice might involve the class in a structured activity allowing some degree of choice and creativity. In one activity of this kind, each student is given the material below and asked to write "The story of _____". Each student does this by first choosing a person for the story to be about, selecting one word from the pair in each sentence, and then putting the sentences together in any sensible order (e.g. chronological, reverse chronological, topical) to make the person's life story, beginning with the sentence, "This is the story of _____."

Students are then put in small groups to read their stories aloud to each other, line by line. As one group member reads a line of his/her story, the listeners are to make appropriate comments, such as "That's nice", "That's really young", "That's really old", or "That's incredible!" If a listener makes a remark that the reader thinks is not appropriate, then the reader repeats what s/he said in the frame, "No, I said _____."

> S/he got married at 13/30.
> In 6 weeks, s/he lost 14/40 lbs. on his/her diet.
> S/he was a 15/50-year-old mother/father.
> S/he became the president of a company at 16/60.
> When s/he was 17/70, s/he ran a marathon.
> S/he retired at 18/80.
> S/he passed away at 19/90.

D. *Realistic practice*
Using the preceding activities in II A–C as a foundation, develop one or more activities in which students practice the pronunciation point in real or realistic (simulated) communication, as in the two sample activities below.

Example: Realistic practice with "teens" and "tens"

Students work in paired groups of 3 to develop and then perform roleplays, either within their own group or for the class as a whole.

The first two roleplays simulate placing and receiving a large order, where producing and understanding the difference between "teens" and "tens" will be crucial. The third simulates a similar process of planning and negotiation of large quantities of different items and materials for an expedition. The choices of situations are as follows:

Situation 1. Your son/daughter is getting married and you are planning a big luncheon reception for all the wedding guests to take place afterwards at a rented hall. You are working with a catering company to prepare and serve all of the food, and to decorate and set up the hall where the reception will take place. Your roleplay will involve three family members who meet with the head caterer and his/her two assistants to decide on and negotiate the food and other items which will be needed for the wedding reception, how much each will cost and what the total price of the reception will be.

The "family" group will decide in advance on the number of guests and the approximate amount of money they would like to spend. Taking the number of guests and approximate amount of money the "family" would like to spend, the "caterer" group will make a preliminary menu and determination of the number and cost of all food and other items needed for the reception. At the same time, the "family" group will make its preliminary menu and list of all food and other items which they think will be needed for the reception. After these preliminary determinations have been made, the two groups meet and negotiate until they agree on the menu, the number and cost of all food items and other items for the reception, and the total cost.

Situation 2. A chain of three large and very successful New York Deli shops in a major urban area somewhere in the world (your choice) wants to contract with a major supplier somewhere else in the world (your choice) to obtain all of a certain type of product – such as cheese, ice cream, wine, soft drinks, candy (your choice) – which they will need for their shops over the next six months. If the price is right, the quality of the product is high, and the variety is sufficient, you intend to establish a long-term relationship with this supplier and will give the company all of your business.

First the entire group needs to decide on the area where the deli shops are located, the location and name of the supplier, and a product to focus on. It should be something whose varieties the group members are familiar with. Then you will split into a "product supplier" group and a "deli shop" group.

The "product supplier" group includes the chief buyer, the sales director and an accountant. Together they will decide on the products which they are prepared to sell, in what quantity, and at what price. The "deli" group includes the owner/managers of the three New York Deli shops in the chosen city. Each deli owner/manager should decide on the number of patrons who must be served in his/her shop, the amount and varieties of each product needed or wanted, and the price they are willing to pay for these goods. After each group has met independently to decide these matters, they then negotiate with each other in an overseas conference call until they reach agreement on what will be bought, in what quantity and at what price.

Situation 3. You are part of one of two groups of people going on expeditions to some isolated place for six months, during which time you will have no contact with the outside world. Each group will be provided with a modest cabin or hut with limited space containing three beds, a toilet, a bathtub, a gas stove, a lamp, a refrigerator and a water heater. Other than transportation in and out by helicopter at the beginning and the end of the six-month period, nothing else will be provided for your group.

First, each group should decide where they are going and what they will be doing there in the six-month expedition. Groups can select similar or different locations and purposes for their expeditions. Once the groups have made these decisions, they should work independently to plan what they will take with them and in what quantity for their expedition. Once each group has made a tentative list of supplies to take with them on their expedition, the groups will compare notes and make any appropriate adjustments.

Example: Real practice with "teens" and "tens"

Students work in pairs to ask and answer questions about their lives and experiences using "tens" and "teens" lexis in answer to "how" questions such as the following and giving their honest reactions to the answers:

How many minutes/hours does it take you to. . . ? (e.g. do your homework)
How old were you when. . . ? (e.g. Elvis died)
How old do you think you'll be when. . . ? (e.g. you get married)
Have you ever . . . ? (e.g. climbed a mountain)
If yes: How old were you (the first time)?

Integrating listening and self-monitoring activities in the pronunciation curriculum

Most listening activities used in connection with pronunciation instruction are of the type which, adapting from the categories of listening activities developed by Rost (1991), can be termed **intensive** listening. These types of activities typically involve such exercises as word-for-word dictation and discrimination between two or more similar sounds, sound sequences, words or phrases to learn to hear the differences (see Burns 1992, Morley 1984, for examples). However, other types of listening activities may find a place in the pronunciation lesson. These include:

- **selective** listening, in which only one or a limited number of aspects of the content or form of speech is focused on;
- **extensive** listening, in which the listener seeks to gain a broad and diversified experience through listening;
- **social** listening, in which the listener is attentive to and responds to the social context of listening, comprising the interaction between participants and their ongoing actions and needs.

For example, students might be asked to listen selectively to a particular speaker to hear the way s/he pronounces a certain phoneme or word. They might also be encouraged to listen extensively – e.g. to the radio, television or special tape series – to gain experience with different voice qualities or accents of English.

In addition, students might learn to listen in a socially more attentive and responsive manner when engaged in conversations with native speakers. In particular, they might try to notice the social messages that speakers signal through voice quality, intonation, rhythm and style of pronunciation (e.g. formality or social distance signaled by precise articulation). Part of social listening might also involve listeners actively signaling their reactions by means of intonation in short verbal responses such as "yes", "mhm", etc., as a way to encourage further participation on the part of the others involved (thereby gaining more input from others) as well as to experience conversation in a more interactive and participatory (and hence more natural) fashion. A class activity along these lines is described by Wong (1987a: 23–4).

Listening activities can be fruitfully tied to work aimed at helping students monitor their own production. One technique – similar to the "fluency workshop" activity described by Wong (1987a: 25–7) – is the **Monitored Conversation** technique (which I adapted in the early 1980s when I was the academic coordinator of the English Language

Program at the University of California at Santa Barbara from a technique used in the Los Angeles area English Language Services centers, as described to me by Helena Kirk). This is a technique which works well when students threaten to lose attention or waste time, e.g. as the last activity before lunch period or as a special activity reserved for Friday afternoons.

In the Monitored Conversation technique, students take one of four roles: "Prompter", "Respondent", "Monitor" or "Timer". The activity begins by pairing two students into the conversant roles of a Prompter and a Respondent. This can be one pair in front of the whole class, or several pairs around the room, each in a small group (4–8) of other students. The activity should be performed several times in a row, with conversant roles rotating to different students each time and the former conversants then becoming formal or informal Monitors. The conversant pair are given a time limit for their conversation (1–3 minutes). The pair are to hold a conversation until the Timer tells them their time is used up. (Alternatively, an electric timer may be set to go off after the pre-determined time.)

The Prompter selects a conversation topic or starter from among a set of these written on strips of paper by the teacher or other students (a good resource is Zelman 1983). For example, the Prompter selects the conversation starter "I heard that some of the students are really homesick." and begins by using the starter or asking a related question to try to get the Respondent to speak. Both members of the conversational pair are to keep the conversation going by responding appropriately and drawing the other person out. If conversation breaks down, it is the Prompter's job to try to get the interaction going again, e.g. by asking new questions or introducing any new topic of interest.

All other students (except the Timer) monitor the conversation either formally or informally as it is occurring. The formal Monitors may be one or more students who listen for particular aspects of language or communicative competence – e.g. voice quality, intonation, word stress, consonants, vowels, gestures and facial expressions, responsive listening behavior, presence of grammatical morphemes, etc. The teacher or the conversants may request certain kinds of monitoring to focus on areas of greatest concern. The Monitor roles can be varied for every conversation, or a certain student can become the class expert in a certain area of language or communication and always monitor for that aspect. The formal Monitor(s) can be encouraged to write down words, expressions or other aspects of communication on which they would like to give feedback. The feedback may be given in written form – e.g. by means of a checklist or brief description – or orally at the end of the conversation period. Those who monitor informally are simply invited to watch and listen to the conversation and then later to give feedback on the conversants' performance if they wish.

Another activity that helps practice phonology while building up self-monitoring skills involves having learners prepare written versions of speeches, which they mark prosodically beforehand by indicating pauses and key words and syllables to be stressed (Firth 1992b: 219). The speeches are then tape recorded, and the learners check and critique their performance afterwards, possibly in collaboration with a peer or the teacher, against their marked script. A technique like this has been used, for example, by Browne and Huckin (1987: 54–5) in their course for non-native technical professionals.

An ongoing, interactive type of monitoring and critique can involve an individual learner and a peer or the teacher in a taped variant of the "dialogue journal" activity. In this activity, a student records a speech sample at the beginning of the school year (e.g. a short impromptu speech about his or her family or a passage or speech marked prosodically in advance) and then passes it to another student or the teacher for taped commentary and feedback, including questions and suggestions on the content and the form – especially, for this activity, pronunciation – of the taped speech sample. After commenting, the peer or the teacher passes the tape back to the first student, who then reacts to the commentary and feedback in a continuing dialogue – e.g. on a daily or weekly basis – over the course of the school term.

The student and his/her dialogue partner should be encouraged to keep all of the old recordings, rather than recording over these, and to periodically listen to older segments of the tape, noting areas of improvement and of continuing concern. The dialogue partner should be encouraged to do this as well. The student thereby gains detailed information on performance and a permanent record of improvement that can motivate the long-term and continuing attention needed to effect changes in pronunciation.

An international approach to pronunciation in the language curriculum

This book has sought to present pronunciation in a broad context that allows for English as both a second language and a language of international communication. Where the learner's goal for learning English is not one of assimilation but rather one of expansion of communicative repertoire, it becomes especially important to base pronunciation work on an analysis of learner needs and to target instruction to meet those needs.

A needs-based approach will focus on the learners' specific needs for English in terms of lexical items – e.g. for academic or occupation-related purposes – and type of pronunciation – e.g. for a more or less localized or generalized variety of English. Such an approach will seek to identify the specific functions which the learner needs to perform in English as well as the specific audiences with whom s/he will be inter-acting and their expectations, orientation to and level of proficiency in English. On the basis of such an analysis, it will be possible to deter-mine the necessary forms and functions that are to be the focus of instruction as well as an appropriate goal for English phonological pro-ficiency.

Where the functions which the learner needs to perform are restricted to relatively formal interactions, this will determine a different variety of English as appropriate than if the functions center primarily on con-versation. Where the necessary functions are both formal and informal, the learner's goal is a more ambitious one, as it will require learning a variety of repertoires, speech styles and areas of lexis. Audiences that include people outside the learner's home community dictate different instructional goals than audiences composed of students or peers in the home community. Where the people with whom the learner will need to interact are native speakers of English or native speakers of languages different from that of the learner's native language, it is necessary to aim towards generalized norms for phonology that can be understood by members of other speech communities.

If English is being learned for community-internal purposes, the norms for phonology can be built on those of the local variety, perhaps with attention to style-shifting between vernacular and more general-ized norms. In such cases, as Adegbija (1989) points out in relation to the English spoken in Nigeria, "contrary to widely-held opinions and popular intuitions, in many parts of the world, the best teacher of a second language is not necessarily the native speaker but rather, a speaker versed in the local norms that the language has developed within the community in question" (p. 176). If English is being learned for a combination of community-internal and community-external pur-poses, as for (a) an academic who must function within a local academic community and an international academic community or (b) a businessperson who must communicate with on-site as well as overseas managers, then the learner will need to acquire both community norms as well as a more generalized norm for English pronunciation.

Where English is being learned for instrumental reasons, as a way to expand the learner's access to social goods, whether within or outside the home community, the target will be different than if the learner is attempting to shift identity to that of another culture. In cases where the desire is not to replace but rather to supplement the learner's primary spoken variety or varieties, an approach which defines and works towards specific targets for performance in a contrastive and gradual manner seems most likely to achieve success. Such an approach might compare and contrast different varieties and speech styles within and outside the home community, and provide models and practice for gradually incorporating features of these varieties and styles into the learner's repertoire as needed and desired. Rather than seeking to "correct" a learner's pronunciation, this approach is a multi-varietal one focusing on style-shifting and adjustment under appropriate circumstances.

Both teachers and learners can become involved in determining local features of pronunciation and how these differ from the norms of other speech communities. They might do "TV research" or "radio research" on the pronunciation of well-known media figures locally and internationally to help gain a recognition of the diversity of English accents and a familiarity with the varieties of English spoken at home and abroad. Learners can also help to develop their own goals and targets for pronunciation performance by suggesting the lexical areas and/or specific lexical items they want or need to learn. They might also interview people working in their chosen field to get suggestions as to potential problems and areas of focus in phonology. In addition, the sociolinguistic mini-research projects of this book can be adapted for use with secondary, tertiary or adult groups of second language learners.

In the pronunciation or speaking class, the learner can be encouraged to experiment with new forms of pronunciation which can be refined over time to approach the target that has been set for performance. To motivate performance, the learner's attention can be drawn to the specific context effects of the second language in speaking and listening and the relationship of these context effects to fluency and message content. As noted in Pennington (forthcoming), the pronunciation or speaking class can be established as a safe environment for second language learners to practice new roles and identities in simulations of the kinds of communicative tasks they will need to perform outside of class. Classroom work can also encourage learners to view the phonology of the second language as offering them new communicative resources by:

(1) exposing them to a variety of speakers communicating in different social roles and tasks; and

(2) raising their consciousness of the part played by pronunciation in establishing roles and ensuring communicative success.

To help the learner develop intelligibility and overall information-structuring and message coherence, the more salient and general aspects of phonology – including the intonation of basic communicative patterns such as set types of questions and answers, the rhythmic patterns of sentences, understandable pronunciation of key words and basic pronunciation of phonemes – can be addressed before minor points of articulation. It might be valuable as well to simplify the learner's task by focusing on key words in listening and pronunciation activities, under the assumption that function words and the details of articulation are more likely to be acquired both gradually and in context.

The salience, the memorability and the interest of the phonological aspect of speech or of specific aspects of the phonology of the second language can be increased by interrelating oral, aural and visual modalities in instruction. The salience of pronunciation features of the second language can also be enhanced by the use of instructional activities designed to focus the learner's attention on pronunciation, either preparatory to other activities or retrospectively through reflection and feedback on performance. A contrastive focus for such activities can help to encourage the learner to notice the difference between one phonological feature and another, or the effect that one style of pronunciation or another has on the meaning and communicative force of a message.

In building targets for perception and production of English phonology, not only the salience of input but also the breadth of input is important. As part of this breadth of input, language teachers can expose learners to a wide range of speakers and contexts in the second language, through use of recorded material, conversation partners or guest speakers. Along with plentiful input, learners need opportunities to practice speaking and to receive feedback on their performance, in order to trigger and maintain the creative construction process which continually adjusts perceptual targets and performance in the acquisition of a second language.

Thus, a second language learner can benefit from a combination of:

(1) **pre-production** training of pronunciation features and consciousness-raising about the importance of pronunciation in communication;
(2) **in-production** meaning-oriented input arising in the course of language use and through negotiation in communicative tasks; and
(3) **post-production** input in the form of feedback on intelligibility,

overall communicative success and the extent to which specific phonological goals or targets have been achieved.

In this way, both the natural and the tutored learning processes of the learner will be activated to develop the phonological system of the second language on its own terms, as an autonomous communicative resource alongside the mother tongue.

Curriculum activities

1. Critique of pronunciation syllabus

Below is offered a brief syllabus for a one-month low–intermediate pre-university summer Oral English class meeting for 50 minutes three days per week. The course is intended to work on (1) problem areas in phonology, (2) areas of phonology directly related to spoken fluency and (3) the use of grammar in colloquial English. Each day starts out with 10–15 minutes of focused pronunciation practice on a certain area of phonology, then moves to a 35–40 minute activity in oral grammar that incorporates the pronunciation point in a meaningful or communicative activity. The students who take this course also have classes titled Situations and Roleplays, Listening Comprehension, Idiomatic Expression and Topical Discussion.

In looking over the syllabus, consider the degree to which the pronunciation point for each day ties in with the oral grammar point. Then think about the activities that are shown to integrate the pronunciation points for each week with the grammar points listed for that week. Do you think students would benefit from this type of syllabus? Would you use a syllabus like this one?

Brief syllabus for low–intermediate Oral English course

WEEK	PRONUNCIATION	ORAL GRAMMAR	ACTIVITIES
1	s/z	singular/plural simple present tense	description of students
	t/th	chronological order	instructions with ordinal numbers
	l/r	commands	TPR (i.e. Total Physical Response) with left and right body parts

WEEK	PRONUNCIATION	ORAL GRAMMAR	ACTIVITIES
2	rhythm and reduced words	count/non-count nouns	descriptions of pictures, scenes
	contracted forms	modal verbs	inferencing activities
	basic intonation	future forms	future plans
3	contrastive vs. weak stress	question patterns	checking for comprehension paraphrasing for clarity
	voiceless/ voiced stops	simple past tense	story-telling; past activities
	contrast of stops in initial, medial and final positions	comparative/ superlative	comparing famous people, places, objects, movies, etc.
4	vowels	present progressive	descriptions of ongoing events
		present perfect	What've you done? (one-upmanship)
		have/get	life experiences: 1st car, job, kiss

2. Critique of pronunciation component of a Speaking/Listening course

The structure shown below was followed in a high–intermediate Speaking/Listening class in a pre-university intensive English course in the U.S. Critique the organization of the course and the treatment of pronunciation in the context of other speaking and listening skills.

High–intermediate Speaking/Listening course

Course goals
In this course, you will learn how to:

(a) express yourself clearly in English in describing
    • facts • ideas • opinions • feelings
(b) express your meaning in different manners, such as

- logically
- emotionally

- directly
- indirectly

- politely
- impolitely

(c) get information by
  - questioning

- listening actively

Course activities

The focus of the course is on a variety of speaking activities in pairs and small groups, such as discussion of topics of interest and information-gap activities. It also includes regular listening practice and daily work on pronunciation. In addition, students present three speeches during the semester on the topics below. The emphasis in all activities is on producing and comprehending fluent English in conversational and lecture styles.

Approximate time per activity

Pair/group speaking practice – 40%
Pronunciation – 20%
Listening – 30%
Speeches – 10%

> *First speech* Give a brief autobiography and then focus on something unusual or especially interesting about yourself (2–3 minutes).
> *Second speech* Tell about the most unusual, exciting or frightening experience of your life (4–5 minutes).
> *Third speech* Describe something which you really like or which you are really interested in (8–10 minutes).

You will prepare for each speech by making a tape recording of your topic and turning it into the teacher one week in advance for feedback on the topic, its organization, your style of presentation, pronunciation, grammar and choice of words.

Daily schedule (class period 50 minutes)

Monday	*Tuesday*	*Wednesday*	*Thursday*	*Friday*
Pronunciation	Pronunciation	Pronunciation	Pronunciation	Pronunciation
Pair/group speaking practice	Speeches Listening practice	Listening practice Pair/group speaking practice	Listening practice Pair/group speaking practice	Speeches Listening practice

3. Curriculum decision-making in relation to pronunciation

Describe whether you would or would not teach pronunciation explicitly under any of the educational circumstances described below. If you would, describe the type of instruction that might be appropriate and how it would fit into the overall structure of the curriculum. If you would not, describe what you would teach instead.

(a) a secondary (high-school) level English course designed for students whose home (native) language is not English and offered as part of the normal public education program for residents in a non-English speaking country

(b) a secondary level English course designed for students whose home language is not English and offered as part of a public bilingual education program for residents in an English speaking country

(c) a primary (elementary) level language program for children in grades 1–8 whose home language is different from the school language

(d) a three-week vacation conversational English course in Hawaii for Japanese students aged 17–18

(e) a three-month, four-hour-per-day intensive language and academic preparation course for intermediate and advanced students intending to pursue university studies in an English speaking country

(f) a mixed-nationality, six-week intensive Business English course meeting six hours per day on weekdays

(g) an adult education night course meeting three nights a week and designed for non-literate adult immigrants who have recently arrived in an English-speaking country

4. Description and classifications of pronunciation activities

Describe and then classify according to the scheme of Figure 6.2 the types of teaching/learning activities characteristic of the following approaches to pronunciation:

	DESCRIPTION	CLASSIFICATION
Audiolingual		
The Silent Way		
Community Language Learning		
The Natural Approach		

As an additional or alternate activity, classify the pronunciation teaching activities of a published text (e.g. Gilbert 1984) or article (e.g. Pica 1984) – or a group of these – according to the scheme of Figure 6.2.

5. Classification of sample pronunciation activities

Categorize the following activities according to the activity types shown in Figure 6.2. Consider any ways in which the activities might be modified, improved, expanded or integrated with other activities to increase effectiveness or adapt them for a particular audience of second language learners.

Example 1: Final voiced/voiceless stops

First, a word is selected from among minimal pairs in sentences. Then a response is selected from among two possibilities according to the meaning of the sentence just spoken. This type of exercise works well in an alternating pair format in which Partner A speaks and Partner B responds, then B speaks and A responds, etc. Partner A may be the teacher or a student. If the respondent makes a response that the speaker thinks is not appropriate, then the speaker repeats what s/he said in the frame, "No, I said _____." For example:

PARTNER A'S CHOICES

(a) He (hid/hit) the ball.

(b) Does he write poems?
     Does he ride horses?

(c) There's the (cab/cap).

(d) I'm glad you caught it!
     Help me catch it!

(e) He's a (bad/bat) boy.

(f) Put this one on.
     What do you need it for?

PARTNER B'S CHOICES

(a) Where did he hide it?
     Where did he hit it?

(b) He (writes/rides) well.

(c) Let's get in.
     Why don't you put it on?

(d) There's a mouse in the
     (bag/back).

(e) Are you going to hit him?
     Then throw him the bat.

(f) I need a (robe/rope).

Example 2: vowel pairs

In this exercise, A pronounces a word in a minimal pair choice. B uses the word that s/he thinks s/he heard in an original sentence. B should be instructed to make sentences which express his/her knowledge or real feelings or opinions. If A thinks that B used the wrong word in his/her sentence, A makes a selection from the same minimal pair and B responds again to the word selected. This sequence is continued until A thinks that B has given the correct response. Then A is free to select a different item. In this way, the two speakers must work together to practice the sounds until both are consistently making the same distinctions.

The teacher or a student can be A. B can be one student or a circle of students who respond one by one as B to each of A's pronunciations of one of the words. Examples for this type of exercise are given below. The progression of the activity, which begins when A says *sheep* and B responds *I prefer.* . . , is indicated by the starred answer choices. For example:

PARTNER A'S CHOICES	PARTNER B'S CHOICES
(a) (*sheep/ship)	(a) Sheep's wool makes warm sweaters.
	* I prefer traveling by plane rather than ship.
(sheep/*ship)	* Sheep usually smell bad. I get seasick when I travel by ship.
(*sheep/ship)	* Australia was built on the back of a sheep. The Titanic was an unlucky ship.
(b) (*cop/cap)	(b) A cop protects us from bad guys.
	* A cap protects us from the sun.
(cop/*cap)	Eddie Murphy is not a cop.
	* Eddie Murphy often wears a cap.

Example 3: final voiced/voiceless stops

This activity simulates the retelling of a story and the recall of information by second and third parties, illustrating the difficulties that arise when the original words are not correctly pronounced or comprehended.

One person tells the story below by choosing one of the alternatives for each pair of words in parentheses and then telling the story aloud in the present tense.

A (bat/bad) boy steals a (cap/cab) and a silk (robe/rope), which he puts in the (back/bag) on the seat of his vehicle. Later, feeling guilty, he (writes/rides) aimlessly for hours. The next day, his partner (hits/hides) him until he gets hysterical, a neighbor hears the screams and calls the police. The police find him with the stolen goods and arrest him.

A second person then retells the story using past tense in the frame: "Did you hear about the (bat/bad) boy who stole a. . . " A third person then recapitulates the key points of the story in the format: "It was about a boy who takes care of the bats on a baseball team, who stole a taxi and a silk dressing gown. . . " The original storyteller (the first person) then attempts to correct any misinformation of the third party version of the original story, using the original words, in the format: "No, it was about a bad boy who stole a cap and a rope. . . "

6. Connecting work on phonology with work on grammar

How might the material below be used to tie in work on reduced stress with grammatical work on articles and prepositions?

Articles

Key examples
  (1) Give me *a* pen.
       Which pen?
       The one on *the* paper.
       The red one.
  (2) *A* man stood up and *a* man sat down.
       A man stood up and *the* man sat down.
  (3) Where's *the* teacher?
  (4) Could you open *the* door?
  (5) *The* women in *the* class like *the* men in *the* class.
       Women like men.
  (6)   *the* English class
  (7) Where's *a* library?
       Where's *the* library?
  (8) *the* moon, *the* sun
  (9) Hi, my name is Lenny Kravitz.
       Are you *THE* Lenny Kravitz?
  (10) Don't be *a* Madonna!
  (11) I'll have *a* Big Mac to go, please, and *a* fries, too.
  (12) I'll have *the* filet mignon au poivre, medium rare, please.

Cloze passage
_____ man bought_____ parrot that could speak five languages for ten thousand dollars. _____ pet shop owner said that he would deliver _____ bird that afteroon. When _____ proud owner got home, he asked his wife

if ____ parrot had been delivered. "Yes," she answered. "Where is it?" he asked. "In ____ oven," she answered. "But he could speak five languages." "Well," asked ____ wife, "Why didn't he speak up?"

Prepositions

Where do you LIVE?
_____ the planet EARTH.

WHERE on the _____?
_____ ASia.

WHERE in _____?
_____ Hong KONG.

WHERE in _____?
_____ KOWloon CITY.

WHERE in _____?
_____ ARgyle STREET.

WHERE on _____?
_____ the SOUTH SIDE.

WHERE on the _____?
_____ number EIGHT HUNdred.

WHERE at _____?
_____ Building C.

WHERE in _____?
_____ the TENTH FLOOR.

WHERE on the _____?
_____ the NORTH END of the HALL.

In which _____ on the _____?
_____ flat 10-01 (TEN OH ONE).

7. Design of a pronunciation unit or lesson

Select one of the Teaching Ideas from other chapters or from a published text and use it as a jumping off point for designing a pronunciation lesson or unit that includes the steps I A–B (Background to lesson preparation) and II A–D (Lesson components) as illustrated in this chapter.

8. Sociolinguistic mini-research: older learners who achieve native-like pronunciation in a second language

Design and carry out an investigation yourself or with the aid of your students as researchers or subjects that seeks to shed some light on the question of why some learners (adolescents or adults) have more success in developing a native-like accent in a second language than others. One way of investigating this question is to identify one or more older learners who have native-like pronunciation and then try to uncover factors which might account for their superior achievement, such as their learning approach and strategies, the circumstances under which they learned the language, their relevant personal characteristics and their attitudes towards the language and its speakers. A questionnaire might be designed for this purpose or an interview schedule made up to question subjects directly. If time permits, a questionnaire plus follow-up interview will probably yield the most complete information.

It might be easier to isolate the factors involved if you compare and contrast a speaker or speakers who exhibit native-like pronunciation in a second language with one or more speakers whose age is the same or younger and whose amount of experience with a second language is the same or more, but whose pronunciation is not native-like.

Note that in order to identify speakers in terms of their pronunciation proficiency, some sort of assessment will have to be made. As you design your research project, consider the best way to assess pronunciation proficiency in light of the discussion of this chapter. You may also wish to evaluate other aspects of subjects' communicative competence to supplement and complement the assessment of their pronunciation.

9. Action research: diagnosis and feedback on pronunciation

Have each of your students make a short recording in which they talk about their family in English. Then apply the analytical system of Appendix A to diagnosing and giving feedback on their phonology. Ask the students to give you feedback on the same tape as to the effectiveness of your feedback and any aspects of it that they did not understand. Use your students' comments to improve your feedback techniques.

10. Action research: classification of student errors

Place a tape recorder in the middle of a group of 3–4 students and record them as they discuss the problems they have experienced with English. Then use the categories of Appendix B to classify and prioritize their pronunciation problems and errors for remediation. Have another teacher listen to the tape and respond to your analysis, offering a different perspective and new ideas, and revise your classification accordingly. Use the classification as a basis to design one or more of the following:

- a pronunciation syllabus for a semester or whole year;
- a pronunciation lesson or unit to address a particular problem or group of problems;
- pronunciation activities to supplement other class activities;
- self-help activities for individual students.

Appendix A: Hierarchical analysis of student pronunciation

The following is intended as a guide for analyzing student pronunciation. It can be used to diagnose areas for attention and to give appropriate feedback, e.g. following students' oral presentations or on a tape-recorded sample of individual students' speech. The points to listen for are listed in descending order of generality and importance. This means that if you have only limited time to work on pronunciation, it is probably best to spend time on the features which occur earlier rather than later in the hierarchy.

I. Level 1

Listen for general characteristics and overall voice quality which interfere with intelligibility or make the accent sound especially non-native, i.e. non-English or non-standard. In particular, listen for:

A. *Transsegmentals*

(1) *Intonation* (pitch contour on phrases and sentences) which is:
   (a) Relatively flat (monotonic), that is, which does not show sufficient variation in the range or in the regular alternation of high and low pitches.
   (b) Unusually high or low throughout or in certain parts of the discourse (e.g. very high pitch on the first word of a sentence).
(2) *Stress* (force of articulation) which is relatively even (monotonic), that is, which does not show sufficient variation in the range or in the regular alternation of strong and weak syllables. Also listen for stress which is unusually strong or weak throughout.

B. *Segmentals*

(3) *Pervasive features* of segmental articulations, such as:
   (a) A tendency to *open* articulation throughout speech.
      [1] Changing non-continuant sounds to continuant sounds:
         [a] changing sibilants to shibilants, e.g. /s/ as [š]; or

      [b] changing stops to fricatives, e.g. /t/ as [θ], /d/ as [ð], /b/ as [β] or [v], /p/ as [ɸ] or [f].

  [2] Lowering of vowels to ones with a more open jaw position, e.g. /i:/ as [ɪ], /ɛ/ as [æ], /ʌ/ as [a], /u:/ as [ʊ].

  [3] Leaving off the final syllable or phoneme(s) of words.

 (b) A tendency to *close* articulation throughout speech.

  [1] Changing continuant sounds to non-continuant sounds:

    [a] changing shibilants to sibilants, e.g. /š/ as [s]; or

    [b] changing fricatives to stops, e.g. /θ/ as [t], /ð/ as [d], /f/ as [p], /v/ as [b].

  [2] Raising of vowels to ones with a less open jaw position, e.g. /ɪ/ as [i:], /ɛ/ as [e:], /ʊ/ as [u:], /ɔ/ as [o:]).

  [3] Raising the tongue in the pronunciation of stops, e.g. /k/ as [kʲ], /t/ as [tʲ], /b/ as [bʲ].

 (c) A tendency to articulate sounds *far forward* in the mouth.

  [1] Articulating alveolars as dentals, e.g. /t/ as [t̪], /d/ as [d̪], /s/ as [s̪].

  [2] Articulating velars as palatals or alveolars, e.g. /k/ as [kʲ] or [t], /g/ as [gʲ] or [d], /ŋ/ as [n].

 (d) A tendency to articulate sounds *far backward* in the mouth.

  [1] Articulating dentals or alveolars with a retroflex tongue position, e.g. /t/ or /θ/ as [ʈ], /d/ or /ð/ as [ɖ], /s/ as [ʂ], /z/ as [ʐ].

  [2] Articulating sounds with tension in a back area (velar or pharyngeal) of the vocal tract.

II. Level 2

Listen for individual sounds which are regularly mispronounced or individual words and phrases pronounced in a way hampering intelligibility or naturalness. In particular, listen for:

A. *Transsegmentals*

(1) Words or phrases pronounced with *an incorrect pattern* of stresses or intonation, such as:

  (a) A strong stress on the wrong syllable.

  (b) All syllables equally stressed or pitched.

  (c) Syllables which are stressed too weakly.

  (d) Over-strong stress (i.e. over-loud voice or over-high pitch) on particular words, giving an impression of emphasis or focus not intended.

B. *Segmentals*

(2) *Phonemic substitutions*, i.e. where an English or a native language phoneme is substituted for the correct phoneme.

(3) *Allophonic substitutions*, i.e. where the phoneme is mispronounced by using the wrong allophone (phonetic variant) for that phoneme.

(4) *Slight mispronunciations*, i.e. where the phoneme is pronounced almost, but not quite, correctly.

III. Feedback

The analytical categories above provide direction for giving students oral or taped feedback on their pronunciation, focusing only or first on higher level concerns. The feedback in each area can follow a four-step process, starting with the Level 1 concerns and moving later to the Level 2 concerns using the categories and terminology above as a guide.

(1) *Compliment the student's performance*
e.g. "I found your tape very interesting, particularly the part about your father and his job. Your voice sounds very good overall in this recording, with lots of variety of pitch and stress."

(2) *Describe a problem*
e.g. "I notice that your pronunciation is too open in some words and sounds."

(3) *Give examples of the problem*
e.g. "For example, you open your lips when you say the [b] in *able*, so it sounds like you are saying [v] instead of [b]. When you say the [p] in *applied*, your lips are also rather open, so it sounds like [f] instead of [p]. The opening in your mouth behind your teeth is also rather large as well when you say *super*; it sounds like [š], not [s], when you say it this way. Your mouth is also quite open when you say [a] rather than [ə] in *bird*.

(4) *Give instructions for remediation*
e.g. "To correct this problem of open pronunciation in /b/ and /p/, put your lips together more tightly when you pronounce those sounds. When you pronounce [s], make only a small space between your teeth. The tip of your tongue should be up just behind your top teeth with only a small opening for the air to go through. To pronounce *bird* with a less open vowel sound, do not open your mouth all the way as for [a] but make it somewhat less open as for [ə]."

Appendix B: Pedagogical classification of pronunciation errors and problems

I. *Most important pronunciation errors or problems*

A. *Those which occur most frequently*
(1) pronunciation of a particular phoneme (e.g. /r/ as [rr])
(2) mispronunciation of a common morpheme (e.g. past tense -*ed* as [əd] after voiceless stops, as in *worked, stopped*)
(3) mispronunciation of a common lexical item (e.g. *she, can't*)

B. *Those which are the most serious, i.e. have the greatest effect on intelligibility*
(1) stress placed on wrong words or syllables of words
(2) misleading intonation (e.g. high pitched intonation on old information; a sharp rise or fall, or a separate intonation pattern on each word)
(3) loss of one or more final consonants (e.g. in *can't, sent, dusk*)

II. *Pronunciation errors or problems that will benefit most from remediation*

A. *Those whose improvement will have the greatest effect on performance*
(1) a very soft or monotonous voice
(2) incorrect stress or intonation
(3) loss of final consonants in lexical items

B. *Those for which there is the greatest chance of successful remediation, i.e. those which will be easiest to correct*
(1) a very soft or monotonous voice
(2) misleading intonation
(3) stress on incorrect word

III. *Errors or problems identified by the learners themselves as aspects of their language needing attention*

A. *Stereotyped errors*
(1) unreduced vowels
(2) substitutions such as /l/ and /r/, /s/ and /š/, /i:/ and /ı/
(3) loss of *-ed* and *-(e)s* endings

B. *Errors causing embarrassment or obvious miscommunication*
(1) incorrect stress or intonation
(2) mispronunciation of common words (e.g. *she, his*)
(3) unintential profanity caused by phonemic substitutions (e.g. opening of the initial consonant in *sit* or lowering/laxing of the vowel in *sheet*)

C. *Items they would like to pronounce correctly*
(1) new words, phrases or sentences which they have recently encountered in their reading or picked up from friends or the media
(2) common or favorite expressions
(3) key words in their field of specialization

IV *Errors or problems in areas of language that are of particular importance for the learner's social, academic, or professional needs*

A. *Errors or problems in communicational pragmatics*
(1) inappropriate voice quality (e.g. talking on the telephone socially or professionally, disagreeing with someone in different social, academic or professional circumstances)
(2) incorrect or misleading intonation
(3) failure to use prosodic backgrounding and foregrounding to indicate the informational structure of messages

B. *Errors or problems related to specialized areas of language*
(1) stress placed on the wrong syllables of key words in the learner's field of specialization
(2) lack of elision and other coarticulatory effects in commonly used or key phrases
(3) commonly mispronounced words or expressions needed for social, academic or professional encounters

Appendix C: Sample unit plan for teaching the /r/–/l/ distinction

Structure of the unit plan: Four lessons, moving from mechanical and controlled to free practice, in a one-week period, 45 minutes each; plus two follow-up activities for 1–2 weeks later.

Goals of unit: (1) To increase student awareness of the /r/–/l/ distinction; (2) to increase intelligibility of student pronunciation of /r/–/l/; (3) to continue to develop phonological concepts introduced in unit one; (4) to continue to develop a consciousness of and interest in pronunciation.

Audience: Japanese, Korean and Chinese students, ages 18–20, taking a ten-week conversational English course in the US. All students are high school graduates; some have 1–2 years of university study.

Background of unit: The class meets daily at 9:00 am for one and a half hours, with 45 minutes four times per week devoted to pronunciation and the rest of the time on those four days devoted to various types of speaking and listening activities. The teacher has designated certain areas of phonology as problems for the students in this class, including certain consonant and vowel phonemes. A persistent problem for this group has always been the /r/–/l/ distinction.

This is the second unit of the term. The course includes ten units of four lessons each. The first unit was devoted to working on general aspects of pronunciation such as the voiced/voiceless distinction, stops vs. continuants, lip shapes and tongue positions. The third unit is on stops, the fourth on the interdentals, the fifth on the sibilants, the sixth on consonant clusters, the seventh on vowels, the eighth on stress and rhythm, the ninth on coarticulation and contracted forms, the tenth on intonation.

Lesson 1 (Monday): Presentation and controlled practice

Lesson objective

To recognize and produce the difference in lip shapes associated with the /r/–/l/ contrast in a small set of minimal pairs illustrating this contrast in initial position.

Pre-lesson

The teacher will tie this lesson in with previous work on differences in lip shapes for English sounds. She has assessed the students as having a lot of trouble producing /r/–/l/ through observation of their speech in pair work.

Classroom arrangement

Students start out all seated and facing the blackboard. Later, they will move into groups of three.

Materials and aids

A chart on which is written in large letters:

	LIST 1	LIST 2
	read	lead
	red	led
	rap	lap
	row	low

Lesson activities

(9:00–9:45 Students interview each other about things they like – movies, books, rock stars, music, songs; they prepare for Friday a 5-minute oral report on the person they interviewed. On Wednesday, they bring in a tape-recorded preliminary version of this report, so that the teacher can give feedback before they present their report in front of the class. NOTE These activities are not part of the Pronunciation Unit but rather general speaking activities also covered in the class.)

9:45 *Focus – visual modeling*: The teacher holds up the chart and silently models the lip shapes of the words in each list, first going down the columns and then across the rows, pointing each time to the word being modeled.

9:48 *Focus – visual discrimination*: The teacher displays the chart so that it is clearly visible to the students. Still silent, she holds up one finger, then two, then shrugs. She repeats this routine, then beckons a student to come up to the chart. She motions the student to watch her lips and then silently mouths one of the words in one of the lists. Following the modeling, she holds up one then two fingers, then shrugs. The student indicates the correct answer, either by holding up the correct number of fingers (one or two) or by pointing to the word on the chart. This routine is repeated several times for three different students brought up to the board to work with the teacher while the other students look on.

10:00 *Focus – discrimination practice*: The teacher beckons another volunteer up to the board but this time sits down. The new volunteer is then to take the role of the teacher, continuing the exercise with 2–3 more students that s/he beckons up to the board.

10:15 *Controlled discrimination practice*: Students are told to count off beginning with the number one. The teacher then instructs them to find two partners who are each odd numbers if their number is odd, even numbers if their number is even. After students have formed groups of three, the teacher says that they should decide who will be the "Judge" and the two "Players", and who will go first. She then gives the directions that the first student will pick five words from among the two lists. The first Player writes the five words down on a piece of paper and shows them to the judge. The first player silently dictates the words to the other Player, who will hold up one or two fingers to indicate which list the word is taken from. If the student holds up the wrong number of fingers, then that pair loses one point. The Judge subtracts points from an initial score of ten points. After the first member of the pair has completed all of his/her five words, the second member of the pair selects five words from the two lists and repeats the procedure.

10:30 Lesson over.

Lesson 2 (Tuesday): Presentation and controlled practice (cont'd)

Lesson objective

To recognize and produce the contrasting sounds of /r/ and /l/ in initial, final and medial positions in a small set of minimal pairs, building from those which were introduced the day before.

Pre-lesson

The teacher will tie this lesson in with the previous lesson and with the song activity of the first part of the day (see below).

Classroom arrangement

Students start out all seated and facing the blackboard. Later, they will move into groups of three.

Materials and Aids

A chart on which is written in large letters:

LIST 1	LIST 2
read	lead
red	led
rap	lap
row	low
dear	deal
fair	fail
mare	male
fear	feel
worry	woolly
gentry	gently
fearing	feeling
dearer	dealer

Another chart on which is written the words to the song, "Row, row row your boat":

Row, row, row your boat
Gently down the stream
Merrily, merrily, merrily, merrily
Life is but a dream.

Activity sheets with an A and a B side with the numbers 1 to 12 written spaced out on each side. For each side of the sheet, A or B, each item 1–12 lists three words from one row in the chart. The same numbered item may or may not have the identical listing on side A and side B. For example:

A 1. read	2. led	B. 1. read	2. led
read	red	lead	red
lead	led	read	led

Lesson activities

(9:00–9:45 Students listen to several popular songs and complete cloze exercises on the songs.)

9:45 *Focus – silent and oral modeling*: Using the chart, the teacher pronounces the words in columns and then in rows, first silently then out loud.

9:48 *Focus – aural discrimination*: The teacher tells students to take out a piece of paper and to write a column of a, b, c, etc. up to i. She then says "a" and then one of the words in each row of the lists, telling the students to write down the number of the correct list for that word. She repeats the same procedure for b, c, etc. She then tells the students the correct answers and has them repeat chorally after her for each word.

10:00 *Controlled discrimination practice*: Students are to work in the same groups of three as in the activity for the day before, with the same roles of Players and Judge. The Players complete a pair activity using the activity sheets, beginning with the first Player. The Judge is to use a separate piece of paper, making a column of numbers 1–9. The activity is conducted as follows. The first Player is A, and the second Player is B. The two Players must sit facing each other, and the activity sheet should be held up between the two of them so that the first player sees only the A side and the second Player only the B side. The Judge should sit at a right angle to the two Players or with his/her back turned, so that s/he cannot read either side of the sheet. The first Player and then the second Player read the three words written on his/her side of the activity sheet for number 1. The Judge then writes down "same" if s/he thinks they each read the same list of words in the same order. Otherwise, s/he writes "different". After all nine items have been read and judged, each group checks their answers.

10:15 *Contextualization*: The teacher calls upon individual students to silently act out one of the words in each row on the list. After the last demonstration, the teacher acts out rowing three times. She repeats this action until the students say "row, row, row" in chorus. She then places the chart with the words to "Row, row, row your boat" in a place visible to all students and sings or chants the song slowly several times, inviting students to join in. She then teaches them how to do the song as a round, in which one singer or group begins the line "row, row, row" just after the previous group has begun this part of the song. She then has each group of three take one part in the round, until every group has sung the song through at least twice.

10:30 Lesson over.

Lesson 3 (Wednesday): Structured communicative practice

Lesson objective

To continue the objectives of preceding days, to add communicative practice and to prepare students for the activity of the next day.

Pre-lesson

The teacher will emphasize the same features of pronunciation as she has focused on in previous lessons in this unit.

Classroom arrangement

Students begin facing the board and later move into pairs.

Materials and aids

Two activity sheets, one for Partner A and one for Partner B (after Celce-Murcia 1983):

PARTNER A

	CAROL	LAURA	SHIRLEY
AGE	19		18
HEIGHT		5' 6"	
WEIGHT	125LB.		
SUBJECT	ART	ENGLISH	
EYES		HAZEL	GREEN
HAIR	BLONDE		

PARTNER B

	CAROL	LAURA	SHIRLEY
AGE		20	
HEIGHT	5' 3"		5' 1"
WEIGHT		130LB.	118LB.
SUBJECT			BIOLOGY
EYES	BLUE		
HAIR		BROWN	BLACK

Lesson activities

(9:00–9:45 Students work in small groups to transcribe the words of songs on cassette tapes they have brought in to class.)

9:45 *Review and preparation*: Choral repetition of ra–ra–ra and la–la–la after teacher. Then teacher models a set of names, each of which includes both /r/ and /l/, writing each name on the board as it is pronounced.

| Carol | Laura | Shirley | Charles | Darryl | Alexander |
| Carl | Larry | Stanley | Charlene | Darlene | Alexandra |

The teacher then calls on individual students to say all of the names until they are producing the names with relatively error-free pronunciation.

10:00 *Structured communicative practice*: Students pick a partner and work in pairs to fill in the missing information on their respective answer sheets. The two partners are seated back to back. Partner A holds the Partner A activity sheet, and Partner B holds his/her activity sheet. Partner A begins the activity by asking Partner B a *wh*-question to obtain one piece of missing information on his/her sheet. For example, Partner A might ask Partner B, "How old is Laura?" Partner B answers, and Partner A fills in the information. Then Partner B asks Partner A a *wh-* question to obtain a missing piece of information such as, "How old is Carol?" The two partners alternate turns until all of the information on each activity sheet is filled in. When finished, the students check their answers.

10:30 Lesson over.

Lesson 4 (Thursday): Structured/free communicative practice

Lesson objectives

To integrate and extend the material of previous lessons.

To communicate using previously practiced vocabulary in a creative activity utilizing the /r/–/l/ contrast.

Pre-lesson

Students have now had considerable practice on the /r/–/l/ distinction and are comfortable working in the pair format.

Classroom arrangement

Students begin facing the board and then move into pairs, moving back to facing front later.

Materials and aids

Paper, pencils
On the board the teacher has written the same names as were written on the board in the previous lesson (see above).

Lesson activities

(9:00 *Review and preparation*: Choral repetition of the names on the board.

9:05–9:45 *Structured/free practice*: Student pairs write a story or dialogue using the characters introduced in the previous lesson or people they know who have the same name as one of those characters or one of the other names introduced the previous day. The activity can be viewed as "structured" if the students write on the model of the activity sheets from the previous day and "free" if they create a dialogue or story that departs from this structure. The teacher may give the students the option to select the more structured or the free activity. When they have completed their dialogue or story, each pair make up 2–3 questions about it to ask the class.)

9:45 *Structured practice*: Student pairs present their dialogues/stories to the class. Students in the audience take notes on content and are then asked to answer the questions orally. The teacher monitors pronunciation and gives feedback after each presentation.

10:30 Lesson over.

First follow-up activity

To be used one week later for review.

9:45 *Review and preparation*: Teacher reminds students of different lip shapes of /r/ and /l/ by modeling the pairs *red/led* and *rip/lip* and then going around the class to check students' pronunciation of the pairs.

9:50 *Structured Practice*: Students are put into groups to create an original story or poem that incorporates the phrases below:

a pure heart
the courage of a lion

ruby red lips
a fair princess
lovely long hair
four prancing horses
an ivory carriage
a golden ring
her father and mother
her brothers and sisters

Each group writes up its story or poem, and then assigns parts of the story/poem to different group members to present to the class as a whole.

10:20 Each group presents its version of the story, and then the stories are handed in to the teacher.

10:30 Lesson over.

Second follow-up activity

To be used two weeks later for review, during the last 20 minutes of class.

(The teacher has previously consolidated the best elements of the students' stories and poems from the week before and prepared one sentence from the story for each student.)

10:10 Students are each given a sentence from the story to memorize.

10:13 Students are told to line themselves up in the correct order to tell the story by reciting their line and listening to other students recite their lines.

10:15 Students tell the story by reciting their lines one by one. If they are in the wrong order, they will discover this and rearrange themselves. The story is then repeated, following the same procedure.

10:25 Students remain standing to sing "Row, row, row your boat" three times all the way through.

10:30 Lesson over.

References

Abdulaziz M H 1991 East Africa (Tanzania and Kenya). *English around the world* ed J Cheshire. Cambridge University Press, Cambridge, pp 391–401.

Adegbija E 1989 Lexico-semantic variation in Nigerian English. *World Englishes.* **8**: 165–77.

Bailey C-J N, Maroldt K, 1977 The French lineage of English. *Langues en contact – pidgins – creoles – languages in contact.* TBL Verlag Gunter Narr, Tu"bingen, pp 21–53.

Bansal R K 1969 *The intelligibility of Indian English.* Central Institute of English, Hyderabad. Cited from Wells 1982, p 631.

Bansal R K 1990 The pronunciation of English in India. *Studies in the pronunciation of English: A commemorative volume in honour of A C Gimson* ed S Ramsaran. Routledge, London and New York, pp 219–30.

Bayard D 1991 Social constraints on the phonology of New Zealand English. *English around the world* ed J Cheshire. Cambridge University Press, Cambridge, pp 169–86.

Berry J 1976 Tone and intonation in Guyanese English. *Linguistic studies offered to Joseph Greenberg, II: Phonology.* Anma Libri, Saratoga, CA, pp 263–70. Cited from Wells 1982, p 574.

Bokamba E G 1991 West Africa. *English around the world* ed J Cheshire. Cambridge University Press, Cambridge, pp 493–508.

Bolinger D L 1985 The inherent iconism of intonation. *Iconicity in syntax* ed J Haiman. John Benjamins, Amsterdam, pp 97–108.

Bolinger D 1986. *Intonation and its parts: Melody in spoken English.* Stanford University Press, Stanford, CA.

Bolton K, Kwok H 1990 The dynamics of the Hong Kong accent: Social identity and sociolinguistic description. *Journal of Asian Pacific Communication.* **1**: 147–72.

Brazil D, Coulthard M, Johns C 1980 *Discourse intonation and language teaching.* Longman, Harlow.

Brend R M 1975 Male–female intonation patterns in American English. *Language and sex: Difference and dominance* ed B Thorne, N Henley. Newbury House, Rowley, MA.

Britain D 1992 Linguistic change in intonation: The use of high rising terminals in New Zealand English. *Language Variation and Change.* **4**: 77–104.

Britain D, Newman J 1992 High rising terminals in New Zealand English. *Journal of the International Phonetic Association.* **22**: 1–11.

267

Brown G, Currie K L, Kenworthy J 1980 *Questions of intonation.* Croom Helm, London.

Browne S C, Huckin T N 1987 Pronunciation tutorials for nonnative technical professionals: A program description. *Current perspectives on pronunciation* ed J Morley. Teachers of English to Speakers óf Other Languages, Washington, DC, pp 41–57.

Burns I M 1992 Pronunciation-based listening exercises. *Teaching American English pronunciation* ed P Avery, S Ehrlich. Oxford University Press, Oxford, pp 197–205.

Busà M G 1992 On the production of English vowels by Italian speakers with different degrees of accent. *New sounds 92,* Proceedings of the 1992 Amsterdam Symposium on the Acquisition of Second-Language Speech ed J Leather, A James. University of Amsterdam, Netherlands, pp 47–63.

Carr E B 1972 *Da kine talk: From Pidgin to Standard English in Hawaii.* The University Press of Hawaii, Honolulu, HI.

Celce-Murcia M 1983 Activities for teaching pronunciation communicatively. *CATESOL News.* **15** (May): 10.

Celce-Murcia M 1987. Teaching pronunciation as communication. *Current perspectives on pronunciation* ed J Morley. Teachers of English to Speakers of Other Languages, Washington, DC, pp 1–12.

Chambers J K 1991 Canada. *English around the world* ed J Cheshire. Cambridge University Press, Cambridge, pp 89–107.

Cheshire J (ed) 1991a *English around the world.* Cambridge University Press, Cambridge.

Cheshire J (ed) 1991b The UK and the USA. *English around the world.* Cambridge University Press, Cambridge, pp 13–36.

Ching M 1982 The question intonation in assertions. *American Speech.* **57**: 95–107.

Chomsky C 1970 Reading, writing, and phonology. *Harvard Educational Review.* **40** (2): 287–310.

Chomsky N, Halle M 1968 *Sound pattern of English.* Harper and Row, New York.

Clark J, Yallop C 1990 *An introduction to phonetics and phonology.* Blackwell, Oxford.

Clennell C 1986 Stress: No ESL lesson should be without it. *Prospect.* **2**(1): 89–97.

Collins B, Mees I M 1992 Differentiated approaches for the acquisition of articulatory setting by second-language learners. *New sounds 92,* Proceedings of the 1992 Amsterdam Symposium on the Acquisition of Second-language Speech ed J Leather, A James. University of Amsterdam, Netherlands, pp 76–85.

Cooper F S, Delattre P C, Liberman A M, Borst J M, Gerstman L J 1952 Some experiments in the perception of synthetic speech sounds. *Journal of the Acoustical Society of America.* **24**: 597–606. Reprinted in *Readings in acoustic phonetics* 1967 ed I Lehiste. The M.I.T. Press, Cambridge, MA, pp 273–82.

Crookes G, Schmidt R W 1991 Motivation: Reopening the research agenda. *Language Learning.* **41**: 469–512.

Cruttenden A 1981 Falls and rises: Meanings and universals. *Journal of Linguistics.* **17**: 77–91.

Cruttenden A 1986 *Intonation.* Cambridge University Press, Cambridge.

Cruttenden A 1990 Nucleus placement and three classes of exception. *Studies in the pronunciation of English: A commemorative volume in honour of A C Gimson* ed S Ramsaran. Routledge, London and New York, pp 9–18.

Currie K 1979 Intonational systems of Scottish English. University of Edinburgh, Scotland. Unpublished PhD dissertation. Cited in Macafee (1983).

Cutler A, Mehler J 1993 The periodicity bias. *Journal of Phonetics.* **21**: 103–8.

D'Souza J 1992 The relationship between code-mixing and the new varieties of English: Issues and implications. *World Englishes.* **11**: 217–23.

Donegan P J 1978 On the natural phonology of vowels. The Ohio State University. Unpublished PhD. dissertation.

Dorrill G 1986 A comparison of stressed vowels of black and white speakers in the south. In *Language variety in the south* ed M B Montgomery, G Bailey. University of Alabama Press, Alabama, pp 149–57.

Downing J 1965 *The initial teaching alphabet explained and illustrated.* Fifth edition. Cassell, Heidelberg.

Eagleson R D 1984 English in Australia and New Zealand. *English as a world language* ed R W Bailey, M Görlach. Cambridge University Press, Cambridge, pp 415–38.

Edelsky C 1982 Writing in a bilingual program: The relation of L1 and L2 texts. *TESOL Quarterly* **16**: 211–29.

Esling J H 1987 Methodology for voice setting awareness in language classes. *Revue de Phonétique Apliquée.* **85**: 449–73.

Esling J H 1991 Sociophonetic variation in Canada. *English around the world* ed J Cheshire. Cambridge University Press, Cambridge, pp 123–33.

Esling J H 1994a Voice quality. *The encyclopedia of language and linguistics* ed R Asher et al. Pergamon, Oxford, pp 4950–3.

Esling J H 1994b Some perspectives on accent: Range of voice quality variation, the periphery, and focusing. *Pronunication pedagogy and theory: New views, new direction* ed J Morley. TESOL, Alexandria, VA, pp 51–63.

Esling J H, Warkentyne H J 1993 Retracting of /æ/ in Vancouver English. *Focus on Canada* ed S Clarke. Varieties of English around the world, G11. John Benjamins, Amsterdam/Philadelphia, pp 229–46.

Firth S 1992a Pronunciation syllabus design: A question of focus. *Teaching American English pronunciation* ed P Avery, S Ehrlich. Oxford University Press, Oxford, pp 173–83.

Firth S 1992b Developing self-correcting and self-monitoring strategies. *Teaching American English pronunciation* ed P Avery, S Ehrlich. Oxford University Press, Oxford, pp 215–19.

Flege J E 1981 The phonological basis of foreign accent: A hypothesis. *TESOL Quarterly.* **15**: 443–5.

Flege J 1988 The production and perception of foreign language speech sounds. *Human communication and its disorders* ed H Winitz. Ablex, Norwood, NJ, pp 224–401.

Flege J 1990 English vowel production by Dutch talkers: More evidence for the 'similar' vs. 'new' distinction. *New sounds 90*, Proceedings of the 1990 Amsterdam Symposium on the Acquisition of Second-Language Speech ed J Leather, A James. University of Amsterdam, Netherlands, pp 255–93.

Gardner R, Lambert W 1972 *Attitudes and motivation in second language learning*. Newbury House, Rowley, MA.

Gibbons J 1987 *Code-mixing and code choice: A Hong Kong case study*. Multilingual Matters, Clevedon, England.

Giegerich H J 1992 *English phonology: An introduction*. Cambridge University Press, Cambridge.

Gilbert J B 1984 *Clear Speech: Pronunciation and listening comprehension in North American English*. 2nd edition. Cambridge University Press, New York.

Giles H, Powesland P F 1975 *Speech styles and social evaluation*. Academic Press, London.

Guy G, Horvath B, Vonwiller J, Daisley E, Rogers I 1986 An intonation change in progress in Australian English. *Language in Society*. **15**: 23–52.

Hancock I F, Angogo R 1984 English in East Africa. *English as a world language* ed R W Bailey, M Görlach. Cambridge University Press, Cambridge, pp 306–23.

Harris M M 1969 The retroflection of postvocalic /r/ in Austin. *American Speech*. **44**: 263–71.

Hindle D 1978 Approaches to vowel normalization in the study of natural speech. *Linguistic variation: Models and methods* ed D Sankoff. Academic Press, New York, pp 161–71.

Holder M 1972 Word accentual patterns in Guyanese English (GE) compared to British English (RP norm). *Proceedings of the 7th International Congress of Phonetic Sciences*. Mouton, The Hague, pp 897–9.

Horvath B M 1985 *Variation in Australian English: The sociolects of Sydney*. Cambridge University Press, Cambridge.

Hymes D 1974 *Foundations in sociolinguistics: An ethnographic approach*. University of Pennsylvania Press, Philadelphia.

James E, Mahut C, Latkiewicz, G 1989 The investigation of an apparently new intonation pattern in Toronto English. *Information Communication*. Speech and Voice Society and Phonetics Laboratory, University of Toronto. **10**: 11–17. Cited in Britain and Newman 1992.

Kachru B B (ed) 1982 *The other tongue: English across cultures*. Pergamon Press, Oxford.

Kachru B B 1984 South Asian English. *English as a world language* ed R W Bailey, M Görlach. Cambridge University Press, Cambridge, pp 353–83.

Kandiah T 1991 South Asia. *English around the world* ed J Cheshire. Cambridge University Press, Cambridge, pp 271–87.

Kanyoro M R A 1991 The politics of the English language in Kenya and

Tanzania. *English around the world* ed J Cheshire. Cambridge University Press, Cambridge, pp 402–19.

Kenworthy J 1987 *Teaching English pronunciation*. Longman, London.

Knowles G O 1978 The nature of phonological variables in Scouse. *Sociolinguistic patterns in British English* ed P Trudgill. Edward Arnold, London, pp 80–90.

Kroch A 1978 Toward a theory of social dialect variation. *Language in Society.* **7**: 17–36.

Labov W 1966 *The social stratification of English in New York City*. Center for Applied Linguistics, Washington, DC.

Labov W 1972 *Sociolinguistic patterns*. University of Pennsylvania Press, Philadelphia.

Labov W 1988 (August) The causes and consequences of linguistic diversity. Linguistics Department lecture. University of Hawaii, Honolulu, HI.

Labov W, Yaeger M, Steiner R 1972 *A quantitative study of sound change in progress*. Final Report on National Science Foundation contract NSF-GS-3287. US Regional Survey, Philadelphia, PA.

Ladefoged P 1982 *A course in phonetics*. Second edition. Harcourt Brace Jovanovich, New York.

LaFerriere M 1977 Boston short *a*: Social variation as historical residue. *Studies in language variation* eds R Fasold, R Shuy. Georgetown University Press, Washington, DC, pp 100–8.

Lanham L W 1990 Stress and intonation and the intelligbility of South African black English. *Studies in the pronunciation of English: A commemorative volume in honour of A C Gimson* ed S Ramsaran. Routledge, London and New York, pp 243–60.

Lass, R 1990 A 'standard' South African vowel system. *Studies in the pronunciation of English: A commemorative volume in honour of A C Gimson* ed S Ramsaran. Routledge, London and New York, pp 272–85.

Laver J 1980 *The phonetic description of voice quality*. Cambridge University Press, Cambridge.

Laver J, Trudgill, P 1979 Phonetic and linguistic markers in speech. *Social markers in speech* ed K R Scherer, H Giles. Cambridge University Press, Cambridge, pp 1–32.

Lawton D L 1984 English in the Caribbean. *English as a world language* ed R W Bailey, M Görlach. Cambridge University Press, Cambridge, pp 251–80.

Li J, Lim J, Wong M (forthcoming). Variation in postvocalic /r/ among Hong Kong bilinguals. *Perspectives*, Working Papers of the Department of English, City University of Hong Kong.

Liberman A M, Ingemann F, Lisker L, Delattre P, Cooper F S 1959 Minimal rules for synthesizing speech. *Journal of the Acoustical Society of America.* **31**: 1490–9. Reprinted in *Readings in acoustic phonetics* 1967 ed I Lehiste. The MIT Press, Cambridge, MA, pp 333–42.

Lieberman P 1967 *Intonation, perception and language*. MIT Press, Cambridge, MA.

Lieberman P 1986 The acquisition of intonation by infants: Physiology and neural control. *Intonation in discourse* ed C Johns-Lewis. Croom Helm, London, pp 239–57.

Lindgren H 1969 *Spelling reform: A new approach.* Alpha Books, Sydney.

Lindsey G 1990 Quantity and quality in British and American vowel systems. *Studies in the pronunciation of English: A commemorative volume in honour of A C Gimson* ed S Ramsaran. Routledge, London and New York, pp 110–18.

Luke K K, Richards J C 1982 English in Hong Kong: Functions and status. *English World-Wide.* **3**: 47–63.

Macafee C 1983 *Varieties of English around the world: Glasgow.* John Benjamins, Amsterdam.

Malmberg B 1955 The phonetic basis for syllable division. *Studia Linguistica.* **9**: 80–87. Reprinted in *Readings in acoustic phonetics* 1967 ed I Lehiste. The MIT Press, Cambridge, MA, pp 293–300.

Milroy J 1982 Probing under the tip of the iceberg: Phonological normalization and the shape of speech communities. *Sociolinguistic variation in speech communities* ed S Romaine. Edward Arnold, London, pp 35–47.

Milroy J 1991 The interpretation of social constraints on variation in Belfast English. *English around the world* ed J Cheshire. Cambridge University Press, Cambridge, pp 75–85.

Milroy J, Milroy L 1978 Belfast: Change and variation in an urban vernacular. *Sociolinguistic patterns in British English* ed P Trudgill. Edward Arnold, London, pp 19–36.

Milroy L 1980 Language and social networks. Blackwell, Oxford.

Mitchell A G, Delbridge A 1965 *The pronunciation of English in Australia.* Revised edition. Angus and Robertson, Sydney.

Morley J 1984 *Listening and language learning in ESL.* Language in Education: Theory and Practice. Center for Applied Linguistics, Arlington, VA.

Morley J 1991 The pronunciation component in teaching English to speakers of other languages. *TESOL Quarterly.* **25**: 481–520.

Naiman N 1992 A communicative approach to pronunciation teaching. *Teaching American English pronunciation* ed P Avery, S Ehrlich. Oxford University Press, Oxford, pp 163–71.

Pennington M C 1982 The story of S or everything you ever wanted to know about sibilants but were afraid to ask. Linguistics Department, University of Pennsylvania, Philadelphia. Unpublished PhD dissertation.

Pennington M C 1989 Teaching pronunciation from the top down. *RELC Journal.* **20**(1): 20–38.

Pennington M C 1994 *English on the world stage: A cross-language view of code correspondences and their effect on language contact and language learning.* Research Report No. 36. Department of English, City University of Hong Kong, Hong Kong.

Pennington M C (forthcoming) Phonology in language teaching: Essentials of theory and practice. *Beyond methods: Companion components in language teacher education,* ed K Bardovi-Harlig, B S Hartford. McGraw-Hill, New York.

Pennington M C, Richards J C 1986 Pronunciation revisited. *TESOL Quarterly.* **20**: 207–25.

Pica T 1984 Pronunciation activities with an accent on communication. *English Teaching Forum* (July): 2–6.

Pisoni D B Auditory and phonetic memory codes in the discrimination of consonants and vowels. *Perception and Psychophysics.* **13**: 253–60.

Platt J T 1984 English in Singapore, Malysia, and Hong Kong. *English as a world language* ed R W Bailey, M Görlach. Cambridge University Press, Cambridge, pp 384–414.

Poynton C M 1979 Attitudes towards Australian English. Department of Linguistics, University of Sydney. Unpublished ms. Cited in Horvath 1985.

Pride J (ed) 1982 *New Englishes.* Newbury House, Rowley, MA.

Rickford J 1985 Ethnicity as a sociolinguistic boundary. *American Speech.* **60**(2): 99–125.

Romaine S 1978 Postvocalic /r/ in Scottish English: Sound change in progress? *Sociolinguistic patterns in British English* ed P Trudgill. Edward Arnold, London, pp 144–57.

Romaine S 1984 The English language in Scotland. *English as a world language* ed R W Bailey, M Görlach. Cambridge University Press, Cambridge, pp 56–83.

Romaine S 1985 The problem of short /a/ in Scotland. *English World-Wide.* **6**: 165–97.

Rost M 1991 *Listening in action:* Prentice-Hall, New York.

Russ C V J 1984 The geographical and social variation of English in England and Wales. *English as a world language* ed R W Bailey, M Görlach. Cambridge University Press, Cambridge, pp 11–55.

Sahgal A 1991 Patterns of language use in a bilingual setting in India. *English around the world* ed J Cheshire. Cambridge University Press, Cambridge, pp 299–307.

Sampson G 1985 *Writing systems: A linguistic introduction.* Hutchinson, London.

Scherer K R 1979 Personality markers in speech. *Social markers in speech* ed K R Scherer, H Giles. Cambridge University Press, Cambridge, pp 147–201.

Schiffrin D 1987 *Discourse markers.* Cambridge University Press, Cambridge.

Schmied J J 1991 National and subnational features in Kenyan English. *English around the world* ed J Cheshire. Cambridge University Press, Cambridge, pp 420–32.

Scovel T 1988 *A time to speak: A psycholinguistic inquiry into the critical period for human speech.* Newbury House, Cambridge, MA.

Scragg D G 1974 *A history of English spelling.* Manchester University Press, Manchester.

Selinker L 1972 Interlanguage. *International Review of Applied Linguistics.* **10**: 209–31.

Selinker L 1992 *Rediscovering interlanguage.* London: Longman.

Singleton D 1989 *Language acquisition: The age factor.* Multilingual Matters, Clevedon, England.

Smith P K 1985 *Language, the sexes and society.* Basil Blackwell, Oxford, England.

Stevick E W 1978 Toward a practical philosophy of pronunciation: Another view. *TESOL Quarterly.* **12**: 145–50.

Strevens P 1960 Spectra of fricative noise in human speech. *Language and Speech.* **3**: 32–49. Reprinted in *Readings in acoustic phonetics* 1967 ed I Lehiste. The MIT Press, Cambridge, MA, pp 202–19.

Stubbs M 1980 *Language and literacy: The sociolinguistics of reading and writing.* Chapter 3, Some principles of English spelling. Routledge and Kegan Paul, London, pp 43–69.

Todd L 1984 The English Language in Africa. In *English as a World Language* eds R W Bailey, M Görlach. Cambridge University Press, Cambridge pp 281–305.

Trudgill P 1974 *The social differentiation of English in Norwich.* Cambridge University Press, Cambridge.

Trudgill P, Hannah J 1985 *International English: A guide to varieties of Standard English.* Second edition. Edward Arnold, London.

Vanderslice R, Pierson L S 1967 Prosodic features of Hawaiian English. *Quarterly Journal of Speech.* **52**: 156–66.

Vihman M M 1993 Variable paths to early word production. *Journal of Phonetics.* **21**: 61–82.

Welkowitz J, Bond R N, Feldstein S 1984 Conversational time patterns of Hawaiian children as a function of ethnicity and gender. *Language and Speech.* **27**: 173–91.

Wells J C 1982 *Accents of English.* Cambridge University Press, Cambridge.

Wells J C 1990 Syllabification and allophony. *Studies in the pronunciation of English: A commemorative volume in honour of A C Gimson* ed S Ramsaran. Routledge, London and New York, pp 76–86.

Werker J F, Polka L 1993 Developmental changes in speech perception: New challenges and new directions. *Journal of Phonetics.* **21**: 83–101.

Wolfram W 1991 *Dialects and American English.* Center for Applied Linguistics and Prentice-Hall, Inc., Englewood Cliffs, NJ.

Wolfram W, Christian D 1976 *Appalachian speech.* Center for Applied Linguistics, Arlington, VA.

Wong R 1987a Learner variables and prepronunciation considerations. *Current perspectives on pronunciation* ed J Morley. Teachers of English to Speakers of Other Languages, Washington, DC, pp 13–28.

Wong R 1987b *Teaching pronunciation: Focus on English rhythm and intonation.* Prentice-Hall, Inc., Englewood Cliffs, NJ.

Woods H B 1991 Social differentiation in Ottawa English. *English around the world* ed J Cheshire. Cambridge University Press, Cambridge, pp 134–49.

Zelman N 1983 *1001 conversation topics.* Alemany Press, San Francisco.

Zuengler J 1988 Identity markers and L2 pronunciation. *Studies in Second Language Acquisition.* **10**: 33–49.

Index

Dear Reader,

When I think back to my teenage years, the most vivid memories are those of depression. Of the many times I cried myself to sleep, of the self-harm, and the periods of complete numbness. I grew up in a very traditional Bengali Muslim family, similar to that of my character Mehreen. In our culture, there is little understanding of mental illness. I remember assuming I was abnormal, that there was no one who could understand me. It was also around this time that I found YA literature. I grew obsessed with books on the topic of mental health, becoming overwhelmed at the notion that someone understood what was happening, someone felt the same (even if they were fictitious). But I noticed that all the protagonists of these books were white. No one had that extra layer of feeling their culture and religion were at odds with their mental illness. Which is why I wrote *All The Things We Never Said*. I wanted Muslim teens who suffer from depression and anxiety to feel seen, to feel understood, to know they're not alone. It's the book I wish I'd had as a teenager.

It's also a homage to my best friend. Emily and I have been friends since we were twelve, but neither of us knew the other suffered with a mental illness until our twenties. Emily is my support group. I don't know where I'd be without her, without the books I read, without the strangers I've connected with on the Internet who deal with the same problems. Such discussions have been my saviour, and I think the more we talk about mental health, the more we can help those in need.

yasmin

Please note that this book deals with sensitive issues that some may find triggering. Turn to page 434 for a list of topics included and links to helpful resources.